Famous Violinists
FOR
Young People

Famous Violinists FOR Young People

BY GLADYS BURCH

Biography Index Reprint Series

BOOKS FOR LIBRARIES PRESS
FREEPORT, NEW YORK

Copyright, 1946, by
A. S. Barnes & Co., Inc.

Reprinted 1972 by arrangement with
Dodd, Mead & Company

Library of Congress Cataloging in Publication Data

Burch, Gladys, 1899-
　Famous violinists for young people.

　(Biography index reprint series)
　SUMMARY: A brief introduction to the violin--its history, construction, and music--accompanies biographies of fourteen famous violinists.
　1. Violinists, violoncellists, etc.--Juvenile literature. [1. Violinists. 2. Violin] I. Title.
ML3930.A2B855　1972　　787'.1'0922 [B] [920] 75-38316
ISBN 0-8369-8118-9

PRINTED IN THE UNITED STATES OF AMERICA
BY
NEW WORLD BOOK MANUFACTURING CO., INC.
HALLANDALE, FLORIDA 33009

TO

BETTY FLO

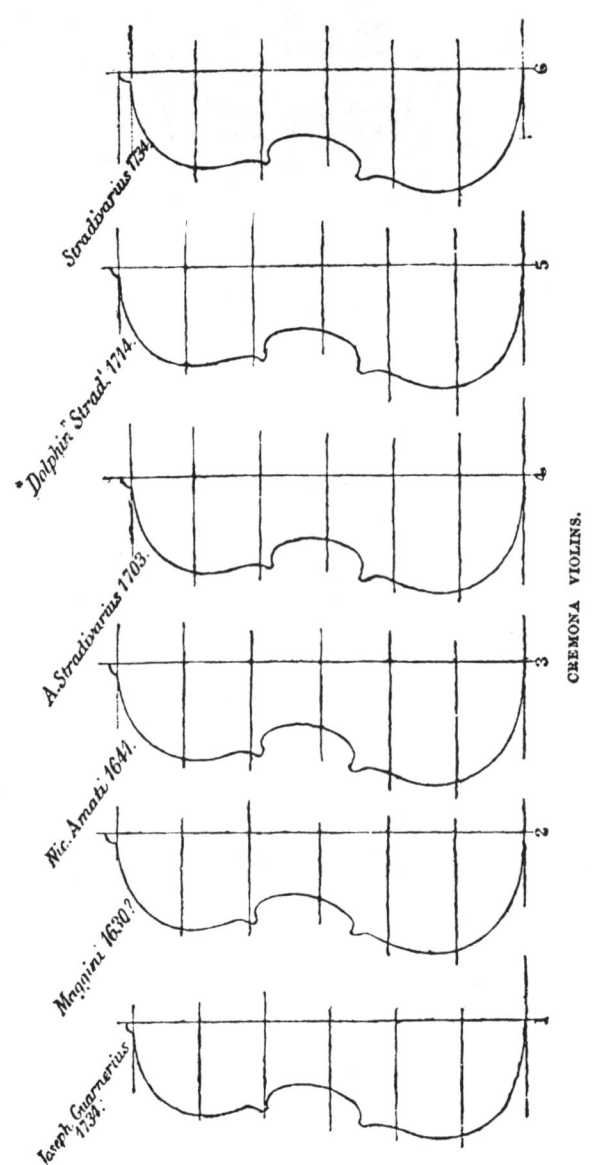

CREMONA VIOLINS.

CONTENTS

How Did the Violin Begin? 3

What is a Violin? 9

Violin Makers, 23

Violin Music & Violin Players, 35 ✗

Arcangelo Corelli, 49 ✗

Antonio Vivaldi, 57 ✗

Giuseppe Tartini, 63 ✗

Giovanni Battista Viotti, 71

Niccolo Paganini, 79 ✗

Louis Spohr, 97

Ole Borneman Bull, 109

Joseph Joachim, 137

Henri Wieniawski, 153

Pablo De Sarasate, 161

Leopold Auer & His Pupils, 169

Eugène Ysaÿe, 191

Fritz Kreisler, 201

Albert Spalding, 213

The pictures on pages 2, 8, 34 are reproduced by courtesy of the Metropolitan Museum of Art, New York, that on p. 200 by courtesy of Louis Lupas, and on p. 168 by courtesy of Mme. Auer

An Instrument Maker's Workshop in the Eighteenth Century.

Famous Violinists
FOR
Young People

LYRA REBEC

HOW DID THE VIOLIN BEGIN?

The violin—that miracle of simplicity! Despite page upon page written to explain its origin, the mystery of the violin's beginning remains unsolved. Various countries claim credit for its birthplace; various instruments have been named as its ancestor; but of one thing only are we certain: such miraculous simplicity resulted from a combination of ancient ancestry and infinite thought.

A true child of the Renaissance, the violin, as we know it, came into existence during the first half of the sixteenth century. Long considered the offspring, or cousin, of the stately viol—which it did eventually surpass in favor—the violin has now turned its back on any such relationship. Documented justification for this position rests largely on the scholarly efforts of Gerald R. Hayes—author of several valuable books on early musical instruments—and Arnold Dolmetsch—famous maker and player of this type of instrument.

Careful investigation has revealed that three families of bowed instruments lived more or less peacefully together, in Europe, at the period made famous by Columbus's discovery of America: the viol, the lyra, or lira, and the rebec. Their respective histories may be traced for several centuries previous to 1500, revealing certain changes in their development without infringement on one another's distinct characteristics.

The viols had long been held in high esteem in aristocratic circles and thus remained for another two centuries; the lyras held forth for another century; while the poor rebec, once the companion of angels, as depicted by the artist Fra Angelico, had now become the instrument of disgrace, played only by wandering minstrels, tramps, jugglers, and other lowly folk.

Soon was to appear a new instrument—the violin—partaking of certain features of both lyra and rebec, and, destined, after a stubborn struggle, to eclipse entirely the highly respected viol.

Let us imagine for a moment that we are visiting a museum where early bowed stringed instruments are displayed. We shall not linger long with the members of the viol family; for we soon discover that the viols, with their characteristic sloping shoulders and flat backs, differ at every important point from the violin. We immediately notice that there are six strings instead of four; and that there are gut frets upon the finger board to designate the semitones. This latter observation is particularly important; for the violin has never in any period of its history had frets.

We also learn the following facts: the tuning of the viols is different; the viols are held downward for overhand bowing; their strings are lighter, longer and looser; the wood in their construction is consistently thinner; and the ribs, or sides, are usually deeper.

We turn away from the dignified, yet friendly-appearing viols, reluctantly convinced that they are not the forebears of that fiery, spirited, instrument—capable of arousing infinite extremes of emotion—the violin.

We approach the next case of early bowed instruments. *What quaint looking violins!* Looking at the card attached to the exhibit, we find that they are listed as two distinct types of fiddles, used in Europe during the Middle Ages; one, the lyra, or lira, the other the rebec. Curiously enough looking at these early instruments—late replicas though they are, for early ones do not exist—we notice immediately their resemblance to our violin. Although peculiar in appearance to our eyes, accustomed to the perfect symmetry and sheen of the lovely violin, both the lyra and rebec display unmistakable relationship—country-cousinship, shall we say—to the universally beloved queen of instruments—the violin!

Let us examine first the half pear-shaped rebec with its sickle-shaped peg-box and pegs inserted laterally in the manner of the violin. Its primitive appearance—although definitely "violinish" in spirit—reminds us of that ancient legend concerning the fleet-footed God, Hermes: Finding a tortoise one day, he is supposed to have made holes in the opposite edges of its shell, have drawn linen cords through the holes and thus have made the first stringed instrument

How Did the Violin Begin?

Looking back into the rebec's history, we find, that it is indeed ancient, that it is one of the earliest of bowed stringed instruments; but there is a difference of opinion as to where it actually originated. All are agreed, however, that it came from the East; and most scholars believe that it was introduced into Europe by the Moors at the beginning of the eighth century, when, pressing through Egypt from Arabia, they invaded Spain.

Dating from the tenth century we find many pictorial examples of the rebec but little written evidence. A few early illustrators show it with a single string; but, for the most part, it is shown in its elongated half-pear shape, held always upon the shoulder or against the breast, with its characteristic three strings. At first the rebec had no finger board, but sometime in its European existence it gradually acquired one. It was tuned in fifths like our violin; and certain characteristics of the smallest member of its family—the poche, or pichette—can be seen in the tiny violin known as the dancing master's kit.

Let us leave the jolly rebec: apparently borne into Europe on the wings of war, then espoused by the religious world as the companion of angels, and later consigned to its dry-as-a-rebec role of providing music for the dance and wayside merriment.

We turn now to the mysterious lira, or lyra, about which so little is known, but, about which there is fascinating speculation. Perhaps the first thing that we notice, in looking at a replica of a lyra, is the position of its pegs. They are inserted from the rear into a leaf-shaped head. Glancing once more at the neighboring rebec, we are reminded that its pegs, like those of the violin, enter from the side. Otherwise the lyra, in shape, looks more like the violin than does the rebec.

Examples of a type of lyra, or lira, sometimes called the Turkish fiddle, are still found in the Balkan countries where the lyra is supposed to have been introduced into Europe from the East many, many centuries ago.

Searching further into the lyra family, we come upon the lyra da braccia, examples of which are very rare, but, evidences of which abound in art and literature of the sixteenth century and the centuries just previous to the violin's capture of the string-world. Studying a picture of one of these instruments, we see that it looks somewhat like a large flattened-out, squarish viola.

Straight off, we notice its vertical pegs, set in a leaf-like head, and, a strikingly different—to our violin-accustomed eyes—number and arrangement of strings: There are seven strings instead of four, including the two bass strings set outside the finger board. These extra strings are known as bourdons, or drones.

Like the rebec and the violin, the lyra da braccia we find, was held under the chin or against the breast and played upon with a long bow. Although it is occasionally pictured with frets, written evidence such as "the positions must be found by touch and ear," indicate that frets were not a practical feature of the instrument.

Much in evidence in sixteenth century art, literature, and instrument-listing, the lyra da braccia, shortly after the beginning of the seventeenth century, finds no place in history. But Gerald Hayes in his book on viols and other bowed instruments has expressed the belief that the lyra da braccia possesses a long pre-history of its own with predominantly Western and harmonic influence.

Now we come to the lyra da gamba, a younger and larger member of the lyra family, first mentioned—as the "bass of the lyra da braccia"—in the mid-sixteenth century. Again we must depend upon pictures, writing, and art for examples of the instrument. Like the lyra da braccia, the lyra da gamba had two bourdon strings outside the finger board; but, it always had eleven strings, and, sometimes as many as sixteen. This larger instrument with frets, broad neck, and long, flat bridge, apparently dropped out of existence toward the middle of the seventeenth century.

Thus we see that both the rebec and the lyra—each bearing kinship and differences—may have contributed to the violin, which mysteriously appeared on the scene in Europe at the beginning of the sixteenth century. The lyra, held overarm, constructed fundamentally like the violin, and usually tuned in fifths, has against its claim for violin-parenthood its greater number of strings—as well as the bourdons—necessitating the use of a flat bridge and long bow. The rebec, held upon the shoulder or against the breast, tuned in fifths like the violin, and rhythmically akin to it in its playing, must disclaim violin-ancestry in tone; for its half-pear shape body and flat belly permit of no sound post.

But despite all documented conjecture, as well as romantic tales concerning the Italian towns of Cremona and Brescia, historical facts do not permit us to say, "The violin was invented by Mr. 'A' at the village of 'X'." For the plain truth of the matter is, that, insofar as recorded facts are concerned, at one date there was no such thing as the violin; then lo! there it was—a fully developed being—living a lusty life!

This much we know: Martin Agricola—a German musicologist whose real name was Martin Sore—living in the first half of the sixteenth century, described an instrument prevalent in Poland at the beginning of his century bearing the marked characteristics of the violin; pictorial evidence reveals the violin's existence in Italy during the first half of the sixteenth century; while various references justify our assuming its use in France midway in that century.

Still, we are forced to ask: *Where did the violin begin? Where did it actually originate?*

Who knows? Perhaps, Poland.... Perhaps Russia—great Mother of Secrets—may one day reveal the story. Perchance some unsuspected Italian master, pushing aside his accustomed colors and brush, conceived the violin's comely contours. But, until time unfolds the mystery, the violin—like Topsy—just grew!

STRADIVARIUS VIOLIN
(One String Missing)

WHAT IS A VIOLIN?

Now that we have arrived at the conclusion that, apparently, prior to 1500 there was no such thing as a violin, and, soon thereafter there was a violin, let us examine the distinguishing characteristics of the violin family: a resonant body made up of sound board, or belly, and back separated by means of ribs or sides, usually fitted with four—though possibly three—strings, always tuned a fifth apart; a neck with no frets, and the smaller instruments held, when played, either upon the shoulder or against the breast.

More specifically, let us consider in detail the construction of the violin as we know it, the principle and outline of which have never changed; although the fittings, as we shall soon see, have been altered by various circumstances.

So simple in appearance, and weighing about one pound, the violin consists of sixty-eight or seventy pieces, depending upon whether the back and belly are cut in one or two pieces; and it is so constructed that it can withstand a strain of approximately ninety pounds.

These parts, variously divided as to number, consist of back, belly, blocks, sides, linings, bass bar, purfling, tailpiece, tailpiece rest, tailpiece fastening, tail pin, pegs, finger board, bridge, nut, sound post, strings, neck and scroll. The neck and scroll are at times separated into two pieces; and the purfling, or decoration which follows the instrument's outline, is occasionally set in place in thirty-six pieces instead of the usual twenty-four. These variations increase the number of pieces, but the normal number is either sixty-eight or seventy.

The violin box in itself, with its proudly curving shoulders, gently nipped-in waistline, rounded bottom outline, and graceful F-shaped sound holes, is thirteen to fourteen inches in length, eight and a half inches across at its widest point, four and a half at its waistline, and about two and a half inches deep in its deepest section.

On studying the violin's construction, we learn that no detail arrived there by accident: the length of the violin is best suited to the action of the arm when the instrument is held for playing; the inward curves of its sides—the center bouts—provide the means of bowing the individual strings, as well as contributing to the acoustics; while the sound holes—contrary to popular belief—are not put there to let the sound out but to help the gradually-arching belly to vibrate freely.

Continuing with this cause and effect situation: The FF holes are cut in their characteristic fashion because of the curved line of the belly; and as to their position, they are thus centered not alone for symmetric beauty, but for scientific effect on the instrument's vibration. And, when we study the inside of the violin, we see that the outer sides, or ribs, have a purpose beside that of holding the back and belly together: they help transmit the vibrations.

Likewise, the wood, in addition to looking beautiful, is chosen for specific reasons. Maple is considered best for the back, although pear and sycamore are sometimes used; and white pine and deal are the first choice for the belly.

But, if you were making a violin, do not think for a minute that you would step into a lumber shop and simply ask for so many feet of maple and pine. The wood must be properly seasoned, preferably sunbaked for five or six years; and according to F. J. Fetis, the French musical historian, previous to that, the wood should have been chosen from the *south* side of trees growing on the *south* side of the forest!

This may be carrying matters a bit too far but the fact remains, that, despite various attempts to season wood for violin making artificially—including baking, steaming and acid-bathing—no quick method has been discovered; for nature alone, apparently, holds the secret.

Nor are we finished with wood-choosing. In addition to being seasoned, the wood must be sound, free from knots, worm holes, or spots; its grain must run evenly; and it must be neither too soft nor too hard! Then, in making the instrument, the grain should—in both back and belly—run evenly up and down. Again we are reminded that such care is prompted not for the sake of appearance alone but for tone as well.

Now having chosen our wood, it behooves us to use care in cutting and chiseling it. There are no set rules for determining the wood's thickness at any particular point of the back or belly, for much depends upon the texture of the wood. The harder the wood the more it may be chiseled away; but Edward Heron-Allen, an authority on violin making, has said that it is better to leave an excess of wood in an instrument than to err in the direction of skimping. And according to him, it is the mark of a master craftsman to know how to regulate the degrees of thickness, just perceptibly providing the maximum density of the belly at a point above the sound post.

Now that we have the violin's skeleton accounted for, let us consider the remaining outer aspects.

Surely the neck and scroll are chosen for no purpose other than to look beautiful and to cradle the strings!

But once more, our assumption is wrong. True, this part of a violin must be carefully proportioned, for, it is after all the instrument's countenance, and might easily ruin the appearance of an otherwise beautiful being; but in addition, the choice of wood, and proportion in the neck and scroll, influence the violin's tone, through acting as a vibratory messenger between strings and body.

The other vibratory messenger—equally innocent of utility in appearance—is the little maple or boxwood two-legged bridge, set atop the violin's belly midway between the FF holes. We can plainly see, that, notched in four places, it provides a suspension spot for the gut strings; and unless we investigate we are doubtless satisfied that the little curlicues simply add to the general loveliness. Not at all! We find that any change in the original design alters the tone of the instrument. This is all the more remarkable when we realize that the bridge is not fastened down in any way except by the strings' pressure.

It is, however, in the matter of the bridge that the most noticeable changes have been made in violin making; changes, to accommodate the raising of the standard pitch in the nineteenth century; and changes, to increase the brilliance of tone. To accomplish these ends the bridge has been raised and arched, which, in turn, has necessitated the slight raising of the end of the finger board and the thrusting backward, in consequence, of the neck. In some cases the finger board has also been lengthened.

But it must be emphatically emphasized that scholars are in disagreement as to whether these changes have been an "improvement"; one, taking the view that no benefit to true power of tone has resulted; another, that these "improvements" are only the beginning of what might be accomplished if a good engineer took the matter of violin making in hand. Time may decide this issue.

Meanwhile, before leaving the bridge-saga, suppose we turn aside from such scientific speculations to the warmer realm of the bridge-experience of an ardent violin lover, H. R. Haweis, who, in his delightful book, *My Musical Life,* has written so glowingly about the violin.

Mr. Haweis, convinced that bridge and violin must unite in harmonious marriage, states, "All old violins have had many bridges in their time, but there is no reason why the union, if happy, should not last for forty or fifty years." And then he goes on to deplore the mating of crude new bridges with instruments mellowed by age; stating that he does not believe in the theory of bridges wearing out. "Glue, mend, patch!" he advises.

And to justify his conviction, he tells a delightful tale about his own grand pattern, 1712, Stradivarius violin:

Soon after the violin was given to him, deciding that the newish-looking bridge was hopelessly choking the lovely violin's vibrations, Mr. Haweis substituted a very old, delicately built bridge from another instrument. The improvement was instantaneous! He writes, "I thought its build too slight, but clapped it on at once, and the old violin waked as out of a long sleep, like a giant refreshed with wine."

Not completely satisfied with its position, off and on he "fidgeted about with the bridge," until one day he snapped it. After experimenting in vain with several other bridges, he glued the old one together, put it back in place, and lo! All was well again!

But the poor little bridge was destined to endure further misery before finding lasting solace with her adopted partner: the Strad having been put aside for a number of years its joints became loosened, due to dampness, necessitating a visit to a violin-doctor. And as Mr. Haweis reports, "he 'fixed it up' again, but sent it back with a new bridge, and sounding—well, like flies and vinegar!" Forthwith recovering the old bridge, cast aside by the "doctor,"

Mr. Haweis restored it to its rightful place. Henceforth "husband" and "wife" lived happily ever after!

Now before discussing that ever-mysterious element of the violin—its varnish—let us see what an opened-up violin reveals.

Surely, there cannot be much inside or a violin would be heavier!

And we do not find *much*, but what we do find proves of vital importance; such as, what is probably the most important minor item of this magic-instrument, its sound post, called by the French the violin's soul. A little round piece of pine, held firmly—but not too firmly—between belly and back, about a quarter of an inch behind the right foot of the bridge, the sound post helps to regulate and sustain the vibrations within the arched interior. And it must be very carefully cut and inserted, for its effect upon the violin's tone is similar to that afforded by the relative thickness of belly and back.

Closely allied to the sound post is the bass bar, or sound bar, the other half of, what Edward Heron-Allen calls, "the entire nervous system of the fiddle." A strip of soft even-grained pine—in modern times, about ten and a half inches long—the bass bar extends along the inner belly, at a slightly oblique angle, beneath the left foot of the bridge. Its purpose is to communicate—and to help sustain—the vibrations transmitted to it by the left foot of the bridge.

Thus we see that these two nerve centers—the sound post and the bass bar—do, in fact, control the very breath of the violin; and we can better understand that the ill-adjustment of either will produce what violinists call "wolf-notes."

Now we come to the finishing touches of the instrument's structural foundation—the blocks and linings. A violin without them will hold together and "play"; but if you want to be rewarded with the sound of genuine music, coming from an instrument of your making, it ill-behooves you to disregard these extra pieces of wood. There are six blocks, usually made of pine—though the great Stradivarius often used willow—set at the top, bottom, and corners of the violin. They contribute to a firm foundation for both structure and vibration. Connecting the blocks are twelve strips of like-wood called the linings, fitted carefully piece to piece, usually just touching, but, in certain exceptions, running into the blocks.

In the top block we see where the neck is fastened; in the bottom one, the tail pin. And now, having seen all that there is to see inside, we shall figuratively glue belly, back, and sides together and ponder over the glowing exterior of a fine old fiddle.

Many an hour has been spent in experimentation; many a book has been written expounding theories, but the secret of the Cremona makers' varnish remains buried with its makers.

One of the most intelligent discussions of the subject was written by Charles Reade, in the form of letters to a London newspaper. Selecting a brilliantly-colored Stradivarius as his varnish-guinea pig, Mr. Reade began to study its finish with a mind uncluttered with previous premises. As he expresses it: "Look at this dark red varnish, and use your eyes. What do you see? A red varnish, which chips very readily off what people call *the bare wood*. But... what *is* it? It is *not* bare wood. Bare wood turns a dirty brown with age: this is a rich and lovely yellow." Then he goes on to say that it is wood, highly varnished with oil and some transparent gum; and judging from the tendency of oil to run into the wood, probably four coats.

Then turning to the chipped red surface, and throwing away preconceived notions that it was the same sort of varnish of *another color*, he decided, on the contrary, that because the outer varnish *did* chip off, it was chemically different from the under varnish; for as he points out, oil upon oil would blend; whereas, the chipping-away aspect of the red finish indicated to him that it was a spirit varnish.

Thus Charles Reade reached the sensible conclusion that Stradivarius "laid on several coats of red varnish, made by simply dissolving some fine red unadulterated gum in spirit; the spirit evaporated, and left pure gum lying on a rich oil varnish, from which it chips by its dry nature and its utter want of chemical affinity to the substratum." And summing up his decision, he states, "The first is a colorless oil varnish, which sinks into and shows up the figure of the wood; the second is a heterogeneous spirit varnish, which serves to give the glory of color, with its light and shade, which is the great and transcendent beauty of a Cremona violin."

Today various methods are used to provide a beautiful varnish; thought by some to contribute to the violin's tone; by others, to contribute only to its beauty. But the mystery of the Cremona makers' varnish continues to tantalize. Did Charles Reade strike the right trail? Is time the answer? Will Mr. "A" or Mr. "B" one day *really* solve the riddle?

Since no violin could function without its fittings—pegs, nut, finger board, and such—let us briefly concern ourselves with them. We find that the pegs are made of ebony, boxwood, or rose-wood, and, that ebony is the most generally satisfactory; boxwood, being too hard; rose-wood—although ideally suited to the purpose—too easily worn out. The nut, that tiny grooved intersection between peg box and finger board, is made of ebony. The finger board—so vital to violin playing—should preferably be made of ebony; and its length must be carefully proportioned to the height of the bridge. The tailpiece, with its four holes cut to receive the strings in a parallel line, usually made of ebony, is attached to the tail pin by means of a looped gut string. The tail pin, firmly ensconced within the bottom block—as we previously observed—is made of ebony or boxwood; and the small piece of wood called the rest, over which the loop of gut passes from the button to the tailpiece, is also usually made of ebony.

Having examined the violin from top to bottom, and having even peeked inside, we must not overlook the various appliances tucked away in every fiddle-case. There we shall find such things as chin rests, mutes, rosin, string box, tuning forks, gauges for measuring the thickness of strings, scissors, and tweezers. And if it is the residing-place of a particularly fine instrument, we shall probably find a soft, silken handkerchief, or a genuine fiddle blanket, to enfold the precious one!

Two more essential items now attract our attention: the bow and the strings. First let us consider the four strings, often erroneously referred to as "catgut." We find, once more, that great care is the important factor; care, in their making; and care, in their choice for a particular instrument and player. Once a player has found strings of a size that best suit both his style of playing and his instrument, it is well for him to measure their diameter carefully with the little string gauge, previously mentioned; for the violin—a very sensitive and temperamental creature—does not respond graciously to tampering.

Also, in choosing the strings, care must be taken that the four be relatively akin; the first string, known as the *chanterelle*, or melody string, should be chosen first; the others, in proportion to it. We can plainly see that the guiding principle of the violin is the "fitness of things"—perfection of relationship—the relative thickness of the strings, the nature of the force brought upon them, and the quality of the sounding body itself determining the character of the tone produced.

The prime requisite, in a string, for producing good tone is its *trueness*. A string must be of even thickness throughout its length or squeaky tones will result at just the moment when the sweetest of harmonies are intended. Though there are scientific means of determining this factor, the process is too complicated to prove practical for today's hurried purchaser or shopkeeper. Consequently the string-buyer must depend upon his eye for guidance. He will soon learn that a true string is transparent and blotchless from end to end. Pliant and elastic, it will spring back into position, like a watch spring, when uncoiled; if too white, it has been improperly or over-bleached and will prove brittle and false. In short, "consistent transparency" is the mark of a good violin string.

Fully aware—after our experience thus far with the violin's heritage—that such transparency arrived not by accident but intention, let us investigate the process of achieving it. We find that violin strings, as well as those of nearly all stringed instruments, are made from the small intestines of sheep. The best strings come from sunny Italy where the lambs will have frolicked in the dry mountain air; and we learn that September is the proper month for string making!

The intestine chosen consists of three membranes; the middle, or muscular one, being destined for music making. Highly skilled workmen scrape clean the selected intestines while warm, in order to avoid their being discolored by foreign matter in the cooling process. Then tied in bundles, the intestines are carried in vessels to the string maker's, where, tied in bundles of ten, they take their first step toward stringdom.

Their first *step* proves to be a cold *bath,* lasting twelve to fifteen hours in running water, or, in a vat of spring water treated with soda. Then follows a four- or five-hour bath in warm running water; after which, the membranes can be more readily separated. This separation is chiefly attained by scraping the soaked intestine with a split cane on a sloping slab, down which flows a steady stream of water.

Still the bathing process continues: the retained fibrous membranes, fastened into bundles of ten and placed in a stone jar, are now soaked for three or four hours in a carefully proportioned lye-solution. Taken out, they are then gently rubbed between the first finger of the left hand, covered with a gutta-percha protector, and the thumb, encased in a copper thimble. This rubbing procedure—for the purpose of removing any remains of the discarded membranes—is repeated three times during the day at two-hour intervals; after each of which, the membranes are placed in another stone jar containing a solution of permanganate of potash. Following their fourth period of rubbing, they are dropped into a weak solution of sulphuric acid.

This operation, repeated in exactly the same way, continues for two or three days; at the end of which time, the much-bathed and polished membranes are ready for sorting as to quality, length, thickness, and strength.

Then when the uneven ones have been split by means of a special knife, and their thick and thin ends set alternately in a jar, they are ready for the spinning, which takes place on a frame about three times as long as a violin. A varying number of strings—depending upon what string is being made—are used; the first, or E string usually requiring three or four fine strands; the second, or A string, three or four strong ones; the third, or D string, six or seven strong ones. The fourth, or G string, we learn, is usually made of gut, then covered with either copper or silver wire.

When the spinning frames are filled with fiddle strings, spun by means of a rapidly revolving fly-wheel process, and sulphur has been put on the strings, the loaded frames are put into a sulphur chamber where jets of sulphur are ignited. The chamber then made air-tight is left sealed over night, during which time the strings undergo a continuous bleaching process.

The next morning, after being exposed to the air until nearly dry, the strings are once more moistened, twisted on the frames, and replaced in their sulphur bath. This process continues from two to eight days depending upon the size of the string.

But they are not ready to go to market until they are polished. This is done by means of hair cushions, occasionally soaked in an alkaline potash solution, while the strings are still on the frames. Then wiped of impurities, they are moistened with clear water, replaced in their sulphur bath for another night, after which they are dried and twisted again. When dry—with the optional exception of the E string—they are in store for one last polishing!

This extra-special polish takes place—with the frames lying flat—by means of little gutta-percha cushions, immersed in olive oil and pounce or whitening, pushed up and down the strings by hand or machine. Then wiped dry, and slightly moistened with olive oil, they are permitted to dry thoroughly for the last time. Cut from the frames, carefully rolled into coils and made up into bundles of fifteen or thirty, they are sent out into the world to find *their* waiting violin!

Now we come to the last, but by no means the least important, accompaniment to the violin—the bow. Needless to say, without a bow, there would be *no violin;* but it is not so well known that without rosin on the bow there might as well be *no bow.* Let us look into that matter, as well as others, concerning the bow.

As with the violin itself, we find that the bow's origin is clouded in mystery. Some authorities declare it to be the most distinguishing factor in the development of stringed instruments; others believe that its importance has been exaggerated; while most historians are content to say that it came from the Orientals. Be that as it may, judging from various early illustrations, it remained for many centuries a primitive affair, not unlike a bow-and-arrow bow.

Gradually the outward-curving stick appears to have flattened down until the one shown in Raphael's famous "St. Cecilia"—painted in the sixteenth century—although still sling-and-arrowish, foretells the bow familiar to us. Sometime, somewhere, there developed a proper nut and head for fastening the hair; later, a means of regulating the hair's tightness was added; and then in the eighteenth century, there appeared the "Stradivarius" of the bow—a Frenchman—who is responsible for the bow that Kreisler, Heifetz or the lowliest student uses. His name was François Tourte.

Long known as François Tourte, Jr., being the younger son of one who had greatly improved the existing bows—he was born in 1747 at Paris. His father, already having one apprentice in his eldest son, arranged for young François to take up the trade of clockmaking. After eight years spent in this fashion, during which time the youth became increasingly dissatisfied with his lot, he returned to the fold of bow making. And, although he could neither read nor write, he brought to his chosen craft the benefit of his experience in clockmaking, which contributed greatly to his remarkable skill of hand.

It so happened that at this time greater demands were being made on the violin: violinists, eager to make their instruments "sing," sought bows with greater lightness and elasticity. Young Tourte, inspired by the challenge, began to experiment. In order to save precious material, he used staves from sugar casks for his first efforts; then, after testing various woods, he decided upon fernambuc as combining the proper stiffness and lightness. This wood had to be imported in the midst of maritime wars of the period; and since it sometimes took as many as ten tons of fernambuc wood to provide suitable pieces for a few bow sticks, Tourte was forced to charge enormous prices for his bows.

He is also credited with the fixing of the bow's length, which is approximately twenty-nine and a half inches; and, with establishing the heat-method of bending the stick. By this process bows are shaped to the required inward curve—distinguishing difference from the early outward-curving bow—preserving at the same time unbroken fibers the entire length of the stick. Great care must be exercised to make certain that the heat penetrates to the inner fibers; otherwise, these unheated fibers will eventually force the outer fibers back to their original position. Then a bow becomes a "fiddle-stick," indeed!

Tourte also perfected the nut and head; and innovated first, the use of a ferrule, or bracelet, made of tin or silver, to keep the hairs of the bow flat; and then invented the little slide of mother-of-pearl, which covers the hair at the nut. And the care with which he or his daughter selected, washed, and scoured the horsehair—preferring that from France—rivals the long string-making process with which we are now familiar.

Now just a word about the all-important rosin, and then we shall turn from the mechanics of the violin to a study of some of its famous builders. Having observed that rosin on the bow is necessary for sound, it is interesting to learn the reason: were it not for the rosin, the pressure of the bow would be continuous so long as it touched a string and, consequently, no sound would result; but the presence of rosin on the horsehair causes a series of intermittent shocks, which produce continuous-sounding vibrations. And again, *care* is the watch-word; for an excess of rosin will call forth a raucous tone.

Thus we see that wood, gut, glue and varnish—with a bit of metal wire—miraculously combined, comprise the fiddle; and wood, metal, mother-of-pearl, and horsehair—with bits of rosin on it—the bow. Unite fiddle and bow with an artist's touch and MAGIC results!

GASPARO DUIFFOPRUGCAR
Etching by Pierre Woeiriot

VIOLIN MAKERS

AFTER LOOKING into the history of early stringed instruments, we came to the conclusion that the violin shows characteristics of both rebec and lyra. After study of the violin's miraculous construction, we decided that only time and care could have produced such perfection. Upon searching the records for the first violin maker, we are faced with confused contradictions.

Going back for a moment to our hinted-at-suggestion that one of the Italian masters of the Renaissance may have had a hand in perfecting the violin's contours, let us remind ourselves that one of the greatest artists of all times—Leonardo da Vinci—lived, worked, and dreamed at just the time when we *believe* the violin was evolving. Born in 1452 at Vinci, between Pisa and Florence, Leonardo da Vinci died in 1519—several years before any certain evidence of a violin—though we shall soon see that there exists a possibility of some violins having appeared shortly before this death.

Leonardo da Vinci may never have made such an instrument himself—he in all probability did not—but when we study his notebooks and scattered writings, we find that there was little his mind did not hit upon, and nothing it did not enhance. Take for example his statement, "One may make of wood thin grained boards, which will seem like camlets and watered silks and with various fixed marks." Is this not a good description of the wood in a beautiful violin? In another note, Leonardo refers to his having learned from a miniature-painter, whom he admired, how gum-lac was dissolved.

Eager for knowledge himself, he was equally eager to share with others the fruits of his study. Consequently, knowing that he was particularly concerned with acoustics, may we not be forgiven—in a situation where the facts are not known—for surmising that Leonardo da Vinci had "a finger in the pie" of violin evolution?

This surmise of ours is precariously linked to an exceedingly controversial subject, that of the two Gasparos—Gasparo Duiffoprugcar and Gasparo da Salò—each of whom has been credited with being the "first violin maker."

For many years, Gasparo Duiffoprugcar, a famous instrument maker—supposed to have been born Gaspar Tieffenbrucker in Bavaria, established as an instrument maker at Bologna in Italy, and taken to France as instrument maker to the French court by Francis I—was credited with making the first violins.

We *do* know that in 1516, the young French King, following a series of wars, did rob Italy of some of her finest craftsmen including Leonardo da Vinci whom he established in the chateaux of Cloux near his castle, Amboise. Consequently, when we read that at the same time Francis I brought Gasparo Duiffoprugcar from Italy as court instrument maker, and that Duiffoprugcar, because of his health, subsequently settled at Lyons, the story sounds plausible.

Then when we learn that six Duiffoprugcar violins—bearing labels assigned respectively to the years 1510, 1511, 1515 and 1517—turned up, we are inclined to believe that Gasparo Duiffoprugcar was indeed the first violin maker.

Add to this, the unmistakable presence of a violin in the famous painting of him by Pierre Woeiriot, in which Duiffoprugcar is surrounded by instruments of his making, and we are convinced.

Lo, and behold! At the end of the nineteenth century, along came a complete refutation of these facts by a Frenchman, Henri Contagne, who claimed that Gasparo Duiffoprugcar was born about 1514—instead of 1469, as previously supposed—near Munich. Settling directly at Lyons, on his arrival from Germany, without benefit of Italian tutelage—according to Contagne—Duiffoprugcar became a French citizen, and died in poverty about 1570. He further claimed that the Woeiriot portrait was painted in 1562 when Duiffoprugcar was forty-eight!

Now this is indeed confusing. "What about the unmistakable Duiffoprugcar violins with their early labels?" we ask. Immediately those who are inclined to credit Contagne's findings tell us that there was a period when labels were cleverly forged: these are probably an example of such infamy, with the dates thus arbitrarily and mistakenly recorded.

Irrespective of the dates involved in the controversy, there are these significant facts favoring the original assumptions concerning Gasparo Duiffoprugcar: the violins attributed to him bear unmistakable likeness in workmanship to his splendid viols; and as to his name being recorded as Duiffoprugcar rather than Tieffenbrucker at Lyons, it would appear that he brought his Italianized version with him after a period spent in Italy, for it is in no sense a French variant of the original German name.

Turning from these fascinating speculations, we find less confusion— although few facts—in the other Gasparo's record. Born Gasparo Bertolotti in about 1542 at Salò, in Lombardy, he took the name of his birthplace when he settled down to instrument making at Brescia. Consequently we know him as Gasparo da Salò, the first maker of violins, or at least *one* of the first makers of violins. It is believed that he may have served as apprentice to Hierolimus Divirchi, a noted Brescian lute maker of the time, although it was as a maker of viols that da Salò first established himself.

Gasparo da Salò's violins, now exceedingly rare, are worthy competitions in tone with later, more beautiful instruments. Usually referred to as "tubby" or "bulgy," they are large in design with short, shallow bouts, long parallel FF holes and exceedingly crude scrolls. Their varnish is a rich amber brown; their labels are never dated, and read, "Gasparo da Salò, In Brescia."

Probably the most famous Gasparo da Salò violin—one ornately decorated, possibly with the help of Benvenuto Cellini—was owned by the famous Norwegian violinist, Ole Bull.

Gasparo da Salò died in the first decade of the seventeenth century, leaving the rapidly developing mantle of violin making to his pupil, Giovanni Paola Maggini, who was born about 1580.

Although Maggini violins are occasionally mistaken for those of his master, they bear distinguishing features of their own. Large like the Gasparo models, with similar FF holes, their scroll is decidedly less primitive, their ribs lower in height, and their tone grand with a touch of melancholy in it. The varnish is either a light yellow or a rich brown, the latter considered a mark of the best Maggini instruments. A particularly fine one was owned by the Belgian violinist, Charles Auguste de Bériot. Maggini labels read either "Gio Paola Maggini in Brescia" or "Paola maggini in Brescia."

Now we come to a name familiar to all of us—CREMONA! Is it a beautiful word because we know that beautiful violins were born there, or is the very word in itself beautiful?

Lying in the fertile valley of the River Po, bathed in the southern sun, and protected from cold northern winds by high snow-capped mountain sentries—whether by accident or choice—Cremona became the cradle of violin making. And the first Cremona maker was a man whose name goes hand-in-hand with the town's—Amati, Andrea Amati.

He was born between 1520 and 1530, and though believed by some to have been a pupil of Gasparo da Salò at Brescia, the dates of their respective births tend to discount such a possibility. He may have been influenced by Brescian-made violins, but common sense prompts us to surmise that *both* makers benefited by patterns from an original source—be it Gasparo Duiffoprugcar or one the world does not yet know about!

Be that as it may, Andrea Amati contributed characteristics of his own to violin making. His instruments are usually small, highly arched toward the center, fairly thick of belly, with broadish FF holes, and produce what has come to be known as the Amati-tone—sweet, delicate, and mellow, without brilliance and carrying power. Their varnish is either a lovely light brown, or rich golden in color; and their labels read: "Andreas Amati Cremona, fecit 15—."

Andrea Amati violins are exceedingly rare although a rebec of his, dated 1546, was long preserved in Milan. Undoubtedly some of his finest violins were among the famous twenty-four—twelve large, and twelve small—commissioned in 1566 by Charles IX for the Chapel Royal at Versailles. These violins must have been unusually beautiful, judging from the description of two that survived the ravages of the French Revolution, a bit more than two hundred years later. Their backs, variously decorated, included paintings of the French arms and the motto, "PIETATE et JUSTITIA."

It is believed that Andrea Amati lived until about 1611. He left both his workshop and craft to his two sons, Antonio and Hieronymus, known to us by their English names, Anthony and Jerome. The brothers, working together for a time, at first followed their father's pattern, but soon developed distinctive characteristics; particularly Jerome, who, when he married, separated from his brother and set up a workshop of his own. Their combined label reads, "Antonius & Hieronym Fr. Amati Cremonen Andrea fil. F. 1587."

Anthony's instruments were for the most part like his father's, except that the whole model was somewhat flatter; the sides, being lower in height; the center, remaining fairly high in proportion to the entire instrument. His FF holes followed in the Brescian tradition; and the tone of his violins was delicate and pure.

Jerome's independent model—bold, yet graceful—was built on the "grand" scale. The FF holes were distinctive, although, on the whole, the finishing touches were rougher than those of his brother. But Jerome could afford to be a bit reckless himself; for he gave to the world a son—Nicolaus, or Niccolo—born to make the name of Amati immortal and to "father" the prince of violin makers—Antonio Stradivari—or Stradivarius, as he is usually known.

Until about 1625, Niccolo Amati followed quite faithfully in the footsteps of his father and uncle, making the characteristic, small violins. Suddenly he burst forth with a much larger model—known as the Grand Amati—to which he henceforth adhered. These violins are regarded as practically the acme of perfection; in choice of wood, design—although the corners are thought by some to be too pronounced—workmanship, finish and tone. And their golden yellow varnish glows like enlivened amber! His label reads, "Nicolaus Amatus Cremonen Hieronymi Fil. ac Antonij Nepos Fecit 16—."

Niccolo Amati died on April 12, 1684, leaving one of his sons—Jerome—to carry on the illustrious name. Alas, this Jerome Amati's violins did small credit to the family name, which disappeared at his death. Nevertheless, the Amati tradition was destined to develop to glorious heights through the various branches of the Guarnerius family and the incomparable Antonio Stradivarius!

Andrea Guarnerius, born in 1630, and Antonio Stradivarius, born in 1644, both worked under the guiding eye and hand of Niccolo Amati; but, while Antonio Stradivarius was destined to reach the pinnacle of achievement in his chosen craft, Andrea Guarnerius was to live in the history of violin making through being the *first* Guarnerius and the uncle of the most famous one—Guiseppe Antonio—known as Joseph Guarneri del Gesù from the fact that his characteristic labels include a cross with the letters "I H S" beneath.

Now let us go back in time to that little sun-baked town of Cremona to find out, if possible, what manner of man was Antonio Stradivarius, who, living for ninety-three years, left to the world such a legacy of beauty. We find that he was a man of simplicity, an artist, a worker, one whose days were as beautifully proportioned as the instruments, brought to life by his making.

Antonio, born into a family long active in the public service of the little community of Cremona, is supposed to have begun his apprenticeship in violin making with Niccolo Amati, when he was but ten or eleven years old, and to have made his first violin at the age of thirteen! Working with his master until he was a grown man of twenty-three or -four, Stradivarius at this period made instruments in keeping with the Amati model, and, in fact, used Niccolo Amati's label. Subsequently, some of these violins have been identified and are now known as Amati-Strads.

The conscientious apprentice, having married in 1667, set up his own home and workshop, within the next two or three years, opposite the west corner of the Church of St. Dominic, close by the house of Niccolo Amati. Next door, lived the Guarnerius family. Thus within a stone's throw of one another lived the Amatii, the Guarnerii, and Stradivarius!

Now a strange thing occurred. During the following fifteen or twenty years, Stradivarius produced only a limited number of instruments, and, though signed by him, these reveal little to set them apart from the Amati tradition. Looking back on this period, in light of subsequent developments, we realize that it was a maturing time for Stradivarius; though we do not know whether, through traveling, he benefited by seeing many of the magnificent fruits of the Renaissance in Rome, Florence, Venice, or Naples; or whether, judging by the light of his own intellect, he matured. But we do know that in about 1690, a new Stradivarius appeared, a fore-shadowing of his triumphant self!

Although the Amati-relationship remained, distinctive characteristics made their appearance: the entire instrument became flatter, every inch of the arching was carefully determined, the FF holes snuggled gracefully to the natural contours, the purfling became a delicate line, and the varnish glowed in a fiery golden, or light red. And at the end of this period, there appeared what is known as "Long Strads," thus called because the FF holes, being placed fairly close together, gave the violins a lanky appearance.

From 1700 to 1725, Stradivarius created the violins that defy description or comparison. Nothing like them came before; nothing like them has appeared since. Beautiful to look at, they harbor a tone that seems to emerge from a fathomless sea; the wood gives evidence of having been chosen for its acoustical properties; the model is definitely flatter, with thicker wood throughout, though measuring at its deepest point—under the bridge—only about half an inch; the waist and other curves are more gracefully rounded; the FF holes are bold, yet graceful; and the varnish is a transparent red-gold.

Yet each instrument of this glorious period bears its own individuality; sometimes through the choice of wood; sometimes in general design; sometimes by means of the purfling forming a corner of its own instead of following the curved outline. But, regardless of the variations, they bear the stamp of their master-maker whose label reads, "Antonius Stradivarius Cremonensis faciebat Anno 17—."

The evening-tide—or last thirteen years of his life—although productive, showed a lessening of the wizard-skill. In fact, the violins of this period hark back in design to his apprentice days, as though he were carrying out the old adage of "returning to one's childhood." On the other hand, some of these instruments were doubtless finished by his pupils, none of whom ever acquired the magic touch.

Looking at a picture of Stradivarius's workshop, set atop the roof, open to the sun's blessing, we can imagine: Stradivarius, stooped with age, white of hair, wearing his traditional white leather apron, helping a pupil at this bench—another one, there—and fondly touching an instrument hung to dry on a special hook in the rafter.

There he lived, and worked—one day like the next filled with loving care—up to one year before his death, which occurred in 1737 when he was ninety-three years old. Buried in the Church of the Rosary, his body remained in death as in life within the small orbit of his workshop, but his spirit has traveled to the far corners of the earth on the wings of his glorious instruments.

Although none of Stradivarius's pupils developed the skill of their master, several of them were worthy followers, including his two sons—Francesco and Omobono—Carlo Bergonzi, and Lorenzo Guadagnini.

Carlo Bergonzi, born in 1690 at Cremona, the most noted, is supposed to have rented the Stradivarius house and workshop, where he and, subsequently, his two sons, Niccolo and Michaelangelo, worked.

Bergonzi's violins, although Stradivarian in character, display certain distinguishing characteristics of their own and are highly prized by violinists for their tone, which is both noble and refined. His instruments are flat, and broadish at the lower part; their scrolls are bold; the FF holes are set lower in the belly and closer to the edge of the violin than those of Stradivarius. The varnish is always rich and transparent, but it varies in color from amber to light or deep red. The labels read, "Anno 17—. Carlo Bergonzi fece in Cremona."

Now before leaving Cremona we shall pause for a moment with the last of the Amati-Stradivarius-Guarnerius trio—Joseph Guarnerius del Gesù. Unlike Stradivarius, Guarnerius did not live his days in beautiful proportion, but, on the contrary, worked fiendishly one day and squandered the next. One side of his nature blazed with the fire of genius; the other, with an urge of destruction.

Born on October 17, 1686, the son of Joannes Guarnerius—brother of Andrea who studied with Niccolo Amati—Joseph Guarnerius del Gesù did not grow up from the cradle in fiddle making, for his father was never connected with the craft. In fact, thus far there is no proof that the famous Guarnerius ever had a teacher, though it was thought for many years that he was a pupil of Stradivarius. Modern authorities discount this assumption: inasmuch as Guarnerius's first violins are too crude to show the slightest relationship to so great a teacher; and his later—magnificent ones—are too completely original.

Be that as it may, living as they did—the Amati, the Stradivarius and the Guarnerius families—within a stone's throw of one another, it seems likely that young Joseph took a peek now and then into the great Antonio's workshop!

Mystery envelops Guarnerius's entire life; and his work was practically lost to the world until Paganini, in 1820, discovered Joseph Guarnerius del Gesù violins. Looking into the few facts known about this great violin maker, we find that he was man-grown before violins appeared under his label; and these, as has been indicated, were decidedly inferior affairs, poor, both in choice of wood and workmanship. Genuine improvements appeared in the second period. The model was small and gently sloping, with a long narrow waist; the scroll bold and well cut; the FF holes conspicuously curled; and the varnish of a warm golden brown.

Then Guarnerius came into his own for a brief and glorious period, during which time his instruments—whether large or small—were of an unrivaled brilliance both in tone and workmanship. These violins are fairly thick in both back and belly; broad in the waist with long, elegant inner bouts and long, perpendicular FF holes. The scroll is magnificently curved, and the varnish—like the tone—brilliant, beyond compare.

A blight then seems to have fallen on this glorious fiddle maker; for the violins made during the last years of his life are carelessly wrought and imperfectly finished. Legend has it that, thrown into prison for debt, he was befriended by the jailer's daughter, who, taking pity on his plight, smuggled tools and materials into his cell in order that he might continue his work. Thus these last badly cut violins with their stiff scrolls, irregular purfling and awkward sound holes are called "Prison Fiddles," "Drunken Josephs," or "Servant Violins."

Henri Poidras, however, in his *Dictionary of Violin Makers* asserts that it is much more likely that Guarnerius retired to a monastery—a supposition in keeping with the maker's signature—and as Mr. Poidras remarks, "The appellation 'Monastery Violins' would certainly be more respectful to his memory."

The famous label reads, "Joseph Guarnerius fecit, Cremonae, Anno 17—." +
I H S

Bidding good-by to Cremona, we shall briefly consider the one early fiddle maker outside of Italy—with the exception of Gasparo Duiffoprugcar—whose name belongs to the Immortal Ones. This is Jakob Stainer, born on July 14, 1621—twenty-three years before the birth of Stradivarius—at Absam in the Austrian Tyrol.

Almost as much mystery surrounds the life of Jakob Stainer as does that of Joseph Guarnerius del Gesù. Born into the humble home of poor mountain peasants, he began, as a shepherd-boy, first, to make unusual wood-wind instruments and, then, violins.

Although it was thought for some time that Stainer studied, perhaps briefly, with Niccolo Amati at Cremona, there is no proof that he ever went farther from Absam than Innsbruck, the Tyrolian capital beyond Hall, the nearest town to his birthplace; with the exception of one visit to Salzburg, the year before the birth of Stradivarius, to deliver an instrument of his making.

Was he then just a born-instrument maker? Did the songs made by the rustling leaves, mountain streams, and chattering birds inspire his efforts as he watched the sheep as a boy? Was the finished craft suggested to him by hearing and seeing the glorious violins from Cremona played at the Court of the Archduke Leopold at Innsbruck? Questions these must remain.

At all events Jakob Stainer was soon making violins in great numbers that recalled those of the Cremonese masters. Attracting the attention of the Archduke Leopold, these instruments so greatly impressed him that he made Stainer his court violin maker.

But poor fellow, he was destined to enjoy little comfort from his title and prodigious work. Having married at twenty-three a woman, who, legend has it, was more of a burden than a help-mate to him, and having become a father of nine children, Jakob Stainer found himself hopelessly in debt. Some accounts say that he was thrown into prison where he made the famous "Elector Stainers," so called from the fact that they were supposedly sent to the Electors and Leopold—now the Emperor—in a vain attempt to secure their help. Some historians claim that these "Elector Stainers" were not even made by Stainer; others, that he made them in a monastery; but at any event, there seems little doubt that his last days were spent as a raving maniac. And there is a stone bench at Absam where he is supposed to have been bound during his periods of violence.

Thus he is supposed to have died—a pitiful artist, bereft of the blessings of work—at the age of sixty-two.

Stainer violins—more widely copied than any others—are highly individual. "Tubby" is the word often applied to them, for their arching is particularly high in the center of the belly; their scrolls, sometimes finished with an animal's head, are at other times, made broad and short; the FF holes are narrow, and rounded at top and bottom; the workmanship is excellent; and the varnish of a beautiful rose-color. Most authorities speak of the tone as being pure and lovely, and at the same time, powerful; but the Stainer-tone has occasionally been described as "Screaming." We shall suppose that the instruments responsible for such a disgraceful appellation were copies and not genuine "Stainers."

The label reads, "Jacobus Stainer in Absam, prope Oenipontum 16—."

Now we have come to the parting-of-the-way with the glorious violin makers of the past. Other makers have appeared, in every country in the world, since this Cremona period; fine violins have been made over the intervening years; and, as we have indicated, engineers may one day turn out super-efficient fiddles; but when all is said and done, the cradle of violin making remains—Cremona!

ONE OF THE TWENTY-FOUR VIOLINS OF THE KING

VIOLIN MUSIC AND VIOLIN PLAYERS

CREMONA AND CORELLI! Two names known by anyone familiar with the violin's background; but, in the case of Corelli, as well as that of Cremona, facts contradict the common conception of violin-pioneering.

Corelli was, indeed, the founder of the Roman School of violin playing, which is directly linked with performers of today, but, since he was not born until 1653, and, as we know, the violin had appeared at least one hundred years previous to that, *something* must have been played on this upstart-instrument and *someone* must have done the playing!

Facts about the violin's earliest music and players have remained clouded in mystery largely because of the instrument's lowly beginning: strolling players, jugglers, tavern musicians, and the like nurtured the seed of violin's Stradivarius-state.

We do know, however, a few violin-pioneers previous to Corelli; and others come to light with the years. Andrea Gabrieli—an organist and chorister—born about 1510 at Venice, is credited with having first used the violin specifically in any composition; Claudio Monteverdi—pioneer in various musical fields, particularly opera, born in 1567 at Cremona, when Andrea Amati was establishing the Cremona School of violin making—used the violin for dramatic effects in his opera, or music drama, *Orfeo*, performed in 1607 at Mantua, Italy; Biagio Marini—a pupil of Monteverdi—born in 1597 at Brescia, is credited with writing the earliest violin sonata; and Carlo Farina—born in the early seventeenth century at Mantua—composed in 1627 a *Cappricio Stravaganta*, known as the first genuine violin piece.

It was, in fact, so *genuine*—in its use of the violin to imitate realistically various animal sounds and extraneous noises—that it set for some time, unfortunately, the standard for violin music.

Looking further we find that Giovanni Legrenzi—born in 1626 at Clusone, near Bergamo, Italy—an important composer of chamber music, was one of the first to write for two violins and violoncello; and Tomasso Albinoni, violinist, born in 1674 at Venice, composed—in addition to nearly fifty operas—excellent music for the violin.

Then we are reminded that France was interested in the violin from its beginning. We find that some time during the latter half of the sixteenth century she attracted to her country as court musician to Catherine de Medici the greatest violinist of his day—an Italian with a number of wonderful names. He is listed in Grove's *Dictionary of Music and Musicians* as: "Baltzarini," followed by "Baldassaro da Belgioioso." But we learn that when he arrived in France he changed his name to Balthasard de Beaujoyeulx. This jolly gentleman—in addition to fiddling away to his heart's content—contributed to the creation of the *Ballet comique de la Reine*, a dramatic ballet, given in 1581, considered the forerunner of French opera.

Three German names stand out in the history of the violin's early days: Thomas Baltzar—born about 1630, at Lübeck—considered the greatest violinist of his time; Heinrich Biber—born on August 12, 1644, at Wartenberg, Bohemia—one of the founders of the German School of violin playing and a composer of distinction; and Johann Jakob Walther, violinist and composer, born in 1650 at Witterda, near Erfurt, who, according to modern scholars—though remembered chiefly because of the technical demands in his compositions—merits consideration for some of his violin sonatas.

In 1655 Thomas Baltzar migrated to England where he made a sensational impression, according to various contemporary reports including one that refers to him as running his fingers up to the end of the finger board and quickly back again—"and in very good tune"—the like of which England had not previously seen.

This remark, incidentally, reminds us that "playing in tune" is still the mark of a good violinist; for the violinist must know how to produce the desired tone without any help except his own natural or practiced-ear. And, like Thomas Baltzar, the good violinist must move upward or downward within three octaves of smooth, rippling tone without offending the *ear* of his listener.

Violin Music and Violin Players

Although Thomas Baltzar did not live to a great age, this German-born "wonder" on the violin was largely responsible for making the violin a respectable instrument in England; and he left some creditable music to honor his name.

Another "foreigner" who contributed to the violin's introduction to polite English society was Nicola Matteis, an Italian violinist and guitar player, who is thought to have gone to England about 1672. According to contemporary reports, Matteis would have provided just competition for the amazing Baltzar: In Evelyn's famous *Diary* the author refers to Matteis's playing as resembling "a consort of several instruments"; while Roger North, in *The Musical Grammarian*, reports that "his Audience was not only pleased but full of wonder at him and his way of performing." And this same author mentions "some books of lessons for his scholars," referring to Matteis's *Ayers for the Violin*, one of the rare and important items in music literature.

England was long reputed to have been reluctant to accept the advent of the violin—that maker of "High-Priz'd-Noise," as described by Thomas Mace in his work, *Musik's Monument*, published in 1676; but scholarly research has somewhat refuted this assumption.

Although no very early English music for the violin as a solo instrument has been unearthed, more and more early part-music is recognized to include the violin in its scheme of things. Some of Orlando Gibbons' music, as well as that of Coperario, is now considered scored to include the violin. Gibbons was born in 1583 and died in 1625; while Coperario, who changed his name from plain John Cooper, after a visit to Italy, was born in about 1570 and died in 1627.

Other early English composers—who used the violin—include: John Jenkins, born in 1592; Henry Butler, born about 1630; Christopher Simpson, a famous violist, born about 1610; and William Young, who died in 1672, about whose early life little is known except that—while in the employ of the Archduke of Austria in 1653 at Innsbruck—he published the part-books of a collection of eleven sonatas.

Who knows but that the ill-fated violin maker, Jakob Stainer, may have been inspired by hearing the music of William Young at Innsbruck!

Returning to England in about 1660, William Young entered the band of

King Charles II as flute player. Appointed violinist the following year, he, henceforth, devoted himself to court duties and composition. His music is often referred to as "Purcellian," though at the time of Young's death in 1672 England's greatest composer—Henry Purcell—violinistically honored for his "Golden Sonata" was but a boy.

Turning our thoughts back to Italy, we find a few more names that deserve attention. Among these are Bartolomeo Girolamo Laurenti, violinist and composer, born about 1644 at Bologna; Antonio Veracini, born about the same time, who wrote violin sonatas that reveal a definite advance in violin technique; Giovanni Battista Fontana, born at Brescia, another pioneer both in violin playing and composing; and Cristano Farinelli, violinist and composer, born about 1650, famous, particularly in England, for a "Follia."

One of the most significant pioneers of this period was Giuseppe Torelli, regarded as the originator of the solo concerto for violin. Born about 1650 at Verona, Italy, he spent a great part of his life in Germany where he helped lay the foundation of the German School of violin playing.

Then we must not forget Jean Baptist Lully—born on November 29, 1632, at Florence, known as the founder of French grand opera—whose violin playing and conducting at the French court, where he was taken as a young boy, set the standard of precise performance taken for granted in our modern orchestra. First admitted to the famous orchestra, *Les 24 violons du roi*, then under Louis XIV, Lully later gained permission to organize his own corps, *les petits violons*, soon regarded as the finest orchestra in France.

An outstanding feature of the group was the *premier coup d'archet*, or first stroke of the bow; Lully, having trained the players to begin in unison—like the twentieth century "Roxettes." And although one hundred years later Wolfgang Amadeus Mozart was to write to his father that this feat inaugurated by Lully amounted to nothing unusual—writing, "they begin well together as they do in other places"—it was in Lully's time a genuine innovation.

Twenty-one years after Lully's birth there was born that violinist whose name is directly linked to the violin players of our own day—Arcangelo Corelli. Born on February 17, 1653, at Fusignano, in the district of Bologna, Corelli, after appearing as violinist in various other cities—including Munich—settled in Rome where he founded the Roman School of violin

Violin Music and Violin Players

playing. In both playing and composing Corelli appears to have been the first to realize the violin's distinguishing feature—its ability to *sing*—the quality so perfectly demonstrated in his familiar *La Follia*.

Pupils flocked to Corelli from far and near, a few of whom contributed links in the chain of violin development. The one whose influence stretched the furthest was Giovanni Battista Somis, born in 1686 on Christmas Day at Piedmont, who, after studying first with Corelli and later with Antonio Vivaldi at Venice, founded the Piedmontese School of violin playing.

Other Corelli pupils were: Francesco Geminiani, born in 1687 at Lucca, who, later settling in London, published the earliest known violin method—*The Art of Playing on the Violin*—based on Corelli's principles; Pietro Locatelli—probably the first violin-virtuoso—born on September 3, 1693, at Bergamo, who, after studying with Corelli and making many sensational concert appearances, settled at Amsterdam, having established himself as the "Paganini" of his day; Baptiste Anet, who carried the Corelli method in about 1700 to Paris; and Pietro Castrucci, born in 1689 at Rome, who, in 1715 went to London as leader of Handel's opera orchestra.

Thus we see that Corelli's pupils, going their separate ways, spread afar the master's gospel of the *singing* tone.

Meanwhile let us pause for a moment with Antonio Vivaldi with whom Corelli's pupil, Giovanni Battista Somis, studied. Born between 1675 and 1678 at Venice, Vivaldi studied the violin; first, with his father, a violinist at St. Mark's in Venice; and later, with Giovanni Legrenzi. A man with a very colorful personality, Vivaldi pursued many paths including that of the priesthood, violin teaching at a girls' school, concert-giving, and opera-composing; but above all, he is remembered as an instrumental composer, one whose concertos served as models for the great Johann Sebastian Bach.

Another important pioneer was Francesco Maria Veracini—nephew of the earlier Veracini—born on February 1, 1690, at Florence. Brilliant violinist and composer, Veracini greatly influenced the next violinist to attract our attention: Giuseppe Tartini, founder of the Paduan School of violin playing and composer of the famous sonata, *The Devil's Trill* and the important work, *Art of Bowing*, consisting of fifty variations on a theme by Corelli. The story goes that Tartini—born on April 8, 1692, at Pirano in Istria, Italy—largely self-taught on the violin, gained the impetus for his remarkable achievements by hearing Veracini play at Venice.

We shall learn more about Tartini later, but meanwhile let us concern ourselves with a few of his pupils. Pietro Nardini, Tartini's favorite pupil, who nursed Tartini in his last illness, was born on April 12, 1722, at Leghorn. His violin playing was highly regarded—as reported by Leopold Mozart and others—and he wrote some distinguished music including the beautiful D major Sonata. Domenico Ferrari, another pupil, born early in the eighteenth century at Piacenza, is credited with being the first to make significant use of harmonics on the violin.

But now we arrive at the link that united the various Italian schools from which sprang the Modern School of violin playing. This key figure is Gaetano Pugnani, born on November 27, 1731, at Turin. The most important pupil of Somis of Piedmont, who, as we remember, was a pupil of both Corelli and Vivaldi, Pugnani, recognizing the value of Tartini's contributions to the art of violin playing, also studied with the Paduan master for a time. Benefiting by contact with both schools, Pugnani became a distinguished violinist and composer, traveled widely, and eventually opened a school at Turin from which were graduated various pupils who did him credit.

Among these pupils were Antonio Conforti, Antonio Bartolomeo Bruni, Giambattista Polledro, and the one who was destined to weave from the combined threads of Italian violin playing a magic carpet spread out to our very doorstep—Giovanni Battista Viotti.

Born on May 23, 1753, just one hundred years after Corelli, Giovanni Battista Viotti brought the violin to a glorious flowering. A gifted virtuoso from boyhood, he traveled widely, making France his home during his most creative years. Fired by the tremendous achievements of his contemporaries, Haydn and Mozart, he wrote music that paved the way for the large violin concerto.

Since we shall devote a chapter to this great violinist, composer, and teacher, we shall only mention here that his most famous pupil, Pierre Rode, born on February 6, 1774, at Bordeaux, France, together with Rodolphe Kreutzer and Pierre Baillot—under Viotti's influence—laid the foundation of the Modern French School of violin playing. Their combined *Violin Method* is known throughout the violin world; while Rode's *Twenty-four Caprices* usually follow—as the night the day—every violin student's study of Kreutzer's famous *Forty Etudes or Caprices.*

Although neither Pierre Baillot nor Rodolphe Kreutzer was actually a pupil of Viotti both were inspired by his playing, and each benefited from association with him. Born on November 16, 1766, at Versailles, Rodolphe Kreutzer when but a child began to study the violin with his father; later, he studied with Anton Stamitz, an exponent of the Mannheim School of violin playing the principles of which are embodied in Leopold Mozart's important *Violin Method*. When sixteen—at the recommendation of Marie Antoinette—Kreutzer was made first violinist of the King's Chapel. Each year brought new opportunities, new honors; and he composed a vast amount of music including many operas.

But the name *Kreutzer* lives eternally through two titles: his own famous *Forty Etudes or Caprices* and Beethoven's "Kreutzer" Sonata; the latter, strangely enough, though dedicated to him, he is supposed never to have played.

Pierre Marie Francois de Sales Baillot, who, fortunately, did not always use this full roster of names, was born on October 1, 1771, at Passy, near Paris. When very young he began to study the violin with an Italian named Polidori. At nine he became the pupil of a French violinist, Sainte-Marie, who laid the foundation of his characteristically sensitive and artistic violin playing. A year later the youth had an opportunity to hear Viotti play one of his concertos, an experience that was to remain a constant challenge; and at the death of his father, Baillot was fortunate in attracting the attention of a benefactor who made it possible for him to study the violin in Italy with Pollani, a pupil of Nardini.

At twenty Pierre Baillot went to Paris where Viotti, impressed with his playing, secured him a place in a theatre orchestra. But, apparently still dubious of earning a living with his violin, Baillot took a minor position in the Ministry of Finance; continuing, fortunately, his violin studies. Finally, having gained recognition as a concert violinist, he was appointed professor of violin at the Paris Conservatory. There he found an outlet for his great talents as artist and teacher.

In addition to the famous "Method," written in collaboration with Rode and Kreutzer, Baillot is chiefly remembered for his *L'Art du Violin* and his contribution to the artistic playing of chamber music. François-Antoine Habeneck, and Charles Dancla were among his pupils.

Here we must remind ourselves that—although Viotti and his associates are credited with founding the Modern French School of violin playing—Pierre Gaviniés—called by Viotti "the French Tartini"—is considered the founder of the earlier French School of violin playing. Gaviniés, born on May 26, 1726, at Bordeaux, largely self-taught, became a popular concert performer and teacher; and in 1795 was appointed violin professor at the Paris Conservatory where he attracted many distinguished pupils. Every modern violin student is familiar with his *24 Matinées*, studies for the violin in all the keys.

Now let us consider that unique type of violin player—the virtuoso—the one who glorifies technique above all else. The first in this category, as we know, was Corelli's pupil, Pierre Locatelli; another, was Antonio Lolli, born about 1730 at Bergamo. Admitted to be a bad musician, Antonio Lolli, traveling from court to court throughout Europe, made light of the virtue of playing music the way it was written. But his listeners were forced to admit that he *could* play the violin; for his tremendous feats of bowing, unheard-of velocity, witch-like imitations of animal sounds, and magnificent tone held them spellbound.

Like his playing, the course of Lolli's life went from the heights to the depths: he died in 1802 in Sicily, a forgotten man.

But the Lolli-legend lived and bore fruit. Time was destined to produce, about fifty years later, the King of Violin Virtuosos—Niccolo Paganini. None who came before had approached his technique; none who followed ever attained or surpassed it. Both a great contribution and a tremendous hazard to the art of violin playing, Paganini's wizardly skill swept all before it.

Fortunately several of Paganini's contemporaries served as balance wheels for this virtuoso-fever. Among these was Louis Spohr, born two years after Paganini at Brunswick, Germany. Able violinist—with a quiet, singing style—romantic composer, and capable conductor, Spohr was also a gifted teacher.

Ferdinand David, born on January 19, 1810, at Hamburg, was Spohr's most noted pupil. Combining the solid virtues of Spohr's training with certain elements of modern technique, David became an outstanding figure in the violin world; and it was for him that Mendelssohn wrote his famous violin concerto.

Among David's distinguished pupils was the virtuoso-violinist, August Wilhelmj, concertmaster of the Bayreuth orchestra, when, in 1876 Wagner's great "Ring Cycle" was given its first performance.

David also exerted a marked influence on the master-violinist, Joseph Joachim, during the latter's stay in Leipzig. It was Joachim—whose career we shall later treat more fully—who became the leading influence in German violin playing after the death of Ferdinand David in 1873. Settling in Berlin, Joachim was responsible for transferring the center of Germany's violin prestige from Leipzig to Berlin.

We must remind ourselves, however, that Joachim's name belongs first of all to what is known as the Vienna School of violin playing; for he was the pupil of Joseph Boehm, born on March 4, 1795, at Pest, Hungary, who, after studying the violin with Pierre Rode and establishing himself as a concert violinist, was appointed violin professor at the Vienna Conservatory. Although the Vienna School of violin playing had long existed, Boehm was destined to give it world renown through the triumphs of his many distinguished pupils.

Among his students, in addition to Joachim, was Heinrich Wilhelm Ernst, born on May 6, 1814, at Brünn, in Moravia. Greatly influenced by hearing Paganini play, Ernst, at sixteen, while on a concert tour, followed the exciting artist from town to town in order to study Paganini's extraordinary feats of technique. Fortunately his own poetic nature, plus Boehm's sound musical training, saved him from becoming a slave to the Paganini tradition: "Paganini's art spiritualised," is the way his playing has been described by Paul Stoeving, an eminent violinist, composer, and author of several important books on the violin.

Still another Boehm pupil was Eduard Reményi, born on July 17, 1830, at Miskolcz, Hungary, who, shortly after finishing his studies with Joseph Boehm at the Vienna Conservatory, was banished from Austria because of his political activities. Going to America, he gave concerts hither and yon. Back in Germany, he took Johannes Brahms with him on a tour; later, fell under the guidance of Franz Liszt at Weimar; and next, became solo violinist to Queen Victoria. Then one triumph followed another, as he eventually gave concerts all over the world. Reményi's style resulted from a sense of color and rhythm—bequeathed him by his Hungarian ancestry—joined to perfect technique.

Before leaving the Vienna School of violin playing we must mention the fact that several modern concert violinists stem from this source. One important link is Leopold Auer, born in Hungary on June 7, 1845, a student of both the Pest and Vienna Conservatories; and later, of Joachim. Establishing himself in Russia, after having filled several important musical positions in several German cities, Auer thoroughly identified himself with the New Russian School of violin playing. A list of his pupils include Mischa Elman, Efrem Zimbalist, Eddy Brown, Kathleen Parlow, Nathan Milstein, and Jascha Heifetz.

Let us now turn back to the violinist—known as the founder of the Modern Franco-Belgian School of violin playing—Auguste de Bériot. Born on February 20, 1802, at Louvain, de Bériot received his early instruction on the violin from a Louvain teacher by the name of Tiby, who, upon the death of the youth's parents, became his guardian. At nine de Bériot successfully performed a Viotti concerto at a public concert; then, while steadily developing in the art of violin playing, he acquired a philosophy of persistence and integrity under the tutelage of a noted scholar by the name of Jacatot.

Going to Paris at nineteen, he came under the influence of Viotti and Baillot—without identifying himself with the classical French School of violin playing—and soon made a tremendously successful Paris début. Following this, he was warmly received in England; and on his return to Belgium, he was made solo violinist to the King of the Netherlands.

Later, after making many concert tours, recognized as one of the outstanding violinists of his time, de Bériot was offered on the death of Baillot, the latter's post at the Paris Conservatory; but he chose, instead, the violin professorship at the Brussels Conservatory: a position he held from 1843 to 1852 when the failure of his eyesight forced him to retire.

Charles de Bériot's violin playing has been described as a blending of the classical and Paganini-style: "grace" and "elegance," being the words most often used to describe it. His influence was wide in his day; and his principles were handed down by many distinguished pupils, including Henri Vieuxtemps and Emil Sauret.

Henri Vieuxtemps, born on February 20, 1820, at Verviers, Belgium, having begun to give concerts at eight, studied with de Bériot at Brussels for a year. Later, while touring, he studied harmony and composition at Vienna and Paris; and eventually he and his many compositions became world famous. For a time he was soloist to the Czar of Russia and violin professor at the St. Petersburg Conservatory. Following a second trip to America, he was made violin professor at the Brussels Conservatory, where his influence was far-reaching. Unfortunately, two years later a stroke necessitated his relinquishing his career as a virtuoso; though, after his partial recovery, he still continued to teach.

Vieuxtemps greatly influenced several violinists, including Jenö Hubay and Eugène Ysaÿe. Jenö Hubay—originally a pupil of Joachim—born on September 14, 1858, at Budapest, attracted Vieuxtemps' interest when he first appeared in a concert in Paris. Having come under the French-Belgian influence, Hubay held for a time the post of principal violinist at the Brussels Conservatory; and then, assumed a similar position at the Budapest Conservatory, succeeding his father who had been his first teacher. A distinguished string-quartet player, Hubay also composed a great deal of music. In referring to one of his pieces, Phyllis Moore Snow, a modern violinist and teacher, has stated, "Hubay's solo 'Hyre Kati'—meaning 'Bad Girl'—is played by every enterprising student."

Joseph Szigeti—the fiery virtuoso—Emil Telmányi, and Eddy Brown were among Hubay's many pupils.

Still another Belgian violinist helped to weave the chain of violin playing—Joseph Lambert Massart—one of the teachers of the much-loved modern violinist, Fritz Kreisler. Born on July 19, 1811, at Liége, Belgium, Massart, after studying with a local teacher, was granted a scholarship by the authorities of his native city, enabling him to go to Paris to study. Following a rebuff from the Paris Conservatory—"because he was a foreigner"—he attracted the attention of Rodolphe Kreutzer who willingly took him in hand.

Excessively shy, Massart—though a genuine artist—never became a popular concert performer; but his talents, fortunately, were not wasted: in 1843 he was appointed violin professor at the Paris Conservatory. This position, enabling Massart to develop to his full capacity, provided inspiration to many distinguished pupils who were destined to gain world renown. Included among these, in addition to Fritz Kreisler, were Henri Wieniawski—whose name is known to every violin student—and Charles Martin Loeffler, violinist and composer, born on January 30, 1861, at Mulhouse, Alsace, who, in turn, became the teacher of Arthur Martinus Hartmann.

Artistically unique among modern violinists, Arthur Hartmann, born on July 23, 1881, at Maté Szalka, Hungary, taken to Philadelphia at an early age, first studied the violin with his father; then, with M. van Gelder; and finally, with Loeffler. Beginning to play in public when but a child, he had, at twelve, mastered practically the entire modern violin literature.

Despite the possible handicap of a career begun as a child-prodigy, Hartmann developed into an unusually mature artist, composer, and teacher; and eventually gave concerts throughout the United States, Europe, and Canada. His critical essay on Bach's *Chaconne*—translated into fourteen languages—is an artistic achievement in itself; and his transcriptions, instead of being mere arrangements, are "original" in the sense that he infused the pieces—chosen with an ear to their violin possibilities—intended for the voice or other instruments, with his own artistic conception.

Claude Debussy, the great French Impressionist composer, pleased with Hartmann's transcriptions of his song, *Il pleure dans mon coeur,* and piano piece, *La Fille aux cheve aux de lin,* offered to write a violin *Poèm* especially for him. The combination of composer and violinist, spiritually akin, held forth promise of a unique addition to the violin repertoire, but Debussy's ill health and early death prevented its realization.

Turning to sunny Spain, we find a name that is glorious in violin history— Pablo de Sarasate. Still another product of the Franco-Belgian school, Sarasate—born on March 10, 1844, at Pamplona, Spain—added luster to its name by carrying his singing-virtuoso playing throughout the world.

To Norway the violin world is indebted for the fantastic, largely self-taught Ole Bull, born in 1810, at Bergen. Rumania is credited with, among others, Georges Enesco, composer and violinist, born on August 19, 1881, at Liveni, teacher of the great modern artist, Yehudi Menuhin. From Greece came the eminent violinist, teacher, and writer—D. C. Dounis—born in 1887 at Athens. The Bohemian violinist, Otaker Sevčik, born on March 22, 1852, at Horażdowitz, carved revolutionary paths in violin playing and teaching, best exemplified in his pupil, Jan Kubelík. And America contributed to violin artistry, among many others, the distinguished violinist—Maude Powell—born on August 22, 1868, at Peru, Illinois, who artistically combined the mingled heritage of study with William Lewis at Chicago, Henry Schradieck at Leipzig, Charles Dancla at the Paris Conservatory, and Joseph Joachim at Berlin.

Thus, like a great family tree, the Roman School of violin playing has spread its branches to all corners of the world; but, more like a snowball rolling, it has gathered up strength and variety in the process.

It is in the matter of repertoire that the concert violinist has moved furthest from his forebears. Never ignoring the vast study-literature left by the great violinists, and frequently including some of their compositions on his programs, the modern concert player draws heavily on the master-composers for his repertoire.

The great Johann Sebastian Bach attracts first attention with his incomparable sonatas for solo violin; while his famous *Chaconne* evokes every artist's best efforts. Then the violinist may choose immortal music from Handel, Haydn, and Mozart; but it is to Ludwig van Beethoven, for his glorious concerto in D that the concert violinist pays highest homage. Nothing has surpassed it, although Mendelssohn's beautiful concerto in E minor belongs in like-company; and Johannes Brahms' concerto in D for violin and orchestra—considered "unplayable" at first—merits comparison.

Also, the following composers are among those who have contributed distinguishing concertos to the violinist's repertoire: Camille Saint-Saëns, Max Bruch, Peter Ilyitch Tchaikovsky, Édouard Lalo, Alexander Glazounov, Antonin Dvořák, Edward Elgar, Jean Sibelius, and Sergei Prokofiev.

But, whether appearing as a solo instrument or as part of a great orchestra, the violin, lovingly known as the fiddle, once the stepchild among musical instruments, now reigns supreme in the concert kingdom!

ARCANGELO CORELLI

Arcangelo Corelli—the founder of the Roman School of violin playing from which all modern violinists stem—was born on February 17, 1653, at Fusignano, near Imola, in the district of Bologna, Italy. Coming about one hundred years after the known-appearance of the violin, Corelli, gathering up all the threads of violin-experience previous to his time and weaving with them his own particular magic, was destined to establish the violin's purpose: He made of it a singing instrument, the lilt of whose voice is "like unto the tongue of angels."

For many years we had been accustomed to read that little was known about Corelli's early life; but, finally, modern research somewhat changed the story. No longer need Corelli be called an "angel" without mortal ties, for, we now know that he had a grandfather whose name was Ippolito Corelli, a father whose name was Arcangelo like his own, a mother whose family name was Santa Raffini, and many brothers and sisters!

Little Arcangelo was among the younger members of a large family. Two of his brothers' names are known—Ippolito and Giancinto—and Giancinto's family tree can be traced to our day.

The future Angel-of-the-violin received his first musical education at Faenza; and since his grandfather was a respected nobleman at Faenza it is reasonable to suppose that "Grandfather Ippolito" early took the young Arcangelo under his wing. As we look back in history how often we must be reminded of the importance of grandfathers—and of grandmothers!

Be that as it may, at thirteen young Corelli went from Faenza to Bologna where he received his first lessons on the violin. Bologna, alive with lore of the violin's beginning! What a wonderful place! What a wonderful moment for an eager young student!

But here we come to one of the controversial spots in Corelli's record: Who were his teachers? One historian after another has stated that he was the pupil of Giovanni Battista Bassani; but since Bassani was at least four years younger than Corelli this does not seem plausible. We do know that, after studying privately from 1666 to 1670, Corelli entered the Accademia Filharmonica. We also know that he studied under two violin teachers—Giovanni Benvenuti and Leonardo Bragnoli—both pupils of a famous violinist, Ercole Gaibara. And Matteo Simonelli has always been credited with teaching him counterpoint.

On leaving the Accademia Filharmonica, Corelli, eventually, went to Rome—the city forever gloriously linked with his name. But historians again differ: Did he go directly there? Or did he see a bit of the world first; Munich, possibly, and Paris, perhaps, where the fabulous Jean-Baptiste Lully was holding forth? At all events, he is known to have been one of four violinists at the Church of St. Louis of France in Rome in 1675.

And then, according to Chrysander, the music historian, Corelli spent some time in the company of Jean Baptiste Farinelli, Concertmaster to the Elector of Hanover in Germany. But sometime between 1681 and 1685 he returned to Rome where he remained, with the exception of visits to the courts of Modena and Naples, until his death.

Shortly after returning to Rome Corelli published his first work, a set of twelve sonatas. Soon the name *Corelli* was unsurpassed in Roman society; for as performer, composer and teacher, Arcangelo Corelli was recognized as the supreme artist. And true to the custom of that time, he came under the protection of noble patronage; first, that of Cardinal Benedetto Panfilio; later, that of Cardinal Pietro Ottoboni in whose palace he lived henceforth.

Cardinal Ottoboni, an outstanding art patron of his day, attracted to his palace artists, particularly musicians, from all parts of Europe; and it was indeed an honor to be chosen a permanent resident of his household. But Corelli more than justified such confidence: The concerts given every Monday at the Cardinal's palace under his direction became the most important musical events in Rome.

Visiting musicians sought out this great artist, pupils came to him in droves, and foreign Royalty, including Queen Christina of Sweden, paid him homage.

Arcangelo Corelli

For her he is supposed to have conducted an orchestra of one hundred and fifty musicians when she visited Rome.

Excessively shy and gentle in manner, Corelli was not always equal to some of the demands made upon him by more boisterous spirits. One such encounter occurred when George Frederick Handel, riding boldly on the crest of Italian hospitality, negotiated performances of two of his compositions at Cardinal Ottoboni's palace.

The story goes that, while Corelli was leading the orchestra for the overture to Handel's cantata, *Il Trionfo del Tempo e del Disinganno*, Handel tried desperately to explain to Corelli the way a certain section of the music should be played. Meeting with no success, Handel finally seized the violin from Corelli's hands and played the passage himself. Completely unruffled, Corelli remarked in his gentlest manner, "But, my dear Saxon, this music is in the French style, of which I have no experience."

Handel, curiously enough, had not written it in the "French Style," but, using two solo violins in his own Handelian version of the *concerto grosso*, had, on the contrary, anticipated commendation from Corelli.

Little did he realize that, though he and Corelli use the same form and instrument, their music would remain alien. Consequently, when his music, intended to be played with fire and vigor, came to life in Corelli's quiet, elegant, and refined style, Handel, being human and a man of action, knew only that he must take matters into his own hands!

Another such encounter occurred at Naples with disastrous results. For some time the King of Naples, impressed by glowing accounts of Corelli, had made overtures to enlist the services of this prince of violinists for his court. Finally persuaded, Corelli went to Naples, taking with him two violinists, and a violincello player, just in case the Neapolitan orchestra did not come up to his standards. Alas! he need not have been thus concerned, for the most competent orchestra in Italy—under the leadership of Alessandro Scarlatti—was at his disposal.

Imagine his surprise and delight on hearing his own music beautifully executed at the first rehearsal! Shedding his accustomed shyness, he impulsively exclaimed, "They can play at Naples!"

But his delight was destined to be short-lived. Although the King displayed mild interest at Corelli's first appearance, in a concert before the court, he was not enthusiastic; and subsequent events at rehearsals completely shattered Corelli's spirit.

They were rehearsing a composition by Scarlatti. Scarlatti was conducting. Cornelli, as guest soloist, was leading the players. All was progressing beautifully when, suddenly in a certain passage, Corelli played one thing and Petrillo, the Neapolitan leader, played another; that is, it sounded like two things! Petrillo, familiar with the music had played it correctly; while Corelli, possibly ruffled by something alien to the violin in the passage, had played it incorrectly.

Then came the final indignity!

When they took up the next piece of music, written in the key of C minor, Corelli, still disturbed by his unfortunate blunder, started it off in the key of C major. Whereupon Scarlatti, recovering from the shock, politely said, "Let us begin again!" Once more, Corelli began in C major. At which Scarlatti was forced to point out the mistake.

Humiliated, Corelli left Naples almost immediately.

Back in Rome, Corelli met with still further sorrow. During his absence a new violinist, Valentini, had won the public's fancy. Under normal circumstances, Corelli, confident of his own artistry and integrity, would have dismissed the newcomer as "just another violinist," but, in his humiliated state of mind, he became immediately convinced that Rome preferred Valentini to him. Although he had already carved a niche for himself in the history of the violin, never to be erased by "newcomers" of any age, Corelli was heartbroken at Rome's apparent slight.

Soon his health began to fail and, not many months after publishing his last work, he died, on January 8, 1713, at Rome. It can be justly said that Arcangelo Corelli died of a broken heart. But the tributes paid him after his death belied the assumption that he had been surpassed in the hearts of his countrymen.

He was buried in the Church of Santa Maria della Rotonda, not far from Raphael's tomb. Cardinal Ottoboni placed a marble monument with the inscription, *"Corelli princeps musicorum"* over his grave. And for many years the anniversary of his death was commemorated in a service of Corelli music, conducted by one of his pupils. Today his statue stands in the Vatican.

But statues and monuments do not, of course, guarantee communion with the Immortals. Time alone does that; time, and the living contribution of the candidate for such glory. Corelli's bid for fame held triple promise; and time has more than justified the claim. A pioneer in violin playing, composing, and teaching, he set a standard in all three, so that when the name *Corelli* appears today we immediately think of the violin, just as when the name *Chopin* occurs, we at once think of the piano.

In calling Corelli a pioneer, we must modify the statement somewhat. It is not that he necessarily *invented* so much, but that he crystalized the various possibilities of his chosen instrument. And it is to his everlasting credit that, probing the depths of the violin, he found its soul which is its voice. After Corelli came stauncher technique, elaboration, but he established the principles of violin bowing and playing so that never again need the violin imitate this thing or that, but live in its own glorious element as a singing instrument!

Attracting pupils from near and far, Corelli distributed the benefits of his conclusions to all parts of Europe; while these pupils in turn passed them on to posterity. Baptiste Anet went to France and Poland; Francesco, Geminiani, influential in England, published the earliest known violin method, based on Corelli's principles, *The Art of Playing on the Violin*; Pietro Locatelli, traveling far and wide, finally settling in Amsterdam, laid the foundation of the world's "Paganinis"; while Giovanni Battista Somis, uniting Corelli's principles with those of Vivaldi from Venice, founded the Piedmontese School of violin playing at Turin, the off-shoots of which are still spreading.

Coming to Corelli's music we find the crystalization-principle particularly well illustrated; for he established the form of the violin sonata and that of the *concerto grosso*, and provided models for the writing of the violin solo.

Before discussing the characteristics of these forms of music, it is well for us to remember that vocal music preceded instrumental music; also, in early times, "good" music concerned itself exclusively with the Church. But within the century previous to Corelli's time instrumental music began to develop an independent form; and secular music, as opposed to sacred, or church, music began to assert itself.

The first major break from the Church—excepting the madrigal, an elaborate vocal composition of several parts—appeared in the secular cantata and opera. The next apparently came about by accident in this way: as madrigals became more elaborate it became the custom to accompany the voice parts with viols; from this practice developed the situation of permitting the viols to make music of their own. These instrumental compositions in one movement, known as canzonas, soon became the natural habitat of the violin.

Then there developed the more elaborate sonata, or sound-piece, as opposed to cantata, or singing-piece. And of these there were two kinds: the *sonata da chiesa*, the church sonata, and the *sonata da camera*, or chamber sonata. At first these were little more than suites of music in which the various parts had little relationship to one another. It fell to the lot of Arcangelo Corelli to develop a general outline, or pattern, that united the separate units into what we know as the violin sonata.

Corelli published at least sixty sonatas, divided into three kinds: twenty-four church sonatas, twenty-four chamber sonatas, and twelve solo sonatas. His church and chamber sonatas usually have four movements; the first one slow; the others alternating, with the fourth the liveliest of all. In the chamber sonatas this movement is usually in the form of a gavotte or gigue. Although some of his sonatas, particularly the chamber sonatas, still bear likeness to the suite-form, especially within the movements themselves, Corelli definitely led the way toward a unified, balanced sonata-form that some of his successors were destined to perfect. And in his solo sonatas Corelli set a standard for all time.

Turning to the background of the *concerto grosso*, we find that a concerted form of instrumental music, with the echo principle of a small group of instruments answering a large one, developed during the close of the seventeenth century. But once again, Corelli was destined to tie the various experiments together. In his twelve *Concerti Grossi, opus 6,* published in 1712, he definitely established the form of the *concerto grosso*.

Add to all of this his famous "La Follia," in the form of theme and variations, and we can plainly see why Arcangelo Corelli's name is eternally linked with the violin.

ANTONIO VIVALDI

Antonio Vivaldi, whose name is forever linked with that of the great Johann Sebastian Bach, was born about 1675 at Venice. Born less than twenty-five years after Arcangelo Corelli, the Roman classical master, Antonio Vivaldi was destined, artistically, to forge forward into the modern world.

Son of Giovanni Battista Vivaldi, an eminent violinist in the Ducal Chapel at St. Mark's in Venice, Antonio began early to study the violin with his father. And judging from a report in the *Visitor's Guide to Venice*, dated many years later, the young boy could not have had a better teacher. This is the way a traveler-to-Venice was introduced to the Vivaldis' playing: "Among the best who play the violin are Giovanni Baptiste Vivaldi and his son, priest."

Reading this recommendation, we are immediately struck with the fact that the younger Vivaldi is referred to as a priest. Looking into the records, we find that he received the first of minor orders in 1693 and in 1703 was admitted to the priesthood.

Meanwhile Antonio the "*prete rosso*," so called because of his red hair, had continued his violin study with Giovanni Legrenzi, the Maestro at St. Mark's, a pioneer in chamber music composition and an innovator in orchestral usage. Legrenzi, by enlarging the orchestra at St. Mark's, and experimenting with various combinations of instruments, had provided splendid opportunity for instrumental development. And it was undoubtedly in this atmosphere that the young Vivaldi found the direction of his own talents, for it was in the field of instrumental music that he was destined to express himself best

Little else is known about Vivaldi's early life except that he had at least three brothers—Francesco, Iseppo, and Bonaventura— for playmates. They, like his father and he himself were referred to as "*rossi*." What a glowing picture of red-heads they must have made! We find that the "red-head,"

Antonio, who became both priest and violinist, acted in the capacity of priest for scarcely more than a year. But contrary to the traditional story, that Vivaldi was relieved of his duties as priest by a church edict for leaving the altar to jot down a musical idea while in the process of saying Mass, he voluntarily relinquished the office of saying Mass because of a physical ailment. This fact is verified in a letter written in his later life, part of which reads as follows:

"I have not said Mass for twenty-five years nor shall I ever again, not on account of any prohibition or order, but by my own choice, because of an illness that I have suffered from birth and which still troubles me. After I was ordained priest I said Mass for a little over a year, and then gave it up, as three times I had to leave the altar before the end on account of my illness. I nearly always live indoors for this reason and never go out except in a gondola or a carriage, as I cannot walk on account of the pain or constriction in my chest.... This is the reason I never say Mass."

Coincident with this decision, Vivaldi apparently began his long association with the Conservatory of the *Ospedale Pietà*, one of four music schools for girls in Venice; for in the school's records, dated 1704, there is a mention of his services. According to further records, we find that he was connected with the school—with the exception of short intervals—for thirty-six years; first, as violin teacher; later, as *Maestro de Concerti*.

This association offered splendid opportunity for musical experiment and growth, for these girls' music schools were an important feature of Venetian musical life at that time. The four schools vied with one another in friendly rivalry at concert-giving, and Vivaldi, in all probability, contributed greatly to the high place achieved by the Conservatory *Ospedale Pietà*, as described, in 1739, by a visitor to Venice:

"The *Ospedali* have the best music here.... Indeed they sing like angels, play the violin, flute, organ, oboe, cello, bassoon,—in short no instrument is large enough to frighten them. They are cloistered like nuns. The performances are entirely their own and each concert is composed of about forty girls. I swear nothing is more charming than to see a young and pretty nun, dressed in white, a sprig of pomegranate blossoms behind one ear, leading the orchestra and beating time with all the grace and precision imaginable."

And the hand of Vivaldi can well be imagined behind the execution that charmed this same writer, as expressed in another letter:

"Where I go most often and enjoy myself most is the *Ospedale della Pietà*.... What well drilled execution! That is the only place to hear a first attack from the strings such as, quite undeservedly, the Paris opera is renowned for."

Thus it can be plainly seen how well this school assignment served Vivaldi's talents; not alone as teacher and violinist, but as composer. Soon after joining the *Pietà's* faculty, he began to compose in much the same part-of-the-day's-work manner in which Joseph Haydn was later to contribute so much to the symphony's development while in the employ of the Esterházy family.

We find that, although permitted various leaves from the Conservatory, Vivaldi was firmly bound, by its authorities, to deliver two concertos a month postpaid!

Smaller wonder that, with an excellent orchestra at his disposal, and a contract, binding him to a congenial task, he should have perfected the form of the concerto!

One leave of absence occurred between 1718 and 1722 when he is supposed to have served as *maestro di capella* to Prince Phillip von Hesse-Darmstadt at Mantua. Then for one year, according to the school's records, he was back at the *Pietà;* but, from the following year until 1735, the records show no mention of him, leading one to believe that this was the time of his greatest travel. To substantiate this assumption still further is his own statement in a letter written in 1737, "For over fourteen years we have traveled together in many European cities."

The points to which Vivaldi traveled are clouded in mystery. We can only put "two and two together," in several instances, thereby supposing him to have been here or there. Certain historical records indicate that he visited France; such as the statement, during the year 1727, in the *Mercure de France*, about "a magnificent instrumental concert which lasted nearly two hours, the music, including the *Te Deum*, was by the famous Vivaldi." An all-Vivaldi concert somehow indicates either his presence in France then, or at some previous occasion.

Then in support of the supposition that he visited France, in addition to the news item, is the fact that the words of two of his cantatas were written in French for French occasions.

Another indication of the direction of Vivaldi's travels has come to light in the Venetian archives. For there, as plain as day, is the statement that Giovanni Battista Vivaldi was granted one year's leave of absence from the Ducal Chapel "to go to Germany to accompany his son." Now, knowing that Johann Sebastian Bach found great inspiration in the Italian method of instrumentation at the Weimar court, particularly exemplified in Vivaldi's music, it is reasonable to suppose that Vivaldi, for one place, visited Weimar, the city destined to be later known as the Kingdom of Liszt.

Then we find that in 1735 Vivaldi was settled once again at the Conservatory of the *Ospedale Pietà*, with every indication of rounding out a useful life in that congenial atmosphere.

Meanwhile, in addition to fulfilling his obligations at the Conservatory and traveling hither and yon, he had written no less than thirty-nine operas. Not only had he written them, but, for the most part, he had acted as director and manager when they were produced over the years in Venice. Long considered unimportant in contrast to his superb instrumental music, they are being revaluated to their greater credit, as modern scholars have an opportunity to study them.

Two years after his apparent settling down for life at *Pietà*, Vivaldi suddenly left Venice for good. There is reason to suppose that the false legend concerning his not saying Mass contributed to this unfortunate departure. The story goes that, having made plans to go to Ferrara to produce one of his operas, he was forbidden to do so by the Church authorities of that city on account of his being "a priest who did not say Mass." At any rate, soon thereafter Vivaldi left Venice—where, as he had once written, he had been *Maestro della Pietà* for over thirty years with never a scandal—for Vienna where several of his musical friends were then situated.

We find no record of any musical activities of his in Vienna. And they cannot have been great, for, in 1741, the man who signed himself *"Musico Veneto"*—and surely he deserved such title—died, a poor man, in Vienna.

He died in the house of a family by the name of Salter, in the Parish of St. Stephan, and was buried on July 28 in the cemetery of the Burger Spital.

Thus Vienna, destined to provide hallowed soil for so many musicians, proved refuge for the non-Mass-saying priest and Venetian master.

But the spirit of Antonio Vivaldi lives—for all the world to enjoy—through his music, chiefly instrumental, and the influence that he exerted upon at least one pupil, Giovanni Battista Somis (also the pupil of Arcangelo Corelli) whose pupils in turn can be traced to our own day.

As far as his music is concerned: what greater tribute could be paid it than that Johann Sebastian Bach thought well enough of Vivaldi's concertos to make them the model of his own! And as we know, Bach also transcribed several of them for clavier and harpsichord.

Today the words Vivaldi and concerto go hand-in-hand for Vivaldi is recognized as the one who molded the concerto into its definitive form. Enlarging the solo passage, usual in the *concerto grosso,* he made of the solo violin the chief instrument, while at the same time he developed the orchestral passages for a legitimate role of their own. Gracefully arguing back and forth, picking up the thread of thought where interrupted by the other, Vivaldi's solo and *tutti,* or orchestral passages, live delightfully together in a balanced whole—the concerto.

GIUSEPPE TARTINI

About seventeen years before Bartolomeo di Francesco Cristofori built the first practical pianoforte, called the *gravicembalo col piano e forte*, at Florence, Italy, there was born nearby at Pirano, in the district of Istria, on April 8, 1692, one of the great pioneers of "Violindom"—Giuseppe Tartini. Founder of the famous Paduan school of violin playing, innovator in bow construction and technique, music theorist, violinist and composer, Tartini scribed well his name on the Roll of Music.

Giuseppe's father—Giovanni Antonio Tartini, a wealthy nobleman—and his mother—whose name had been Catarine Zangando—originally came from Florence; but it was at their beautiful *villa Struegnano*, in Pirano, that their children—Domenico, Antonio, Pietro, Giuseppe and a daughter who died in infancy—were born.

Giovanni Tartini, a generous patron of the Church, planned carefully an ecclesiastical career for his son, Giuseppe. The die was cast for him to become a member of the Brotherhood of the *Minori Conventuali*. With this goal in view, his education was first put in the hands of a priest belonging to the order of *St. Filippo Neri of Pirano*. Next, he was admitted into the *Collegio dei Padri delle Scuole Pie at Capo d'Istria*. Then in 1709, Giovanni Tartini obtained permission from the Bishop, Paola Naldini, for Giuseppe's admittance to the University of Padua; the Bishop, commending and abetting the nobleman's desire to render one of his sons to the Church.

Alas, for such well-laid plans! Having tasted the joys of music, particularly those provided by the violin, at the *Collegio dei Padri delle Scuole Pie*, and having succumbed to the fascination of fencing, Giuseppe could not, somehow, reconcile these delights with the prospects of priesthood. And after long and heartfelt pleas he at last won permission to study law instead of theology at Padua.

Giuseppe, seventeen years old, and bubbling over with the joy of living, found the atmosphere at the University both congenial and stimulating. What glorious vistas opened before him! How wonderful it would be to spend one's life in the world of art and music! So thinking, he conceived, what appeared to him, a remarkable plan. He would go to Naples, open a fencing school—for he was the champion-fencer at the University—and with the money earned thereby continue his violin studies. Yes. He would be a violinist!

Again, alas, well-laid plans went far awry. In his twentieth year—the third at Padua—he fell desperately in love with Elizabeth Premazone, whose welfare lay in the hands of Cardinal Giorgio Cornaro. Distressingly impetuous by nature, Giuseppe, eloping with the young woman, found himself within the twinkling of an eye—a married man, a fugitive from law and a penniless wanderer! For the Cardinal, disapproving the marriage, ordered Giuseppe's arrest; while at the same time, the young bridegroom's family, no less provoked, withheld further support.

Consequently, disguised as a Monk, Giuseppe, not yet twenty, leaving his wife at Padua, set out on the road to Rome, making his way from hand to mouth as best he could.

Fortunately, as he wended his way onward from the Holy City, he met by accident a relative who was custodian in the Monastery of Assisi. Thus it was—through this sympathetic encounter—that young Tartini found refuge at Assisi.

What a time of growth the two years spent there proved to be! Burying himself in serious study, he emerged an accomplished violinist, able composer and theorist. It was, according to some authorities, while studying there that he discovered what he called "the third sound," resultant tones from sound—combinations, a phenomenon in acoustics, later to be more scientifically explained by Hermann Helmholtz in his famous work, *Sensations of Tone as a Physiological Basis for the Theory of Music.*

Tartini also, at this time is supposed to have begun work on his contribution to the development of the violin as an instrument: that is, the bringing about the use of thicker strings and the inauguration of changes in the bow. Under his hand the bow lost its bow-and-arrow outward curve, became lighter, smaller in the size of its head, and developed fluted ridges at its heel to provide firmer grip for the player. Thus he paved the way for the modern bow as later perfected by the French maker of bows, François Tourte.

Meanwhile it was the fugitive violinist's good fortune to study composition with Padre Boëmo, organist at the convent church at Assisi. Returning to his native land, this Bohemian organist and eminent composer, whose real name was Bohuslav Czernohorski, later became the teacher of Christoph Willibald Gluck.

Among the compositions composed by Tartini at Assisi was the celebrated sonata, *Trillo del diavolo*, or *The Devil's Trill*. This is the way he described its conception:

"One night I dreamt that I had made a bargain with the devil for my soul. Everything went at my command; my novel servant anticipated every one of my wishes. Then the idea suggested itself to hand him my violin to see what he would do with it. Great was my astonishment when I heard him play, with consummate skill, a sonata of such exquisite beauty as surpassed the boldest flights of my imagination. I felt enraptured, transported, enchanted; my breath failed me, and—I awoke. Seizing my violin I tried to reproduce the sounds I had heard. But in vain. The piece I then composed, the Devil's Sonata, although the best I ever wrote, how far was it below the one I had heard in my dream!"

At the end of his second year at Assisi another *accident* determined Tartini's fate.

For some time enthusiastic music lovers had been packing the convent Chapel at Assisi to hear the extraordinary violin playing that issued magically from behind the choir loft's curtain. Tartini, the magic-player, chosing thus to hide his identity, relished none the less the congregation's warm approval. This little drama betwixt artist and audience might have continued indefinitely had not a combination of circumstances intervened. On August 1, 1715, when the Chapel was particularly packed with visitors—come from other cities to pay homage at the Tomb of St. Francis—the Deacon, in presenting the incense, inadvertently snatched aside the curtain that provided shelter for the magic-violinist.

Several visiting Paduans among the congregation could not suppress whispers of recognition. "Giuseppe Tartini! It's Giuseppe Tartini!"

Naturally the news spread to Padua where Tartini's young wife, beside herself with grief at his flight, now persuaded the Cardinal to permit Tartini's return.

Arrived back at Padua, Tartini soon established himself in circles of the highest culture through his earned reputation as violinist and his growing renown in philosophy and literature. But, during the year following his return, an event, precipitated by rumors of his wonderful violin playing, proved to be a discouragingly bitter experience.

This unhappy occurrence came about through a custom then prevalent of holding competitive concerts in music, as we do athletic meets. Accordingly, Tartini was overjoyed at an invitation to compete with the noted Florentine violinist, Francesco Veracini at the Palace of His Excellency Pisano-Mocenigo in Venice to honor the visit of Elector of Saxony. But upon hearing the Master, known as "Il Florentino," rehearse at Cremona before the contest, Tartini, overcome with chagrin at what he considered his opponent's greater skill, particularly in the handling of the bow, again decided to run away; this time, not from the law, but his own humiliation. He would study the violin until none remained his equal, let alone his superior!

Leaving his wife in the care of his brother, Domenico, at Pirano, Tartini retired to Ancona for intensive study. Although it is not known whether he had any teacher there, it may have been at Ancona that he studied with a certain Giulio Terni, whom Tartini referred to as his first master.

Be that as it may, the next link in the chain of his career proved a binding one. Developing steadily thereafter, Giuseppe Tartini emerged the Paduan Master. This opportunity presented itself in the form of an invitation to become first violinist at the famous Chapel of the Church of St. Anthony at Padua. The document confirming the appointment, dated, April 3, 1721, refers to him as "Signor Giuseppe Tartini, an extraordinary violinist." And indeed he must have been thus considered; for, disregarding their usual practice of requiring their musicians to take an examination, the Chapel authorities welcomed Tartini at face value. Not only that, but in addition to offering him a splendid salary, they stipulated that he might appear in places other than the Chapel if he so desired.

Completely happy, at last, in his Paduan position, Tartini was little tempted to wander far afield. But in 1723, he was persuaded to accept the invitation of the Chancellor of Bohemia, Count Kinsky, to go to Prague. Taking with him Antonio Vandini, principal violoncellist of the St. Anthony Chapel, Tartini, together with his fellow artist, appeared at the Festival held in honor of the Coronaton of the Emperor, Charles VI, at Vienna. Then settling down at Prague, as conductor of Count Kinsky's band, Tartini, from 1723 to 1725, became the toast of the Bohemian capital.

The honored violinist, unfortunately, felt less enthusiastic about Bohemia. Something there not congenial to his nature, together with family worries, forever turned his thoughts homeward. Prompted to stay by pressing financial obligations only, Tartini, in a letter written to his brother, Domenico, prayed that help be given to both of them, continuing, "and teach me, and help me remain in a place where the air, the food, and the people are equally distasteful to me."

But the day came at last, when bidding many kind friends good-bye, he set out from Prague. Traveling by way of Venice, he visited there an ardent admirer, His Excellency Michele Morosini di San Stefano, who fortunately relieved the financial pressure heaped on the violinist's willing shoulders, by steering the luckless Domenico toward a position in the Public Salt Works.

Welcomed home with fitting tribute, Tartini soon set about establishing the Paduan School of violin playing. Becoming known as the "School of Nations," it attracted students, as honey does the bees; while Giuseppe Tartini, the Master of Nations, became a teacher both honored and loved.

Among Tartini's many distinguished pupils were Pietro Nardini, Pierre Lahoussye, André Noel Pagin, and Maddalena Lombardini Sirmen to whom he addressed an often-quoted letter of instructions, dealing with the bow, the trill, and the various positions in violin playing.

As his reputation increased many opportunities arose to go to other cities. One came in an invitation from Sir Edward Walpole to go to London, subsequent to the Englishman's having heard Tartini play at Padua; but the Master of Nations, after careful consultation with his own conscience, abetted by advice-of-caution from his wife, refused the financially tempting offer, replying, "Although not rich, I have sufficient and do not need more."

Paris, too, repeatedly urged him to appear there, but, persisting in his refusals, he confined concert-giving to occasional tours in his own country. Some ten or twelve years after founding the Paduan School, he visited Rome at the invitation of Cardinal Olivieri, at whose palace he associated with the city's leading citizens. Through this association he met Pope Clement XII who commissioned him to write his *Miserere*, which was performed on Ash Wednesday at the Sistine Chapel.

Meanwhile, on his way to Rome, he had been warmly received at Venice, Milan, Florence, Leghorn, Bologna, Palermo and, particularly, at Naples where the enthusiastic Neapolitans tried to carry him aloft their shoulders!

Returning to Padua after his triumphant pilgrimage, Tartini thereafter avoided travel. Invitations continued to pour in; and in 1755 a rumor to the effect that he would appear on a certain date in Paris nearly caused a riot. Notwithstanding the much-sought-after violinist held firmly to his resolution to remain at Padua.

After forty years of devotion to his Paduan students, together with countless hours spent in research, writing, and composition, Tartini was forced to face the fact of his failing health. Confined to his house for seven months, the indefatigable worker constantly strove to conquer the paralysis that held him captive.

Though he managed to gain strength sufficient to warrant his removal from bed to sofa, the hopes thus aroused were short-lived. On February 26, 1770, following a long illness, during which he was nursed by his devoted pupil, Pietro Nardini, the Master of Nations died at his home in Padua.

He was buried in the Church of St. Catherine of Padua. A Requiem composed by his friend, P. Francesco Antonio Vallotti, known as the "best organist and church composer in Italy," was sung at the Church of St. Anthony. And the Abbé Fanzago delivered an address, bespeaking Tartini's virtues, which was duly published at Padua.

A great master of the violin, a revered teacher, classic composer, author, and scientist, Giuseppe Tartini left a rich heritage. His *Art of Bowing* still serves as a model for violinists. And his compositions, many of them supposed to have been inspired by reading Petrarch, provide constant challenge for artist and student.

GIOVANNI BATTISTA VIOTTI

J UST ONE HUNDRED YEARS after the birth of Arcangelo Corelli, and three years before the birth of Wolfgang Amadeus Mozart, on May 23, 1723, at the little town of Fontanetto, near Crescentino, in the canton of Piedmont, Italy, there was born the violinist who is known as the founder of the Modern School of violin playing—Giovanni Battista Viotti.

Little did the blacksmith Antonio Viotti and his wife Maria Magdalena know that the tiny violin purchased at a fair at Crescentino would project their son, Giovanni, into the company of kings, and, moreover, start him on the road to lasting fame. But from the first minute that Giovanni held the precious instrument in his hands, there was no faltering in his attempts to learn to play it. Fortunately his father, an able horn player, could help him in the rudiments of music; so that, at eight Giovanni managed to play the violin with fair skill.

When he was eleven another circumstance contributed to his destined career: A wandering lute player, a good all-round musician decided to settle down at Fontanetto. Antonio Viotti, impressed with his son's talent, arranged for this new arrival to give Giovanni violin lessons; and the eager student progressed at remarkable speed. At the end of a year, unfortunately, he was once more without a teacher; for the lute player, having been offered a permanent position in another city, betook himself there—leaving at Fontanetto a disappointed young violinist.

Disappointed but undaunted, Giovanni continued to work by himself, until, attracting the attention of Giovanni Pavia, a flute player, he impressed this professional musician so much that Pavia decided to introduce him to Francisco Rora, the Bishop of Strombo. This benevolent patron, who afterward became Bishop of Turin, equally impressed, recommended Giovanni to the Marquis de Vogliera in Turin, as a tutor-companion for his eighteen-year-old son, Alphonso del Pozzo, Prince of Cisterna.

Alas! For a time, it looked as though Giovanni's youth would act against him. But the master-of-his-fate must have been looking over him; for, just when the trip to Turin appeared to have been made in vain, Colognetti, a distinguished musician in the royal chapel chanced to hear him play a sonata at sight.

"Well done, young man!" exclaimed Colognetti.

"Thank you, Sir. It was a small thing to do," answered Giovanni.

Charmed by his modesty, as well as his ability, Colognetti then placed a difficult Ferrari sonata before the aspiring violinist; and, when he heard this skilfully performed, he forthwith persuaded the Prince to reconsider his decision to send Giovanni back to Fontanetto.

Thus it was that Giovanni Battista Viotti, the blacksmith's son, found himself at thirteen lodged in a palace at Turin—soon to come under the influence of one of the outstanding violin masters of all time. For not only did the Prince take the young man into his home, but, now convinced of Giovanni's talent, he arranged for him to study with Gaetano Pugnani, a pupil of both Giovanni Somis and Giuseppe Tartini. Advancing rapidly in violin playing under Pugnani's tutelage, Giovanni also began to compose, though it is not known whether he had a teacher in composition. Be that as it may, at fourteen he composed his first violin concerto.

In 1780 Pugnani took his talented young pupil, then seventeen, with him on a concert tour. They went first to Geneva, thence to Dresden, and from there to Berlin, where the Emperor, Frederick the Great, delighted with Giovanni's playing, often invited the artist-pupil to take part with him in the performance of chamber music; the Emperor, as we know, being a skilled flute player.

During the same year, generously supplied with letters of introduction, Giovanni Battista Viotti, the sensational young violinist, set out for Warsaw. From there he journeyed to St. Petersburg, where he was presented to the Empress Catherine by Prince Potemkin. And then, with wonderful memories of Russian hospitality and friendliness stored within him, wending his way westward through some of the German cities where he had previously appeared, he eventually arrived at Paris, intending to stay a few months.

"I delayed my departure from month to month, and year to year, and remained ten years," Viotti later wrote in his Autobiography.

Appearing first at a small private concert, he completely won the hearts of his Parisian listeners. "I've never heard anything like it!" "What artistry!" "How does he do it?" "Such music is Heaven-inspired!"

The critics were equally enthusiastic after Viotti's public début, which took place on March 15, 1782, at the Concert Spirituel. "A true execution, a precise finish and an admirable quality of tone in the Adagio, have placed this artist amongst the greatest of masters," wrote one.

One sensational success followed another, until, within a year, Viotti was considered the greatest violinist in France. According to one report in the *Mercure de France*, he was received "with triumphs of delight."

But before another year had passed these "triumphs of delight" appear to have lost their charm for Viotti. Suddenly, in the midst of his greatest popularity, he stopped playing at the Concert Spirituel. The exact reasons for this decision are not known; but one of his contemporaries explained it by remarking that the indiscriminate character of the public's applause was repugnant to Viotti's nature.

At any rate, Viotti himself has written, concerning a request by Queen Marie Antoinette in 1784 to play for her, "and when I had determined to play no more in public, and consecrate myself entirely to the service of this Sovereign, she in recompense obtained for me, during the time that Mons de Calonne was Minister, a pension of 150 pounds sterling, though I had given up playing for some time."

But, although he ceased playing at the Concert Spirituel, he by no means disappeared from the music-life of Paris. At one time he was the leader of Prince Gueménenée's band; and another, first violinist in the band of the Prince of Soubise. And all times he was the willing listener or performer where conscientious young students were concerned. It is said that while living with his friend, Maria Luigi Cherubini, Viotti made of their combined-home a veritable conservatory where enlightened musicans gathered for inspiration and encouragement. With them he was ever generous, playing often and long in the company of those who understood and appreciated the extent of his art.

Meanwhile, occupying himself with composition, he had the satisfaction in 1787 of hearing his "Symphonies concertantes" for two violins enthusiastically received when performed by two of his friends at the Concert Spirituel; while, on Christmas Eve of the same year, his Concerto for piano was given at the same place.

Then in 1788, Viotti was persuaded to join Léonard—Queen Marie Antoinette's hairdresser—in the management of the Théâtre de Monsieur. Sponsored by Monsieur le Comte de Provence—the King's brother—this operatic venture was well on the way to fair success when the French Revolution broke out. Viotti described the situation in this way:

"Having placed almost all I possessed in an enterprise for an Italian Theatre, what terrible fears assailed me at the approach of the terrible flood; what cares I had, and what arrangements I had to enter into before I could pull myself out of the difficulty."

But despite "the approach of the terrible flood," Viotti refused to flee the city, as many of his associates were doing. On the contrary, joining the National Guard, he stood by his committment to the opera company as long as it was physically possible, believing that a man should die at his post; good sense having taught him, he said, that if honest men deserted, the wicked gained thereby.

Finally, on the night before the arrest of the King and Queen, Viotti was persuaded to leave Paris. And mid-July in the year 1792, he arrived in London—a refugee from a country that had come to be his own. Then, after a journey to Italy to settle affairs related to the death of his mother, the Italian-French violinist established himself in London, as he said, "for life!"

Putting aside his determination not to appear further in public, Viotti soon found himself a permanent feature of Salomon's concerts; Salomon, being the concert manager, who, only a few years previously, having lured Joseph Haydn to London and having successfully commissioned music from him, had made a name for himself in musical history thereby. But a man of Viotti's talents could not long be satisfied with concert-giving only: He must have his hand in other music-matters!

Such an opportunity presented itself at the King's Theatre, where he began to help in the direction of Italian opera.

Meanwhile, having had the good fortune to find communion of the spirit in the Chinnery household in London, Viotti expanded with happiness. And eventually when Cramer, the manager of the King's Theatre, resigned, Viotti fell heir to the position. He then came magnificently into his own! Here at last it was possible for him to carry out some of his artistic ideas without undue interference. Here at last he found a congenial haven.

Alas! The situation was too ideal to remain long intact.

One evening in 1798, while he was in the company of his dear friends, the Chinnerys, he was, without the slightest bit of warning, arrested by some of the King's officers. *What was it all about?* Viotti didn't know! Certainly the Chinnerys didn't know.

In due course of time it developed that Viotti was suspected—on account of some innocent letters sent to friends in Paris—of being in league with French Revolutionary leaders. This was particularly ironic—since he had left France *because* of the Revolution. But in times of great violence and stress Justice often becomes confused. Poor Viotti, a victim of such confusion, was forced to leave England just when life there was pleasantest for him.

Fortunately he found refuge with some friends at Schönfeldz, a litle place near Hamburg. There he remained for three years, occupying himself with composition and some teaching. Friedrich Wilhelm Pixis, a young violinist, came to live nearby in order to take lessons from him; and some of Viotti's best music resulted from this enforced exile; so that, as he wrote Mrs. Chinnery, "All is not in vain."

In 1801, permitted to return to England, Viotti was warmly received by his friends, but for some strange reason found it impossible to pick up the threads of his musical career. Finally, upon the advice of Mrs. Chinnery, he became—of all things—a wine merchant! Had he made his living thereby the venture might be viewed with more favor, but, alas, it thrust him into hopeless debt.

One bright spot illuminated the darkness of those early winery-days. This was a visit to Paris, where, renewing some of his former friendships, he was gratified to find, that in the company of artists, he was still regarded as the supreme artist despite his enforced wanderings far afield. Among those musicians who listened gratefully to Viotti's compositions written at Schönfeldz was the violinist, Pierre Baillot, who, then violin teacher at the Paris Conservatory, felt deeply indebted to Viotti both for inspiration and for securing him his first important musical post.

But, back again in London, Viotti became submerged once more in the dull business of losing money as a wine merchant; brightened only by musical evenings spent in the company of the Chinnery family. Such a life could not long satisfy a man of Viotti's spirit. Accordingly, identifying himself with musical affairs, he became one of the organizers of the London Philharmonic Society, which gave its first concert on March 8, 1813. Salomon was the leader of the orchestra—occasionally conducted by Viotti; and one of Viotti's quartets appeared on the program during the first year.

Meanwhile he made frequent trips to Paris; each, amounting to a great feast of music; with Viotti, according to Baillot, "like a father among his children." On one of these happy occasions, at the end of a particularly beautiful performance, Viotti impulsively embraced his friend, Cherubini. Those were indeed wonderful moments for the truant wine merchant!

Finally in 1818, thoroughly discouraged with attempts to make both ends meet in his business venture, Viotti decided to return to Paris. Baillot, delighted, arranged a tremendous reception at which Viotti played with even greater skill than his friends anticipated. "Many were reduced to tears," is the way Baillot spoke of the occasion. And soon thereafter fortune appeared once again to have taken the luckless master in hand.

Viotti's former patron, the Comte de Provence now the French Sovereign—Louis XVIII—secured for Viotti the post of Director of the Opéra. And all went well for about a year: with the great violinist once more in his rightful element. Then, one night, the King's nephew was assassinated at the opera house; and the ill-fated theatre was forced to close its doors. After two unsatisfactory attempts at other theatres Viotti was induced to resign, on a pension of 6000 francs.

Returning to London, weary and humiliated, Viotti, to whom the fates had given tremendous talents but little fortune, now an old man, literally gave up the struggle. Two years later, on March 3, 1824, he died at the home of Mrs. Caroline Chinnery.

His will, written two years previously, is a pitiful document; particularly so, in view of the rich heritage that he bequeathed to future violinists. Heartbroken at his indebtedness to Mrs. Chinnery, induced by the demands of his wine business, he asked that everything that he owned—including two violins (one a Stradivarius), and two concertos in manuscript—be sold to pay this debt. The only reservation to this behest called upon the Chinnery family to pay a much smaller sum to his brother, André Viotti, from whom he had borrowed during his darkest days. Two gold snuff-boxes and a gold watch were to go to Caroline Chinnery; while as final witness to his despair, he admonished his friends to reserve nothing for his burial, "a little earth will suffice for such a miserable creature as myself."

But today the great-great-grandchildren, violinistically speaking, of Viotti's pupils pay homage to the art of this "miserable creature": for, he, his distinguished pupils, and followers, it can be justly said, founded the Modern School of violin playing: its principles, having been set down in the famous *Violin Method* by Pierre Baillot and Rodolphe Kreutzer—two of his disciples—and Pierre Rode—his most famous pupil.

In his music, no less than in his playing, Viotti bespoke the modern idiom: dignified and classic in spirit, his concertos, taking full advantage of large orchestral effects, were the first in the large sonata form.

Thus today, listeners, when they frantically applaud a favorite-violinist's playing of one of the great modern concertos, unconsciously applaud Giovanni Battista Viotti!

NICCOLO PAGANINI

Niccolo Paganini—violinist and greatest virtuoso the world has ever known—was born, according to the tablet on the pink-painted house of his birth, on October 27, 1782, at Genoa, Italy. Across the waters young America was about to win her Independence, founded upon the principle of man's inalienable Right to Life, Liberty, and the pursuit of Happiness; while in Europe, twelve years previously, had been born the composer whose name is forever linked with Liberation—Ludwig van Beethoven.

Although Niccolo Paganini was not to concern himself with matters of Revolution in government, he was destined to precipitate a revolutionary movement in musical circles: Henceforth the classic Corelli-Tartini style of violin playing must eternally vie with technical display; while musical composition—particularly represented by Franz Liszt and Hector Berlioz—was long to feel the Paganini-impact.

From the minute that Antonio Paganini—a clerk in one of the shipping companies at Genoa—discerned musical talent in his son, he set out to exploit it. We are forced to use the word *exploit*, rather than *develop;* for, according to most accounts, Antonio's chief thought was to reap the benefits of Niccolo's evident precocity. A good amateur musician, skilled in mandoline playing, he gave Niccolo his first violin lessons. And from morning until night, while other children were playing at marbles or building sail boats to compete with their sea-faring fathers, Niccolo practiced and practiced away!

There was no escaping this enforced discipline, for added to his father's greed was his mother's faith. Frequently interfering when her husband was brutally strict with their son, she, nevertheless, contributed to Niccolo's own determination to become a great violinist. This came about through a dream that she had one night; a dream, which she repeated again and again:

An angel, appearing at the foot of her bed, had promised, "Your son will be the greatest violinist in the world!"

What mother could ignore a vision like that? Accordingly, although it must have been evident that Niccolo's health was suffering thereby, she, by repeatedly reminding him of the dream, held him continually bow-in-hand.

Outgrowing his father's ability to teach him further, he was put in the hands of a violinist in the theatre orchestra by the name of Servetto. Two years later, having far surpassed this musician in skill, he became the pupil of Giacomo Costa, *maestro di cappella* of the Cathedral of St. Lorenzo. Advancing rapidly under Costa's guidance, Niccolo, at nine, made his début at a concert given by two great singers—Luigi Marchesi and Madame Albertinotti—at the leading theatre of Genoa. Not only did his unusual playing delight his listeners but his own variations on the French patriotic air, "La Carmagnole," completely captivated them.

"The little darling!" "He plays like one possessed!" "He appears to be a part of the very instrument!"

Following this initial success quickly with a benefit concert, assisted by the same artists, Niccolo firmly established a reputation in his native city; and, at the same time, further stimulated his father's zeal in his behalf. Consequently, when Giacomo Costa suggested that he play a solo in church each Sunday, Antonio Paganini readily gave his consent, thinking, "That will keep Niccolo before the public."

But what was more to the point, as the mature violinist often stated, was the benefit derived from having constantly to learn new works to satisfy the weekly requirements. It is well that some great good came from such prodigious effort, for the continuous study and practice completely undermined his health.

Meanwhile Costa introduced him to various eminent musicians, including the operatic composer, Francesco Gnecco, who, taking the young violinist under his wing, gave him some sound advice. And only too soon he was to profit thereby, for fast-moving events were to thrust him helter skelter on his own!

When it became evident that Giacomo Costa could teach Niccolo nothing further, Antonio Paganini decided to take his son to Alessandro Rolla, distinguished violinist, composer and conductor at Parma. The elder Paganini, ever practical, hit upon the idea of calling up the Genoese public to defray the expenses of such a venture. Accordingly the following advertisement tells its own story:

"July 25, 1795, Niccolo Paganini of Genoa, a boy already known to his country for his skill in handling the violin, having determined to study at Parma to improve his talents under the direction of the renowned Signor Rolla, but lacking the means to do so, has adopted this plan, and has taken courage to beg his compatriots to contribute towards this object, inviting them to come to this entertainment for his benefit."

Needless to say, the boy who had shown "such skill in handling the violin" attracted a generous audience to his benefit concert. Consequently, with the necessary funds thus supplied, father and son set out for Parma.

Arrived there, they went immediately to the residence of Alessandro Rolla. To their great disappointment, they learned that the master was confined to his bed; but nothing daunted, Antonio Paganini politely asked the sick man's wife, "Is it possible that the master would admit two visitors, come from afar to see him only?"

Moved by the man's evident sincerity and the unusual appearance of the boy, wistfully standing there, Madame Rolla replied, "I shall see."

Inviting them to be seated in a room adjoining her husband's, she disappeared on her kind-hearted errand. Meanwhile Antonio Paganini's opportunity-seeing eyes having fallen upon a violin and a manuscript lying side by side, made a significant motion in his son's direction. Picking up the instrument, Niccolo played the accompanying music at sight without the slightest hesitancy.

Within the sick room, Alessandro Rolla, hearing his newly-written concerto played with such skill, sat up in bed with a start.

"What professor is that?" he eagerly inquired of his wife, completely forgetting his illness.

"No professor, Alessandro," she replied, peeking meanwhile into the adjoining room, "'Tis a child!"

"Never! Bring the artist hither!"

And when having been reluctantly convinced that the "professor" was indeed a child and on being asked to teach this prodigy, Alessandro Rolla exclaimed to the elder Paganini: "I can teach him nothing. Take him to Ferdinando Paër for instruction in composition."

Acting accordingly, Antonio Paganini immediately sought out Paër, the opera composer, only to find that he was then in Germany. Fortunately Ferdinando's master, Gasparo Ghiretti, coming to the rescue, took Niccolo in hand, giving him composition lessons three times a week for six months. During this time Niccolo composed twenty-four fugues without the aid of any instrument and devoted many long hours to the study of instrumentation. The knowledge of various instruments' capabilities, thus gained, subsequently came to his rescue when he was sadly in need of funds. At one such desperate moment in Paganini's later life a wealthy Swedish amateur musician called upon him to write some music for his chosen instrument—the bassoon. And Paganini, by supplying this ambitious gentleman with bassoon music sufficiently difficult to satisfy his highly cultivated taste, profited handsomely thereby.

Meanwhile, during his concentration on the study of composition, Paganini had by no means been neglecting the violin; for, despite Rolla's assertion that he could teach the Genoese youth nothing, he did give him occasional lessons: and moreover, Antonio still kept vigilant watch over the matter of practice.

Then, while still thirteen, Niccolo Paganini began a professional career that was destined to carry his name round the earth. Leaving Parma, accompanied by his father, he gave concerts in one Lombardian town after another, arousing increased enthusiasm at each appearance. With the echoes of the applause ringing in their ears, PAGANINI THE VIOLINIST and his ambitious father returned to Genoa.

For a time the virtuoso-turned-composer buried himself in composition; doubtless realising even then that his forte lay in playing music of his own making. Accordingly, he incorporated such great difficulties in his compositions that he, the creator, was hard-put to master them.

Growing restless, now nearly fourteen, a recognized artist with the enforced rigors of his childhood ever present in his memory, Paganini resolved to become independent. Such a goal was not easily arrived at; his father, being the man he was; but, having made up his mind, the younger Paganini by persistence won out. Through due persuasion, he obtained permission to go with his elder brother to an annual musical celebration of St. Martin's day at Lucca.

This event, at which he played before an audience hysterical with enthusiasm, proved the springboard to his freedom. Encouraged by his cordial reception at Lucca, Paganini continuing on to Pisa and other cities, increased his reputation at leaps and bounds. But with his belated independence came great license in behavior. Freed at last from parental restraint and drive, throwing discretion completely windward, he dashed pell mell into all manner of excess; gambling, proving the keenest temptor. Driven beyond his means, one night at the gambling table, he was reluctantly forced to pawn his violin to cover his losses.

Consequently, PAGANINI THE VIOLINIST, arrived at Leghorn to fill an engagement with no violin! But ever resourceful, he went straight to the French merchant, Livron, stated his story, and soon walked away with a borrowed Joseph Guarnerius of the finest sort! Upon attempting to return the instrument to Livron after the concert, Paganini was greeted with these words, "My hands shall never profane the violin which your fingers have touched; the instrument belongs to you."

Thus it was that Paganini acquired his famous Joseph Guarnerius, his favorite instrument and his choicest possession. Later a painter, Pasini, gave him a fine Stradivarius, upon his playing a difficult violin concerto at sight, and over the years other splendid instruments came his way, but the Joseph Guarnerius remained his favorite.

On one occasion this precious possession came close to slipping through his fingers; the threat of which proved the means of ending Paganini's gambling habits: It so happened that a certain Prince, who had long had his eye on Paganini's Guarnerius violin, appeared with a handsome offer to buy it just at the moment that Paganini was hardest pressed for funds. Desperately in need of a certain sum to pay a debt of honor, Paganini was for a moment tempted. But first, taking his only available money, he set out for the gaming-table. He would try to win at gambling the required amount. In desperation he saw his thirty francs reduced to three. But just when his Joseph Guarnerius seemed to be doomed, the tide turned in his favor. Four, five, six, ten, twenty, fifty, one hundred, one hundred and sixty francs were pushed his way! The precious violin was saved! And at that instant Paganini made a vow never to gamble again; for as he said, "A gamester is an object of contempt to all well-regulated minds."

Shortly thereafter the sensational violinist disappeared from public life. Many weird stories began to circulate in explanation of his sudden retirement; stories, unfortunately, which were to haunt him the rest of his days; in fact, to become legendary after his death. "He was imprisoned for a murder!" "He was in league with the devil; yes, the devil taught him those extraordinary tricks in playing the violin!"

Actually, for three years, he lived in seclusion at the château of a royal lady in Tuscany; during which time he devoted himself to the study of the guitar, composing two sets of duets for guitar and violin. At first glance this little siesta in the midst of so brilliant a career may appear odd; but, when we remind ourselves that Paganini had never enjoyed a minute's childhood with an opportunity to "grow up" like other boys and girls, such behavior becomes plausible.

In 1804 came the call of the violin once again. As much a part of him as his very skin, the violin was bound to win his attention sooner or later. The direct cause of this re-awakening was a chance-introduction to the violin studies of Pietro Locatelli. This pioneer-virtuoso's technical gymnastics both touched a spark of kinship in Paganini and supplied him with a challenge. *There were still other possibilities in his chosen instrument.* He would set about exploiting them!

Returning to Genoa, he buried himself in study and composition for a time, emerging with two sets of three quartets for violin, viola, guitar and violoncello, and a set of virtuoso-variations for violin, with guitar accompaniment.

Beginning to appear in public again the following year, he created more excitement than ever before. Sensationally successful, he soon attracted the attention of Napoleon's sister—Elisa Bacecocchi, Princess of Lucca and Piombo—who invited him to become director of her private music. At first he staunchly refused but eventually he accepted the post; becoming at the same time, conductor of the Opera orchestra and a Captain of the Royal Bodyguard.

It was during this assignment that Paganini developed some of his most characteristic stunts in violin playing; stunts, that came not from the devil's prompting as rumored by his enemies but from his own particular nature and genius. One such bravura-touch, his most famous perhaps—originated in these suroundings. Enamoured of a lady at the court, Paganini wrote for her benefit his *Scene amoureuse,* for two strings only. Delighted with the performance, according to Paganini's own words, the Lady said, "You have just performed impossibilities on two strings; would not a single string suffice for your talents?"

What greater challenge for a man of Paganini's temperament! As he himself said: "I promised to make the attempt. The idea delighted me, and some weeks after I composed my military Sonata for the G string entitled "Napoleon," which I performed on August 25, before a numerous and brilliant court audience."

This was only the beginning of his continuous attempts to plumb the violin's furthest possibilities: for instance, by experimenting with harmonic tones he lengthened the extent of the fourth string to three octaves. And with each discovery he became more secretive, guarding the means by which he achieved his effects as a miser does his gold.

Motivated by the realization of his greater skill, Paganini in 1808 sought permission from Princess Elisa to appear outside her court. The permission granted, he set out for Leghorn where he had previously met with such success. His first concert there on this occasion, in a curious way, provided further impetus for extravagant showmanship. Owing to the unaccountable behavior of audiences, Paganini's initial appearance was greeted with decided ridicule. And strangely enough, this set the key to the whole affair; until, by sheer bravado he won their unrestrained applause.

This is the story of what took place at that bedeviled performance: First of all, having run a nail in his heel, Paganini was forced to limp his way onto the stage, at which the audience screamed with laughter. Undaunted, he began his first number. Both candles in the music-desk dropped instantly to the floor. *More laughter.* No sooner had he once again put bow to string than one of the strings snapped as though possessed. *Hysterical screams of hilarity, followed by a sudden hushed silence.* For not only was Paganini apparently immune to what had befallen him, but to the audience's amazement, he continued to play, undisturbed, on three strings! Then the applause became deafening; while, at the same time, Paganini added another "stunt" to his rapidly developing virtuosity.

The following year the court of Princess Elisa was transferred to Florence; the Princess, then becoming the Grand Duchess of Tuscany. And after about four more years in her employ, Paganini, thoroughly nipped with the fever of virtuosity, broke the restraining ties of a court position and set out on a concert tour.

Following appearances at Bologna and other places, he arrived at Milan, a city that especially appealed to him and one which greeted him with unusual cordiality. During his stay there he gave about thirty concerts, some of them at the famous Scala; and it was from Milan that stories of his extraordinary performances began to trickle to the world outside of Italy.

But once again the weakened condition of his health forced him to retire for a time. On this occasion, after giving some concerts at Romagna, he went to Ancona—earlier, the refuge of Tartini—to rest and regain his health. Soon thereafter, on a visit to Venice, he met the dancer, Antonia Bianchi, who was destined to provide still further complications to an already-checkered life. Desperately jealous, she watched over Paganini with an eagle-eye for many years, but their son Achillino, born eleven years later at Palermo—was to prove Paganini's greatest consolation.

In 1816 Paganini, prompted somewhat by rumors of a rival's accomplishments, revisited Milan in order to hear at first hand this reputed wonder. The violinist, causing this furore, was the Frenchman, Charles Philippe Lafont; and upon hearing him play, Paganini was generous in praise of his skill. In fact, it took some persuasion on Lafont's part to bring about a Paganini-Lafont concert. Finally persuaded, Paganini left all the arrangements to the visiting violinist. But, despite the Frenchman's avowed reputation, Paganini in characteristic fashion, apparently held his own. "Lafont probably surpassed me in tone," Paganini modestly conceded, "but the applause which followed my efforts convinced me that I did not suffer by comparison."

The following year while appearing in Rome, Paganini met Count Metternich, the Austrian Ambassador, who urged him to visit Vienna. Though eager to accept the Ambassador's invitation, Paganini was enforced by the state of his health to refuse. And over ten years were to elapse before he finally appeared in the Austrian capital.

Meanwhile in the winter of 1821 Paganini, once again in Rome, spent a good bit of time with Giocchino Rossini, already the composer of the opera, *The Barber of Seville;* later, to be also forever remembered for his *William Tell*. But the opera that concerned him at this particular time was not one of his major successes. It was called *Matilde di Shabran* and Paganini had quite a finger in its ill-starred launching. Having played each number as it fell from Rossini's pen, he was sufficiently familiar with the score to take over the conducting when the conductor was striken with an apopletic fit at the final rehearsal. And not only did Paganini conduct at the opera's premiere, but, when a horn player, too, fell ill, he played the horn solos on the viola!

Later in the season the two musicians had a merry time during the Roman Carnival. Together with two friends, they hit upon the idea of disguising themselves as blind street-singers. Rossini forthwith composed some music; Paganini and he, dressed as women, solemnly strummed it on guitars. What a picture they must have made: Paganini, tall, thin and angular; Rossini, short, thick and fat.

Intermittently for the next few years the violinist was obliged to go into seclusion in an effort to regain his health; and in 1823 an especially severe attack of the internal malady that was always with him nearly took his life. The year 1826 brought him great happiness in the birth of his son. Two years later the child became his sole responsibility when legal steps were taken for a permanent separation from Antonia Bianchi, little Achillino's temperamental mother.

In March of the same year—1828—Paganini at last made his long-anticipated trip to Vienna. And words are inadequate to describe the reception at his first concert. The audience went wild with excitement; while, Paganini intoxicated by their enthusiasm, out-Paganinied Paganini! For two months the town rang with his praises: the critics extolled him; great posters displayed his likeness; the shops sold pictures, statues and busts of this unique figure; ladies wore hats "a la Paganini," and Viennese society even ate food that was named in his honor.

But it was also at this period that the false stories concerning a jail-term began seriously to plague him; so much so, that on April the 10th he made a public denial, printed both in German and Italian in the leading Viennese papers. This manifesto served, however, only as fuel to the rumors. *His countenance had the look of another world; his figure was like nothing seen in average men; the way in which he played the violin was awe-inspiring. Surely he must be in league with the nether world!*

Notwithstanding Paganini set out from Vienna with the title—"Virtuoso of the Court"—conferred by the Emperor, as well as the city's presentation of the Gold Medal of St. Salvator.

Appearing in various German cities, he everywhere created a furore. At Cassel his contemporary, Louis Spohr, attended both concerts given by Paganini; and the two diametrically-opposed violinists dined together on one occasion. Impressed by Paganini's pure intonation, Spohr was equally puzzled by his apparent lack of taste; this latter quality showing itself, in Spohr's eyes, both in performance and personal behavior.

For three years "The Virtuoso of the Court"—charlatan, though he might be in the minds of some artists—toured the various cities of Austria, Bavaria, Bohemia, Poland, the Rhenish provinces, and Prussia, everywhere triumphantly received. Then in the spring of 1831 he arrived at the city of perpetual delight—Paris!

Picture his consternation at finding billboards posted about the city depicting him chained to a prison wall. Once again he made a public denial; this time, in the *Revue musicale* where he sought to prove that the rumor began through the public's confusing his name with that of the violinist, Durawoski, arrested for the attempted murder of a priest.

Once again, though the published statement did little to lessen the rumors, Paganini's reputation thus flaunted had only the effect of increasing his popularity. His first concert given at the Opera-House was greeted with greater enthusiasm than he had yet experienced, if such was possible. And it was at this time that he acquired one of his two devoted disciples—Franz Liszt—already a renowned pianist at twenty; Hector Berlioz, he was to meet later.

Fascinated equally by Paganini's technique and personality, Franz Liszt consciously set about apeing both. A good bit of a showman himself, he looked and listened with amazement at such virtuosity, and determined to equal it. But Paganini was to render little direct help to the young pianist's resolution, for though flattered by such obviously sincere enthusiasm, he remained characteristically secretive concerning his methods of achieving effects, holding to his maxim, "Everyone has his secrets."

The story goes that at rehearsals the orchestra players would feverishly await Paganini's entrance in a piece of music, hoping thereby to learn some of the Wizard's secrets. Arrived at a solo-section, with a wave of his hand, Paganini would skip his solo, showing by the sardonic smile on his face that he knew full-well what was in the players' minds. The rehearsal over, quick as a flash he would collect each orchestra-part and carry them away himself to avoid their being too carefully studied. Moreover, once he had achieved his recognized virtuosity, he is supposed never to have practiced. Lying stretched out on a couch on the day of a concert, he would speak scarcely at all, and take little nourishment except soup, or camomile tea. Possibly, during the day, he might strum a bit on either mandoline or guitar, but his violin lay untouched.

In the matter of publication he was equally zealous in guarding his secrets. Much of the music that he composed and played was lost to the world; and even in the case of that which he permitted to be published he frequently omitted the significant parts, lest they be copied or imitated. But, finally persuaded to publish his twenty-four Capricci, he gained rather than lost prestige by so doing; for violinists were the more amazed at his execution of them.

These Capricci immediately proved pianistic challenge for Franz Liszt; and he set about transcribing them for his chosen instrument. Though he finished six only, twelve were originally announced and it is probable that at the outset he intended to do all twenty-four. Of these six perhaps the best known is *La Campanella*, the origin of which is actually first found in Paganini's second violin concerto. Not only is Liszt's name forever linked with that of Paganini because of these direct transcriptions, but the violinist's influence is conspicuously evident in Liszt's own compositions of an extravagant nature: such as, the *Faust* Symphony, the *Mephisto Waltzes* and the *Todtentanz*.

Meanwhile Paganini's reputation had traveled to England. Consequently, when he went there in May of the year 1831, he was greeted with more than usual fanfare. He literally could not walk down the street without being followed, stopped in his path, or even touched to see whether he were flesh and blood like other men. For once the curiosity was too extravagant for comfort. It was all very well to have created a spirited interest in his coming-concert but he *did* want to live to give it; and at moments, weakened by his ever-present throat malady, he became actually frightened by this English reception. In addition, this fear was somewhat aggravated by the public's reaction to the announced prices for his initial appearance. The papers, in fact, printed so much adverse criticism concerning the outrageous amount Paganini had demanded for his London début that the concert was postponed until June, at which time tickets were sold at a more reasonable rate.

But despite this "more reasonable rate," when Paganini left for Italy after his final concert on September 11, 1832, at Portsmouth, he took with him a net profit made in England alone of over 16,000 pounds. Long before this, incidentally, the amazing violinist had added the name "miser" to his various other titles.

Arrived in his native land after an absence of six years, Paganini set about investing his money in landed estates; deciding to become a "country gentleman" at one of these newly acquired properties—the *Villa Gajona* near Parma. For a time he then occupied himself with preparing various manuscripts for publication, but he asked such exorbitant prices for the privilege of publication that Rossini's publisher—Troupenas—with whom he was negotiating, refused to come to terms.

Doubtless missing the stimulation of more sophisticated companionship, Paganini returned to Paris that winter. And it was then that he had the greatest influence on Hector Berlioz. Varied stories have developed concerning their relationship, but since one of the two—Berlioz—has written a full account it seems only sensible to credit his version. Following a period of unusual misfortune, Berlioz had arranged a highly successful concert of his compositions at the Paris Conservatory. Overjoyed at the reception of a program which included his *Symphonie fantastique*, Berlioz, while still basking in the orchestra players' shared delight, following the public's departure, was accosted backstage by a man of singularly compelling appearance. This stranger—lean of face, with piercing eyes and long black hair—clasping the composer's hands, poured forth in a broken voice words of unstinted praise for Berlioz' music. And as Berlioz afterward wrote, *"It was Paganini."*

The two were immediately drawn to each other and soon thereafter, Paganini, on a visit to the French composer, made a suggestion that resulted in one of Berlioz' major compositions. The following is an account according to Berlioz:

"I have a wonderful Stradivari viola but no music for it. Suppose you write me a solo. Only you can do it." said Paganini immediately upon his arrival.

Vastly flattered by this proposal, Berlioz replied that he would gladly do so, but for the fact that he did not play the viola, adding: "I fear that I could never write a sufficiently brilliant composition for one of your virtuosity. It seems to me that only you can do that."

But Paganini, insisting, replied: "You will be successful. As for myself, I am far too unwell to think of composing."

Thus Berlioz found himself writing an orchestral piece interwoven with viola solos; justly proud of the fact that he was not neglecting the part of the orchestra for that of the solo instrument. But no sooner had Paganini set eyes on the score of the first movement than Berlioz was forcefully reminded of his initial opinion concerning anyone's attempting to write a piece for the unique virtuoso-player.

Noticing the rests in the viola part, Paganini exclaimed: "That will never do. I am silent far too much of the time. I must be always playing!"

"Exactly!" replied Berlioz. "That is what I said. What you really want is a viola concerto, and only you can write it."

To which, Paganini, obviously disappointed, did not reply.

Following this conversation Berlioz resumed the task of writing the composition; now, completely independent of suiting the style of Paganini's wishes. Using the viola as a melancholy dreamer wending its way through the piece, he produced in a very short time the highly regarded *Harold in Italy* Symphony. Given its performance at the Conservatory, on November 23, 1834, it was immediately successful, but Paganini was not to hear it for another four years. Meanwhile the violinist had returned to Italy, where, he appeared at rare intervals in charity concerts, or played on state occasions—including one at the court of the Duchess of Parma at which time he received the Imperial Order of St. George.

Then, regardless of the fact that long ago he had vowed to put gambling forever out of his life, Paganini found himself in the year 1836 involved in the finances of a gambling-house in Paris, bearing his name. The net result of this "Casino Paganini" for the violinist was the loss of a great deal of money and the breakdown of his already ailing health; for he was obliged to give various concerts to help defray the expenses.

Still another meeting was to take place between him and the always-in-some-kind-of-trouble Berlioz. This one occurred in the late fall of 1838 at a Paris Conservatory concert when Paganini heard for the first time the *Harold in Italy* Symphony. Suffering with bronchitis, but desperately in need of funds, Berlioz had arranged for two concerts to offset an unfortunate production of his opera, *Benvenuto Cellini*, which, incidentally, Paganini had attended and about which he was heard to remark, "If I were manager of the Opéra, I would commission Berlioz to write three such operas; pay him in advance, and make a good bargain thereby."

Equally stirred by the *Harold in Italy* music, Paganini, with his young son Achillino, rushed backstage to congratulate Berlioz. Gesticulating wildly, Paganini tried desperately to express himself. But at this time his throat was so badly affected by the long-endured disease that he could not speak above a whisper. Consequently, owing to a good bit of confusion caused by the dispersal of the orchestra, Berlioz could not hear a word that Paganini said. Finally at a gesture from his father, Achillino got up on a chair, held his ear to his father's mouth and thus managed to hear what Paganini wished to convey to the French composer.

Getting down from the chair, Achillino then turned to Berlioz and delivered his father's message: "My father wishes me to say that he has never before been so moved at a concert. And he is so affected by your music that he can scarcely resist falling on his knees at your feet!"

And before Berlioz knew what was happening to him Paganini, grasping him by the arm, pulled him onto the stage and in front of the astonished musicians, knelt and kissed the composer's hand.

The aftermath of this little drama provided the greatest controversy yet for Paganini's critics. Having gained a reputation for stinginess, Paganini was not believed capable of the generosity soon to be credited to him in some quarters. But since his son was later to verify the story as told by Berlioz there seems no reason for us to doubt it. Paganini, apparently touched by a fellow-artist's financial plight, admiring the man, and only too familiar with the handicaps of poverty, decided to remove such a burden from Berlioz' shoulders.

At any rate, confined to his bed by an attack of bronchitis a few days later, Berlioz was surprised by a visit from Achillino Paganini. "My father will be sorry to learn that you are ill," said the boy. "If he were not ill himself he would have come to see you. Consequently he asked me to bring you this letter."

But when Berlioz began to break the seal of the epistle Achillino stopped him, saying, "My father said that you were to read it at your leisure, for there was to be no answer." And with that he left the room.

Thinking it to be a letter of congratulation, Berlioz broke the seal and read: "My Dear Friend:

Beethoven is gone, and only Berlioz can revive him. Having listened to your divine compositions, so worthy of your genius, I beg you to accept, in token of my homage, twenty thousand francs which will be transferred to you by the Baron de Rothschild on presentation of the enclosed.

Believe me always your affectionate friend,

Niccolo Paganini."

The news of Paganini's generosity spread like wildfire, causing his enemies to say that it was merely a bid for public favor; while some even asserted that Paganini was only the intermediary for an anonymous giver. Notwithstanding Berlioz benefited greatly by the token; and Paganini's obvious admiration for his genius justifies our conviction that he thus generously contributed to its development.

Soon thereafter, on the advice of medical authority, the suffering violinist went to Marseilles in the hope of regaining his health. And for a time it looked as though the change of climate, together with his tremendous will to get well, had restored a certain portion of his native energy. Taking up his violin, he often played for sheer enjoyment's sake, especially moving his listeners by the performance of a favorite-Beethoven quartet.

But the improvement in his health was short-lived. Feeling another severe attack of the old malady returning, Paganini decided to travel to Genoa by sea—hoping to benefit by the voyage. From Genoa he went to Nice, thinking that the warm climate would surely help his throat. Alas, such was not to be the case; he grew steadily worse.

And, one night—apparently aware that it would be his last—the dying violinist reached for his faithful Joseph Guarnerius and played as he had never played before. Thus the most famous of all violinists died—on May 27, 1840—at beautiful Nice.

Due to the devil-communion rumors surrounding him and the fact that he had not received the last rites of the Church, his body was not at once permitted burial in consecrated soil. But five years after the great artist's death, Achillino contrived to obtain permission to hold a memorial service in the burial ground of the little church near his favorite home—the *Villa Gajona*.

Paganini, according to his will, had wanted little attention paid to his passing. After listing a fortune to be paid to his son, certain amounts to his two sisters, and an annuity for Antonia Bianchi, the document reads, "I desire that no musician play a Requiem for me; and I bequeath my violin to the city of Genoa where it may be permanently kept."

Today a visitor to Genoa may see this famous Joseph Guarnerius del Gesù, sealed forever within a cylindrical glass case, hung in a blue, silk-lined recess in the city's museum. At its feet outside the case—but within the niche—lies another violin, looking for all the world as though it had through persistence found its place there. We find that this Stradivarius belonged to Camillo Sivori, Paganini's only pupil with the exception of a little girl by the name of Caterina Calcagno, who, after making a successful debut at the age of fifteen, disappeared soon thereafter from public life.

Paganini, unlike the other great violinists, was descended from no particular school; nor did he found one, except in the sense that no fiddle player after him could ignore his influence. In addition to his dazzling feat of playing such pieces as the *Witches Dance* on one string, changing the tuning of his violin to produce wierd effects, and the countless other tricks of his temperament, Paganini genuinely contributed to the art of violin playing: By pursuing the furthest possibilities of harmonic tones he extended the compass of the violin; by developing the use of double-stops, left-hand pizzicato, and staccato-bowing, he enriched the instrument's color-palette.

By just being PAGANINI he made himself immortal!

LOUIS SPOHR

Louis Spohr—at times referred to as *Ludwig* Spohr, though recorded in his *Autobiography* as *Louis*—was born at Brunswick in Northern Germany, on April 5, 1784, two years later than Niccolo Paganini. Had the fates set out to furnish a striking contrast in violinists they could not have succeeded better. For Spohr, equally as individualistic as Paganini both in playing and composing, lived worlds apart from the Italian virtuoso: Solid, dignified and distinguished—the German violinist; elusive, eerie and indifferent—Paganini!

Born in the house of his grandfather, a clergyman, little Louis was taken when two years old by his father, a physician, to Seesen. Here the future violinist, composer and conductor spent a happy childhood unmolested by over-discipline; though both parents were musical and he early showed a talent in that direction. The young physician, a good flute player, and his wife, both pianist and singer, often spent wonderful musical evenings together and when their son was four he joined his mother in singing duets. At five he began to play the violin; at six he could take part in trios written by Christian Kalkbrenner; and soon he himself was writing violin duets.

His first teachers—whose names were Riemenschneider and Dufour—were both amateur musicians; Dufour, being a Frenchman then living in Germany. And he it was who, impressed with the boy's talent, persuaded Louis' father to send his son to Brunswick for further study.

At Brunswick Louis attended grammar school and continued his varied musical studies, taking violin lessons from Kunisch, a member of the Duke's band, and counterpoint from an organist by the name of Hartung. According to Spohr's *Autobiography*, this was the only instruction in the theory of music that he ever had. Like Wagner and many other composers, Spohr appears to have acquired the technique of composition through studying the scores of the great masters; in Spohr's case, especially, Mozart.

Young Spohr made his first public appearance at a school concert; at which he played one of his own concertos so successfully that he was asked to repeat it at one of the Duke's band concerts. And doubtless at Kunisch's insistance, following this performance, Louis began to take violin lessons from Maucourt, leader of the Duke's band and considered the best violinist in Brunswick.

Then at fourteen encouraged by his steady progress, with a few letters of introduction in his pocket, Spohr set out on his first tour. Alas, after desperate but fruitless attempts to gain a hearing at Hamburg, he was forced to return penniless to Brunswick. Disheartened by this experience, Spohr resolved to appeal to the Duke for help in continuing his studies. And it proved a thoroughly sensible resolution; for the Duke, impressed both by his forthright manner and his talent, not only gave the young violinist a place in his band but offered to defray the expenses for further study under a recognized master of the violin.

True to his word, the Duke set about searching for a proper teacher; and in seeking the best, it was natural that he approach the great Giovanni Battista Viotti. Failing to persuade the violinist-turned-wine-merchant to accept another pupil, the Duke turned to Johann Friedrich Eck who recommended his brother, Franz Eck, then traveling in Germany. Acting upon this suggestion, the Duke at once invited Franz Eck to the court; and pleased with his playing, he arranged for him to take Louis Spohr along on his concert tour, with the provision that the artist meanwhile instruct the eager young violinist enroute; in payment for which, the Duke provided both a salary and one half the traveling expenses.

Accordingly, in the spring of 1802, artist and pupil set out for Russia. Fortunately they made prolonged stays in both Hamburg and Strelitz which provided fruitful periods of uninterrupted study for Spohr. It is well that this happened for once they actually got under way in the matter of concert-giving there was little time for lessons. Notwithstanding the traveling-pupil gained from hearing Eck play, for, though not a good musician, he was an excellent violinist. At the same time—lessons or no lessons—Spohr, a large husky youth, practiced as much as ten hours a day and even found time to do a great deal of composing. His first published violin concerto—in the style of Pierre Rode—was written then, as well as violin duets which were later published.

That winter they spent in St. Petersburg, where Spohr had an opportunity to meet many eminent musicians including the piano-pioneers—Muzio Clementi and John Field. And although he had no opportunity to appear in public, the young violinist gained immeasurably from the Russian experience.

Arrived back at Brunswick in the summer, he found to his great delight that Pierre Rode, Viotti's most famous pupil, was appearing there. Vastly impressed upon hearing Rode play, Spohr eagerly sought to assimilate the master's characteristics, though eventually he was to emerge with his own individual style; as impossible to copy in its way as was Paganini's.

Now a thoroughly equipped violinist and musician, Spohr gave a highly successful concert at Brunswick and then resumed his duties in the Duke's band. Soon thereafter he started on a journey to Paris, the goal of artists in every age. Arrived at the gates of Goettingen, to his great consternation, Spohr discovered that his most precious and essential possession had been stolen. Some one had snatched the satchel containing his priceless Guarnerius violin as the coach jounced through the countryside.

Imagine his dismay! There was no point in continuing the journey to Paris without a violin. And to think that it was his precious Guarnerius, received not so long before from a Russan admirer.

Returning to Brunswick, he soon acquired another violin with the help of his friend, the Duke, but it in no way compared to the one lost. Undaunted by a circumstance that could not be helped, Spohr soon buried himself in preparations for a German tour, which was to include in its itinerary Dresden, Leipzig, Berlin and other cities. He was everywhere successful, his fame steadily preceding him as he went along. And it was at Berlin that he was assisted in a concert by Giacomo Meyerbeer, a young pianist of thirteen, who was to become famous as a prolific opera composer.

Owing to the reputation gained on this tour, Spohr was offered the post of leader in the band of the Duke of Gotha; a position he assumed in the year 1805. While there he married Dorette Scheidler, an accomplished harp player, with whom he often appeared in concerts and for whom he wrote several sonatas for violin and harp, in addition to solo pieces. And having a competent band at his disposal, he began to experiment with the composition of vocal and orchestral music in the larger forms; his first attempt at opera writing being given at one of the court concerts.

In 1807 Spohr, now a well-known violinist, set out on a concert tour with his wife. Revisiting some of the cities, previously cordial, he included several others on this tour. Leipzig, Dresden, Prague, Munich, Heidelberg, Frankfort, and Stuttgart all paid homage to the distinguished violinist and his wife; while at Stuttgart, Spohr had the good fortune to meet Carl Maria von Weber, another coming-musician.

Back at Gotha, Spohr resumed his duties as leader of the band, meanwhile continuing to compose. His second opera, *Alruna*, written at this time, was accepted for production at Weimar by the great Goethe, then manager of the Weimar Theatre; but, for some reason, it never reached the stage. Louis Spohr was not one to be easily discouraged, however, as we shall see in the unfolding of his next venture.

Later this same year came the announcement of Napoleon's projected Congress of Princes at Erfurt. Spohr, curious to see so much royalty thus assembled decided to take the journey to Erfurt for this purpose. It so happened that a French troupe of artists were giving nightly performances for the entertainment of these visiting princes. And it was to one of these affairs that Spohr immediately sought admission. To his great disappointment he found that only a few were permitted to enter the theatre; and, since he was not among the privileged, his trip appeared to have been made in vain.

But the persistent violinist had no intention of returning to Gotha without having seen the assembled monarchs. Believing that where there is a will there is a way, he conceived the idea of persuading the second-horn player in the orchestra to permit him to take his place. What matter that he had never played a horn in his life. He would learn the rudiments in a day! And, though his lips were sore and swollen from the effort, when night came he had sufficiently mastered the instrument to enable his carrying out the little scheme. Fortunately having been forewarned that the musicians were not permitted to face the assemblage, the violinist-turned-horn player carried a pocket mirror with him to overcome the disadvantages of this regulation.

Thus it was, with the tiny mirror placed inconspicuously on the music-rack before him, that the ingenious Spohr saw as plain as day Napoleon and his honored guests sitting close behind him!

During the following year he made another tour through Northern Germany, everywhere received as the nation's foremost violinist. And at Hamburg to his great satisfaction, he was commissioned to write an opera, *The Lovers' Duel;* Spohr, being one of those artists not content with the mastery of one art-form. This opera was subsequently given with gratifying success; while at this time he already had to his credit six violin concertos.

To his growing list of accomplishments he now added conducting. In the year 1809 he was privileged to conduct Germany's First Music Festival— held at Frankenhausen, a small town in the Bach-world of Thuringia. For another one of these occasions he composed his first symphony. Branching out still further, he wrote in 1812, at the invitation of the French Governor of Erfurt, his first oratorio, for performance at a Napoleon Celebration in August of that year. His nature is especially well revealed in his own reaction to this oratorio's presentation: realizing that the composition suffered from his lack of practice in fugue and counterpoint writing, he at once went out, bought himself a copy of Friedrich Wilhelm Marpurg's treatise on fugue, diligently studied it, wrote a few fugues on the author's models and considered himself equipped with another tool!

That winter, after appearing for the first time in Vienna, with remarkable success, he accepted the post of leader of the band at the newly opened *Theatre an der Wien*. While there he met Ludwig van Beethoven but, strangely enough, failed to appreciate fully the great master's genius, although he did admire his quartets and was the first, in fact, to perform some of them. Meanwhile, not neglecting his own composing, he wrote during the next summer one of his most important works, the opera, *Faust,* as well as a cantata to celebrate the battle of Leipzig.

After spending three years at Vienna, where he had added further stature to his steadily growing renown, Spohr, following a disagreement with the management of the theatre, relinquished his position. Genuinely in need of a vacation, he spent that summer at the country home of Prince Carolath in Bohemia; but it is not likely that he sat and twiddled his thumbs for his cantata, *Das befreite Deutschland,* was ready for presentation under his direction at the next music festival at Frankenhausen.

Shortly thereafter Germany's leading violinist and most prodigious composer ventured outside his own country, going to Italy by way of Alsace and Switzerland. Not only did he give various concerts on the way, but he found time to compose a concerto—the *Scena cantante;* writing it purposefully in what he called "the Italian style." Though Spohr would never stoop to Paganini-tricks, such as deliberately using worn violin strings in order to show an audience how well he could play on three, two, or even *one*, he was practical enough to write music deliberately intended to please the Italian taste. Perhaps without doing the great violinist an injustice we might applicably remark of his behavior, "When in Rome do as the Romans do."

Be that as it may, he appears to have been well received in the "Land of Paganini, Stradivarius, and Corelli," playing in all the principal towns and including the recently written concerto on his programs at Rome and Milan. While in Italy he met the jolly Gioacchino Rossini, but, according to his *Autobiography,* was not particularly impressed with Rossini's music. In fact, if Louis Spohr's reputation were confined to the role of critic his name would long ago have disappeared, except for ridicule. Fortunately he was more violinist than critic!

Following his return to Germany, Spohr next went to Holland and soon thereafter accepted the post of opera conductor at Frankfort-on-the-Main. It was here that his opera, *Faust,* was first produced. Fairly successful, it was immediately followed by still another of Spohr's operas—*Zemira and Azor*—at first the greater success of the two. Then again arriving at some disagreement with the management, Spohr, after a two years' stay, left Frankfort.

At the invitation of the London Philharmonic Society, Spohr, in the spring of 1820, went to London for the first time, where he was cordially received in the capacity of a distinguished visiting artist and composer. He played in one of his concertos—*nello stilo drammatico*—at the initial concert and in his solo quartet in E at the second. Then at the third concert he inaugurated a new feature into the Philharmonic concerts, following a good bit of persuasion on his part. According to the custom, on this occasion he should have led the orchestra as first violinist, but, instead, he insisted upon conducting with a baton. Thus it was—by breaking down the prejudice against this innovation—that Spohr is credited with having been the first to conduct a Philharmonic concert with a conductor's stick. Meanwhile, true to his nature, he had finished a new symphony since coming to London; and this, he conducted from manuscript on that occasion.

Still another of his symphonies was performed at the last concert of the season, as well as a small composition for strings and wind. Spohr was especially delighted with the string section of the Philharmonic orchestra; while we, knowing that Viotti had helped in the society's organization, may assume that this great master may have contributed the strings' efficiency.

Spohr's wife played at his farewell concert in London and it also proved to be her farewell appearance as a harpist, for ill-health necessitated her relinquishing thereafter the harp for the piano. Once again rising to the occasion, Spohr began to write piano and violin duets which they often played together at subsequent concerts.

On their way home they stopped at Paris, where Spohr met Viotti, Cherubini, Rodolphe Kreutzer and other eminent musicians. They treated him with marked honor and respect; Cherubini, according to Spohr's report, asking him to repeat one of his quartets three times. At the same time his concert given at the Opéra was cordially received, but, on the whole, Paris and Spohr proved not akin.

Returning to Germany, he settled at Dresden, where he enjoyed the stimulating companionship of Carl Maria von Weber who was then occupied with his lovely opera, *Der Freischütz*. Curiously enough, Spohr had previously entertained the idea of writing an opera on the same subject, but now gladly gave up any such notion on learning of Weber's project; for the composer-violinist greatly admired his fellow-countryman's music. In fact he considered it far superior to Beethoven's!

Weber in turn, admiring the distinguished violinist, recommended Spohr for the post of court conductor at Cassel, when the Elector of Hesse-Cassel offered him the position. Accordingly, on New Year's Day, 1822, Louis Spohr took up his duties—to continue for the rest of his life—at Cassel. It is with this city that his name is traditionally associated. There his reputation grew to its ultimate stature and there he came magnificently into his own.

In addition to his court duties, he found time to do a vast amount of composing; *Jessonda*, his most famous opera, being produced soon after his arrival at Cassel. He himself conducted the first performances of it at Berlin and Leipzig; and it rapidly became part of the standard repertory of other German cities. While in Berlin, during the winter of 1824, Spohr had an opportunity to become well acquainted with Felix Mendelssohn and his distinguished family; continuing an association that had started two years previously when the Mendelssohns spent some time at Cassel.

Two years later he conducted the Rhenish Festival at Düsseldorf, where his oratorio, *The Last Judgment*, met with such favor that it was repeated at a benefit concert for Greek revolutionists. Then for a time he occupied himself once more with opera composing, three operas being produced in rapid succession without receiving the public acclaim of either *Faust* or *Jessonda*. Meanwhile he was also concerned with one of his most important projects—the great *Violin School*, which was completed in 1831. A standard work in violin literature, the *Violin School*, while chiefly valuable as a guide to Spohr's own compositions, provides generally interesting material in both text and music.

For some time after the beginning of 1832, owing to political unrest, opera production was discontinued at Cassel, providing Spohr with more free time for composition. And needless to say, he made good use of the situation, writing among other things his most famous symphony, *The Consecration of Sound*, produced in 1832 at Cassel. The following year he finished his oratorio, *Calvary*, but this was not first given until 1835 on Good Friday. During the previous year his wife died after a long illness; and in 1836 he married the pianist, Marianne Pfeiffer.

In 1839, at the invitation of the directors of the Norwich Festival, Spohr went to England to conduct his *Calvary*. And this event proved the crowning triumph of his career, despite the fact that certain clergymen in England had objected to his oratorio's being given because of its subject matter. Additional evidence of his having won favor in England came soon after his return to Cassel in an invitation to compose an oratorio on a libretto, *The Fall of Babylon*, to be given in 1842 at the Norwich Festival.

Meanwhile, having conducted in 1840 the Festival at Aix-la-Chapelle,

Spohr produced two years later at Cassel Wagner's *The Flying Dutchman* at a time when producing "Wagner" revealed unique perception and a radical spirit. But this year was destined to bring disappointment to the indefatigable composer, violinist and conductor; for the Elector of Cassel, doubtless disapproving of Spohr's radical tendencies in politics and wishing to punish him, refused to permit his going to England to conduct *The Fall of Babylon* at the Norwich Festival. Consequently although various English admirers sent a petition asking the Elector to reconsider, Spohr was forced to enjoy the triumph of his latest oratorio from afar.

But once the first day of his summer vacation arrived, the disappointed royal-employee set out for England; and soon after his arrival he had an opportunity to hear the applause first-hand when he conducted the oratorio at the Hanover Square Rooms in London. It was later given a more elaborate presentation by the Sacred Harmonic Society in Exeter Hall. And on July 3rd the Philharmonic Society devoted its last concert of the season, in great part, to the visiting German's music; including on its program a symphony, an overture, a violin concerto, and a vocal duet by Spohr. Following a special-request concert before Queen Victoria and Prince Albert, Spohr toured triumphantly through Southwestern England and Wales, returning to Cassel refreshed by a vacation both pleasant and profitable.

During the year 1843, an incident occurred that both indicates Spohr's importance and his independence. Enroute to Darmstadt on a concert tour, Hector Berlioz, the French composer, decided to stop at Cassel for the exclusive purpose of seeing the renowned Spohr. But Berlioz relates in his *Memoirs* that *it was seven in the morning; Spohr was asleep and must not be awakened.*

The following year Spohr completed his last opera, *The Crusaders,* and went to Paris for his vacation that summer. There he attended many musical events, including a specially arranged performance of his *Consecration of Sound*. Later in the year at the Beethoven Festival at Bonn he conducted Beethoven's *Missa Solemnis* and great Ninth Symphony.

His next visit to England occurred in 1847 when he went to London to attend a series of three Sacred Harmonic Society concerts devoted entirely to his compositions. Returning to Cassel, he found himself caught up in the great political whirl that was agitating Germany; and he even spent his precious vacation that following summer listening to the debates of the newly organized German Parliament at Frankfort. This interest in political freedom was destined to bring the court musician into disrepute with his Elector-employer. After a busy winter, during which he completed his symphony, *The Seasons*, he met with the Elector's refusal to sign his usual, contracted-for vacation leave-of-absence. Greatly annoyed, Spohr left without the signature thereby cutting out for himself a lawsuit, lasting for four years, which he eventually lost.

Meanwhile having made an adaptation of his opera, *Faust*, to suit the Italian style, substituting singing for spoken dialogue, Spohr went to London to attend its performance at the new Opera at Covent Garden. Generally regarded as a successful undertaking it, nevertheless aroused little genuine enthusiasm, according to the English critic, Henry Chorley, who was present. In his *Thirty Years' Musical Recollections* Chorley refers to "the excellent performance at Covent Garden," praises the incomparable orchestra and chorus, but adds that "even the veritable presence of the composer could do nothing to change our apathetic respect into real enjoyment." Chorley further remarks that while Spohr was a distinguished violinist and composer of violin music he was destined, otherwise, to be little remembered.

That winter, after overcoming the Elector's objections, Spohr produced Wagner's *Tannhaüser* at Cassel; hoping to follow it up with *Lohengrin;* but he was, in this, disappointed. From his first acquaintance with Wagner's operas, Spohr had declared that Wagner was the greatest living dramatic composer, thereby, winning our indulgence for some of his traditionally mistaken judgment.

Later the same season he went to London for the last time. On this occasion he conducted several Philharmonic concerts which included a number of his compositions. But whether he was conducting "Beethoven" or "Spohr," according to contemporary witnesses, the result was always SPOHR. And this seems to be most consistent criticism of him as artist, composer, and man. Thoroughly competent, composer of romantic music, he, nevertheless remained cold and aloof from his fellow beings, unconsciously wrapped within himself.

His opera, *Jessonda*, was in preparation for production at Covent Garden during this last London visit, but the Cassel contract prevented his staying to see the performance. The critic Chorley in referring to the Covent Garden *Jessonda*, says that "it was listened to with respect...."

Four years later, against his wishes, he was relieved from his post at Cassel on a pension. And as though this were not enough to irk a man of Spohr's indefatigable nature, he had the misfortune that winter to break his arm—ending forever his career as violinist.

The following year he vigorously conducted a performance of his *Jessonda* at Prague, in celebration of the fiftieth anniversary of the Prague Conservatory. This proved to be his last public appearance. He died on October 22, 1859, at Cassel: apparently, his life being over when his work ceased.

Louis Spohr will long be remembered as one of the great violinists; his style, revealing breadth of tone rather than brilliance. Where Paganini threw his bow, bounding, at the strings, Spohr held each stroke, firmly marked; while other violinists screamed with the latest feats of technique, Spohr calmly sang in both delicate and sonorous tones. The style and the man live on in his music: some of his violin concertos holding best promise for long life. Unlike Paganini he had many pupils—including Ferdinand David—but like Paganini he left no violinist-heir. The grand, singing tones produced by hands unusually large and inspired by a highly individual mind, can be approximated by studyng his *Violin School* and compositions; but, in the final analysis, only Spohr was SPOHR.

OLE BORNEMAN BULL

OLE BORNEMAN BULL—the Paganini-of-the-North—was born on February 5, 1810, at the *Svaneapothek*, situated in the very center of Bergen, Norway. Passionately stirred by love of his native land, he was destined—violin in hand—to spread the spirit of Norway from the splendid courts of Imperial Russia to the wildest mining town in young America.

The eldest of ten children, "Ole Olsen Viol, Norse Norman from Norway," as he called himself, was the son of Johan Storm Bull, a chemist and apothecary, and Anna Dorothea Geelmuyden Bull of Dutch descent. From his earliest childhood little Ole had "a way" with him that was hard to resist; a quality, which was to increase with the years as people flocked to his concerts in crowds and ladies swooned for love of him.

Those early days were divided between the apothecary's substantial house with the swan, made of wood, hanging over its door and the family's summer home called *Valestrand*, at Osteroy, some twenty miles north of Bergen. It was in the Norwegian countryside that the future violinist found his greatest joy, absorbing into his very being the sound of its streams, the feel of its forests and the smell of its heather. Added to these was the stored up memory of folk songs, dances, and country fiddle playing.

When scarcely three years old the strong-willed little boy showed a significant interest in music and by the time he was five he had mastered the elements of violin playing without any instruction. At this point his Uncle Jens, who played the violoncello, took him in hand. Next he studied with a Dane by the name of Paulsen and finally with Herr Lundholm, a Swede lately settled in Bergen who had been a pupil of Pierre Baillot.

But this precocious talent for music was by no means approved by Johan Bull, the apothecary. How different might have been the career of his extraordinary son had he been given a proper musical education in his youth: Whereas native skill and bravado prevailed in his fantastic career, finished artistry of limitless heights might have resulted from a thorough understanding of the theory of music and wider knowledge of the world's great music. This is, of course, all in the realm of might-have-been; a state of affairs, which could not have brought greater love to Ole Bull than the course he was destined to follow.

The initial step in this career was brought about by Ole's father's determination that his first-born should become a clergyman. Accordingly, Ole was provided with a tutor who was directed to prepare the boy for theological studies and to discourage thoroughly his musical tendencies. In fact, Ole was forbidden to touch the violin! The end-result of this enforced tutor-situation was that Ole, now a strapping youth, crossed by the teacher, gave the latter a sound thrashing, and thereby won his freedom.

He won his freedom from the tutor only to be packed off to Christiania, now known as Oslo, to take examinations for entrance into the University of Christiania. His father's farewell words, *Don't you touch the violin*, rang in his ears throughout the fateful journey, destined to be the beginning of fabulous journeying.

No sooner had he arrived at Christiania than out came his fiddle. He could no more obey his father's command than he could stop eating—and live. Before nightfall he had gathered an impromptu following among the Christiania students and not many days later he had played for Waldemar Thrane, violinist and conductor of the local orchestra. Needless to say, he did not pass his examinations. But undaunted, he persuaded Thrane to let him play in his orchestra; and in the fall, at the conductor's death, Ole became the orchestra's leader.

Gloriously in his element, throwing himself whole-heartedly into the artistic and political life of the community, he soon found congenial friends; among them, Henrik Wergeland, an ardent Norwegian poet and patriot. Here it was that Ole Bull's ardent nationalism took shape. Inspired by Wergeland's efforts in the National Revival movement, he, too, became active in an attempt to bring about the complete independence of Norway. Having been under the domination of Denmark since 1397, Norway had, in 1814, gained her independence from that country; but alas, in the minds of the patriots, she was still not fully independent for she was united with Sweden. Little did Ole Bull and his enthusiastic young friends know that nearly a hundred years were to pass before Norway became her independent self!

Be that as it may, on May 17, 1829, the young patriot-violinist suddenly left Christiania, without his violin, following his participation in a forbidden ceremony celebrating the Independence Day of 1814.

Resolved to become a famous violinist in order to carry the fame of his native land to the far corners of the earth, Ole Bull first considered going to Paris to study with Pierre Baillot; but, instead, he set out for Germany where he hoped to win the attention of the eminent Louis Spohr. Though he had never heard the German violinist play he was aware of Spohr's great reputation; and filled with grandiose hopes for his own future, he naturally sought in a teacher the *best*.

Arrived at Cassel, the exuberant young Norwegian went immediately to Spohr. Words tumbled forth helter skelter as he tried in vain to persuade the austere master to become his teacher. Spohr not only remained indifferent to Ole's pleading but even refused to play for the eager youth, informing him that he might have the privilege of hearing him by traveling to Nordhausen where he was to play at a festival.

Accordingly, disappointed but not discouraged, Ole set out for Nordhausen at the designated time. And naturally enough, upon hearing Spohr play, he was not particularly impressed; he was, in fact, as cooly responsive to the great violinist as the latter had previously been to him. Diametrically opposed in temperament to Spohr, Ole, with his strong, lyric nature could not appreciate the solid, formal manner of Spohr's playing. But once again we are forced to ask whether Ole Bull's career might have been different *if* this situation had been one from which a sound musical education had resulted.

As it was, Spohr's rebuff, together with the reaction on Ole of his playing, served to cement the direction of Ole Bull's career. Henceforth he developed along lines of his own individuality both in violin playing and musical composition. And while in each instance a natural singing-quality produced stirring results, how phenomenal might have been Ole Bull's musical career had he come, for instance, under the guidance of Joseph Joachim, who, was later to say of the Norwegian violinist, "If Ole Bull had gone the right way he would have been the greatest of all violinists."

After a summer spent in Goettingen, where, becoming involved in a duel and knowing nothing about dueling, he nevertheless came out victorious, Ole first returned to Christiania then to Bergen. He now began to wander through the country, picking up folk tunes as he went along; and weaving them into his own compositions he played them for the city dwellers in an attempt to arouse an appreciation for Norway's native music. Although it cannot be said that he was entirely successful in accomplishing this objective, he did succeed in arousing wild enthusiasm for his own playing; Bergen and Trondjem being two cities where he was particularly triumphant.

Then in 1831 Ole Bull, equipped with marvelous fiddle-facility—though it be of his own making—set sail from Bergen for Ostend with his destination—Paris. Seven long years, filled with sensational success, were to go by before he again saw his beloved Norway. But wherever he went there went Norway; for he never once relented in his resolve to become famous not for himself but for Norway!

Arrived at Paris, Ole Bull soon made the acquaintance of various contemporary musicians: the young Chopin, born the same month and year as himself; Ferdinand Hiller, Rossini, Habeneck—the eminent conductor, and Wilhelm Ernst with whom he lived for a time. But sophisticated Paris, then and ever after, was not to prove the scene of the Northerner's great triumphs.

Notwithstanding "the turning point of his life," as he afterwards stated, occurred at Paris: It was there that he first heard Paganini play; and the final spark to his own genius was thereby lit. Throwing himself into technical studies, he emerged with Paganini-like feats of display, colored by his own Ole Bull-exuberance. One of his characteristic innovations was the lowering and flattening of the violin's bridge whereby he could play on all four strings at once.

His lack of theoretical knowledge, however, already in that Paris visit, was the cause of his not securing a post that he sought. Handed a simple piece of music to play when he applied for a place in the Opéra orchestra, the embarrassed violinist defensively asked, "At which end would you like me to begin?" As we can see, nothing ever stopped him; a characteristic which is eloquently apparent from his youthful motto, *Bellum vita, vita bellum,* "Life is Battle, Battle is Life."

Following a severe illness he moved into the home of Madame Villeminot where he was nursed back to health. Madame Villeminot, who declared that he resembled her son who had died, was only the first of many women destined to "mother" him in his long career. Throughout his life, in various parts of the world, the famous "way with him" melted the hearts of women and impelled them to look after him. This particular household proved more than a haven; for in it, lived Félicie Alexandrine Villeminot—Madame Villeminot's orphaned granddaughter and Ole Bull's future wife.

Having completely recovered on April 18, 1832, Ole Bull made his first public appearance in Paris at a concert in which he was assisted by Wilhelm Ernst and Frederic Chopin. Though warmly received he was not by any means granted an ovation. Such an experience awaited him in the not-far distant future.

Setting out for Switzerland in 1833, he began his career in earnest. Thoroughly in stride, his glowing temperament ablaze, the tall, sturdy Norseman, throwing himself heart and soul into his concerts at Geneva, Lausanne, and Vevey, met with correspondent enthusiasm from his audiences. At about this time he hit upon one of his most successful and characteristic gestures: that of incorporating into his concerts the songs of the nation in which he happened to be playing. This never failed to win an audience, for, in addition to the national element involved, there was Ole Bull's incomparable skill in making the violin sing. And generous by nature, he would *sing away* on his fiddle far into the night.

From Switzerland he went on to Italy where his success was enormous. At *La Scala* in Milan, at Trieste and Venice, the Italian people flocked to his concerts. He was indeed one of them! Opening their hearts to him, they received his full homage in return.

But Ole Bull always considered his genuine début to have occurred at Bologna, the scene of a tremendous ovation. There are conflicting stories as to the origin of this particular appearance, but the gist of the situation lay in his being chosen by the celebrated singer, Maria Malibran, to substitute for her future husband, Charles de Bériot, who had been scheduled to appear with her.

Be that as it may, Ole Bull took his Bologna listeners by storm. Wild with excitement, following the concert, they drew him through the streets of their city in a horseless carriage. He was immediately engaged for two more concerts and he was made an honorary member of the Bologna Philharmonic Society.

Leaving Bologna, the Northern Paganini met with one success after another as he appeared at Florence, Lucca, Naples, and finally at Rome, where, his striking figure and violin bathed in moonlight, he played in the famous Colosseum. Surely this was proof that Norway's son had held to his youthful resolution: He was indeed famous; there he stood, enjoying the feverish applause for his playing of Norwegian folk songs intermingled with songs of sunny Italy!

By this time his reputation had traveled to other countries. Consequently, when he returned to Paris in the spring of 1835, he came, no longer an unschooled musician seeking a minor post in the Opéra orchestra, but, the *soloist* with this identical orchestra! And despite the handicaps that beset him on this occasion—stumbling as he stepped onto the stage, and then breaking one of the strings of his violin—he was very warmly received. The critics, too, for the most part, were kind to him; particularly, one by the name of Jules Janin who was to remain Ole Bull's staunch supporter, when, later, some of the critics reversed their opinions regarding him.

After giving concerts in the French provinces, the Viking violinist stopped for a time that summer at Dieppe where Jules Janin, who was spending his vacation there, encouraged him to give further concerts in Paris. Accordingly two concerts took place in December at the Opéra and were sensationally successful. Later Ole Bull could look back at this brief season as his one moment of glory in Paris.

"His magic tones are the most delightful that we have heard since Paganini was here," wrote one critic. Another, "His playing is that of a man of genius." While Jules Janin wrote, "He is an artist who never saw his master; he plays a violin not belonging to any school—there is inconceivable power in it, and something naive and inspiring."

"Naive and inspiring," such was the essential quality of the violinist who now set out on a tour of Europe, traveling in an immense carriage large enough to provide sleeping quarters for himself and servant.

After rumbling through various cities on the continent he went to England in the spring of 1836. And though handicapped by a rumor to the effect that Ole Bull simply imitated Paganini, he completely won the hearts of the Londoners at his English début at the King's Theatre in May. After describing this situation in a letter to Félicie Villeminot, he gleefully reported: "Victoria!!! We have won! ... Wreaths, bouquets, applause!"

The critic of *The Times*, after praising the Norwegian's amazing technique, wrote, "His 'Quartette,' in the ordinary mode of playing, would seem impossible; but he distinctly made out chords of three notes with the bow, and produced the fourth with his finger." And further showing the appreciation of this feat, the critic adds that though Bull was thoughtful enough to play the English national anthem at the close of the concert, their great loyalty notwithstanding, the audience would have preferred that he repeat his "Quartette."

His stay in London was truly sensational: after many concerts at the King's Theater he appeared a number of times at the Drury Lane Theatre, Covent Garden—some times two times a day—and finally with the Philharmonic Society. Artistic circles and English society welcomed this lovable genius, while gifts were literally showered upon him. Among his lavish patrons was the Duke of Devonshire—at whose country place he often visited—who presented him with a cluster of diamonds which he had set in the tip of his violin bow.

Mid-summer in 1836, off he went to Paris: a fantastic God of the North to claim his bride! On July 19, he and Félicie, his "little tigress," were married, and while they were to have their ups-and-downs, chiefly owing to the violinist's insistence upon traveling the earth over, they remained devoted to each other. "My white lamb," as Félicie called her husband, immediately following his marriage, set out on a long tour of the English provinces. Félicie, being left behind, thus experienced early the characteristic feature of being married to a traveling-virtuoso.

Ole Bull was accompanied on this journey by an almost equally fantastic musician, the French harpist, Robert Nicolas Bochsa. Jogging over the English countryside, and on through Ireland, Scotland, and Wales the two artists out-did themselves in their respective stunt-playing. And when their carriage broke down, leaving a waiting audience impatiently seated many miles away, Ole Bull, with that wonderful "way with him," changed the ill-favor of the irked assemblage once he stood on the platform. Noticing the people's dour looks, he made believe that he feared for the safety of his violin, holding it behind his back to evade any missiles directed at him. Before long he was playing away as though possessed, the crowd having completely succumbed to his charm.

From "You wouldn't hurt my violin," his fiddle gloriously sang, "I love every one of you."

And of course they, in turn, loved him.

Then with a new traveling companion, a Danish 'cellist, Ole Bull set out for new territory to conquer—Brussels and the North German cities—everywhere meeting with sensational success. Next substituting runners for wheels on the famous carriage, to enable them to travel over the snow, they started for Russia: Königsberg, Riga, and on to St. Petersburg, where the Czarina presented the violinist with two rings, one of which contained eighty diamonds; the other, one hundred and forty! Ole Bull loved Russia and the Russians loved Ole Bull.

Following five public concerts at Moscow, he was off by way of Finland to Stockholm. Called to the palace of the King, he delighted that monarch with his playing, but, all but landed himself into a good bit of trouble by speaking his mind about Norwegian independence. Characteristically Ole Bull emerged from the little argument victorious; king and violinist shaking hands as they parted.

In June, 1838, he arrived in Christiania—a returned-hero! There he was joined by his wife and their little son, Ole, born the previous year. Giving several concerts at Christiania, he was insistent on including many Norwegian folk tunes in his programs. And eventually, through his efforts, the people became conscious of their own music.

Then came a short visit with his family at Bergen. His mother, brothers and sisters—his father had recently died—greeted him, Félicie and little

Ole with open arms; but poor Félicie could not feel at home in this Northern country. Although she was later to make her home in Norway, while her husband was gallivanting about the world, her heart remained forever in France.

Henceforth to the end of his days Ole Bull ceaselessly traveled, stopping only now and again for short visits with his family or for the purpose of hatching some great undertaking to further the interests of his countrymen. Little Ole died while still a baby, but eventually there were five children to welcome him home from his wanderings.

After his hurried visit to Bergen in 1838, he set out on an extended tour, which included Denmark, Holland, France, Austria, Germany, Russia, and England. What a wonderful time he had, traipsing about in his great carriage, meeting new people, renewing old friendships, buying old fiddles—and most important of all—playing the violin to his heart's content. For Ole Bull enjoyed every minute that he was on the platform, drinking in the reaction of his listeners with the sensitivity of a Shakespearean actor. Though his programs consisted chiefly of his own compositions there was an occasional Paganini or Spohr concerto; and the rebuffed young violinist, now grown famous, had the satisfaction while at Cassel of being invited by Spohr to play Mozart quartets with him. Never one to harbor ill-feelings, he gladly accepted the invitation and enjoyed himself immensely.

Probably his greatest fault was extravagance; and even this was tempered with generosity: He would—could it have been managed—have taken the responsibility of all oppressed ones on his own shoulders. Old violins he simply could not resist; at Nuremberg he found a lovely Nicholas Amati; at Leipzig, a Gasparo da Salò; at Pest, a Stradivarius. Back they all went to his friend, J. B. Vuillaume, the noted violin maker, in Paris. Some day he would have time to tinker with them himself!

Then while at Prague he bought fifty gold and silver pheasants and sent them off in the care of a man employed for the purpose to *Valestrand* in Norway. For the most part, however, it was not necessary for him to buy things; for presents of the most extravagant sort were everywhere showered upon him.

In 1840, after several fairly unsuccessful concerts in Paris, he appeared once again in London. Playing with the Philharmonic and by special invitation before Queen Victoria and Prince Albert, he became the sensation of the hour; a position, shared only with Franz Liszt with whom a friendly rivalry developed. They appeared together on several occasions, one of which nearly caused a breach in their friendship: The program mentioned Franz Liszt as appearing with the "eminent violinist." The equally eminent pianist was furious.

"So, you are the eminent violinist!" Liszt hurled at Ole Bull.

But, as always, where the sunny-natured Norwegian was concerned, the situation was smoothed out; and, following the London season, Liszt and Bull appeared together in several concerts on the continent.

During the year 1843 a new adventure appeared on the horizon. Urged by his friend—Fanny Elssler, the dancer, who had been in America—he decided to visit the New World. Accordingly, on November 4, 1843, after bidding his family good-bye in Paris, the "eminent violinist" set sail for America from Liverpool on the Royal Mail steamship, *Caledonia*.

Little did he know that he was sailing to a land eminently suited to his temperament. For America then was indeed the New World; young, spirited and extravagant like himself.

"The world's greatest violinist," according to one New York paper, arrived at Boston on November 20th. On the following day another New York paper, impressed by both his artistry and vigor, wrote: "Ole Bull, the prince of violinists, from Europe, is expected here tomorrow, by the steamer. He is the greatest and best of the lot in the old world—and fights like a tiger."

Settling down at the Astor House with his entourage—consisting of Julius Schuberth as manager, a young Norwegian as secretary, and a German valet—Ole Bull proceeded to take New York by storm. He made his American début November 25, 1843, on Evacuation Day, at the Park Theatre. Referring to the day being celebrated, he said, "John Bull goes out and Ole Bull comes in."

And Ole Bull surely "came in!" The theatre, packed to its very doors, rocked with enthusiasm. The *Herald* next day wrote, "We cannot describe Ole Bull's playing—it is beyond the power of language." Everywhere rang the refrain, "Ole Bull—Ole Bull—Ole Bull!" Six concerts were given in a month; and he finally moved to the immense *Tabernacle* to accommodate the eager crowds.

Equally successful concerts followed in Philadelphia, Baltimore, Washington and Richmond. As he traveled the legends about him grew until even *he* lost track of which were based on fact. When asked by one newspaperman, "Who was your master of the violin?" Bull promptly replied, "God the Infinite!" An answer that was later corroborated by a woman critic in New York when a rivalry sprang up between the Norwegian violinist and Henri Vieuxtemps. This lady wrote, "France made Vieuxtemps—and God made Ole Bull."

Following some trouble with his management, the Heaven-taught violinist set out on a tour that extended north to Canada, south to Cuba, and west to and down the Mississippi. Though the way was not always smooth it was, for one of Ole Bull's nature, exciting. As he himself said, in his broken English, "I am always in de heav-ven or in de odder place below." During his trip down the Mississippi a ruffian demanded that he hand over the diamonds embedded in the bow of his violin. For answer, the violinist picking the man up, threw him over his shoulder to the boat's deck; and thereby, in addition to winning the man's respect, added another legend to the rapidly growing saga of his strength and skill.

Ole Bull was wonderfully in his element in the pioneer-country of America: The rough generous spirit of the people greatly appealed to him; and when, peppering his concerts with "Yankee Doodle" and songs picked up along his travels through the country, he played as long as the applause rang out, he was showered with affection.

New Orleans, Havana, Charleston, Columbia, Norfolk, and finally back to Boston for a tremendous concert on May 21, 1844, at the Melodeon, where his reception was nothing short of sensational. Longfellow the poet wrote, "A great violinist." Certain ladies were heard to remark that his playing transported them into another kingdom. Ralph Waldo Emerson wrote, "It was a beautiful spectacle." While Margaret Fuller, usually reserved in her utterances, admitted, "I felt raised above all care, all pain, all fear, and every taint of vulgarity was washed out of the world."

His entire stay in Boston—during which he gave five concerts—consisted of one triumph after another. And at the conclusion of his last appearance the overwhelmed Norseman made a speech, part of which was:

"Ladies and gentlemen, may you sometimes remember one whose feelings of gratitude always shall be synonymous with the name of Boston. I never leave you. When I go, I don't go. I don't come back when I come. Boston shall be what the sunshine is to the little flower! May it be the flower of everlasting benediction to you!"

Then he returned to New York, where, despite his love for Boston, he made his permanent home while in America. During the winter of 1845, having decided to return to Europe, he began giving a series of farewell concerts, including Boston, Philadelphia, and Baltimore in his tour. By this time to the great delight of his audiences he had added several compositions based on American themes to his repertory: *Niagara, Prairie Solitude* and *To the Memory of Washington*.

His last two concerts in New York were in the nature of benefit performances; and at the final one there was a very touching scene enacted to which he responded with characteristic charm: As the last notes of his music died away one of his admirers, a lady who had often expressed her feelings for him, tossed a bouquet of white roses at his feet from her box nearby. Picking up the flowers, Ole Bull made a little speech in which among other things he graciously avowed, "Ladies and gentlemen, these flowers will fade, but the spirit which gives them will never die away from my grateful heart."

After traveling over one hundred thousand miles and giving over two hundred concerts, on December 3, 1845, the sensational art-ambassador from Norway set sail for Europe on the ship *LeHavre*.

Arrived back in the Old World, Ole Bull discovered that he had left his heart in America. The conservative taste of Paris, where he gave his first concert on his return, doubtless contributed to this reaction. He was glad to escape to the French provinces, and was particularly pleased to come upon his friend, Hans Christian Andersen, at Marseilles. The call of travel once again seizing him, he set sail for Algiers and thence to Spain where he happily remained for a year. Cadiz, Seville, Madrid, Valencia, Barcelona, the Balearic Island towns—all loved Ole Bull and he, them. In Spain, as in America, he felt at home. Royalty, as well as everyday folk, paid him homage; particularly, Queen Isabella, at whose marriage at the age of sixteen he played a concert.

Late in 1847, returning to France, he visited his family in the country for a time. But by summer he had settled down in Paris near his friend Vuillaume, the violin maker, where he tinkered away at old fiddles hours on end. Then in 1848, when the Revolutionary spirit was everywhere rampant, Ole Bull became an active participant: Among other things, he marched at the head of a group of Norwegian patriots and presented the colors of his native land to a revolutionary leader; and he gave a benefit concert for the wounded.

That fall he returned to Norway after an absence of five years. This time he was pleased at the developing national consciousness and soon found himself buried in plans to establish it still further. He purchased the Island Andoën, and then sent for Félicie and their children. Henceforth Norway would be their combined home! Reluctantly Félicie complied. And, though Ole Bull was to continue to wander the earth over, Norway was destined to be thereafter his French wife's home.

During the winter the Students' Union at Christiania gave a great celebration in honor of their violin-hero. On this occasion he played a new composition, *Ex Saeterbesög* (A Visit to the Saeter), based on his most popular melody, *Saeterjentens Söndag* (The Saetergirl's Sunday). Next came a great Norway National Festival at which he played.

Then during the summer of 1849 at Bergen a vast dream began to take shape. He would help found a national Norwegian Theatre! Together with Fritz Jensen, a painter, he began to lay the plans for such an institution. Soon he was giving concerts—including a great open-air one to help raise funds and arouse enthusiasm for the project. Excitement ran high, with the people sometimes following him to his lodging and cheering until he would play, to their great delight, his *Saeterjentens Söndag*.

"Long live Norway!" they'd cry. "Long live old Bergen! Long live Ole Bull!"

Finally, after a tremendous struggle, a company for the theatre was got together; the building selected got painted red on the inside with the help of Ole Bull himself; an orchestra was assembled and trained under the violinist, even unto his giving some of the individuals private lessons; and on January

2, 1850, the Norway National Theater opened at Bergen. This was its motto: "Norwegian plays, Norwegian actors, Norwegian music, and a Norwegian ballet." It was a wonderful occasion: a genuine Norwegian comedian was recognized in Johannes Brun who appeared in the play, *Henrik and Pernille*; Ole Bull conducted Mozart's *Jupiter Symphony*, and, at the peak of the audience's enthusiasm, he burst forth on his violin in the *Saeterbesög*.

To Félicie, he wrote, "It is necessary for the national honor to carry out this work—and the work will go on, it is a national monument!"

In June he was off to Christiania by boat, with the crowds cheering wildly as he set forth. Back again in Bergen after a few months, he helped get the season underway at the theatre; then, withdrawing from its active management, he went on a concert tour to Denmark and Germany.

Meanwhile the students of Christiania planned a musical festival for the Theatre's benefit. Occurring in October of 1851, it proved to be a tremendous success and served to introduce Norway's future literary son, Henrik Ibsen, to her illustrious violinist. Ole Bull played; and Henrik Ibsen, who was twenty-three years old, made his literary bow to the world in a prologue of his own writing. Impressed with the young man's sentiments, Ole Bull sought him out after the concert, talked with him at length; and later, appointed him playwright and stage manager at the Berger Theatre. Ever encouraged by the older man, Ibsen was to draw inspiration for his famous play, *Peer Gynt* from Ole Bull's life-story.

Unfitted by nature to concern himself long in the routine-details of an organization, Ole Bull now turned over the management of the Theatre to a board of directors. With another idea already buzzing about in his head, he set sail in January 1852 on the *Asia* for America. He would found a New Norway in the United States, where the poor and down-trodden of his own country might find new hope!

Accordingly, upon arriving in America, he mixed talks-about-this-project with concert-giving; appearing first at Baltimore and later at Lexington, where, finding his friend, Henry Clay, ill, he played the statesman's favorite tune—"The Last Rose of Summer"—outside his door. Then turning back to Washington, he gave two concerts there, taking at the same time onto himself another one of his many "protectors": Living in the home of Charles and

Fanny Eames, he was surrounded with loving care and kindness; and for many years thereafter Fanny Eames sought to keep his Quixotic life out of tangles.

In May of 1852 he went on to New York, where the Swedish Nightingale Jenny Lind was holding forth under the management of the fabulous P. T. Barnum. Notwithstanding Ole Bull drew a tremendous audience—including Jenny Lind herself—when he appeared on May 22nd at Metropolitan Hall. Once again the critics found it difficult to express their evaluation of his playing. George William Curtis of the *Tribune* wrote in part: "Like Paganini he is an exceptional person. Like every man of remarkable and pronounced genius, he is a phenomenon. He is his own standard; he makes his own rules.... We find a purity, a firmness, a sweetness, and breadth of tone which is unprecedented."

After he had appeared in Boston in the month of June, John Sullivan Dwight wrote in the *Journal of Music,* "However one may quarrel with Ole Bull's style of music, it is a very genuine, very real, very earnest thing with him.... He is not a mere mechanism with the bow, not a mere routine variation player. He stands there as if he believed in his music, as if he were making his confession of faith." Then the critic went on to regret the fact that the Norwegian player did not include, say, something of Mozart in his program; and this critic was increasingly to deplore Ole Bull's shying away from music by the great masters.

Following a speedy concert tour ending at Montreal, the patriot-violinist settled down in earnest to his New Norway project. Appointing his friend, John Hopper, agent and attorney, he soon found himself involved with a John F. Cowan who owned a tract of land near Coudersport in Potter County, Pennsylvania. What matter that the land was so wild and rocky that only the greatest effort might produce from it a livelihood in farming; it looked like his native Norway. Yes, it was just the place!

Advancing $25,000.00 as capital, he arranged for thirty hardy Norwegians—carpenters, bricklayers, foresters and the like—to come on to Coudersport from New York. On September the 8th, having arrived at Kettle Creek, the center of this new colonial enterprise, these men, together with Ole Bull and Mr. Cowan, proceeded to lay out sites for a hotel, stores, and other necessary buildings in the founding of a community. At the same time Ole Bull decided upon the location of his own home, finding a glorious spot that was "just like Norway!"

Then came the celebration to dedicate this mighty venture. A tall pine tree was felled to serve as a flag pole. And when having set it up, with a few leaves and branches left in its uppermost part, the celebrants heard some birds immediately break into song from its top, they felt that their little colony had been genuinely blessed. "A good omen!" said Ole Bull. As the flag was raised they gave thirty-one cheers, honoring each state in the Union, and then added three lusty cheers for Ole Bull, as they christened the colony "Oleana."

In the evening their leader gave a heart-stirring speech in which he set forth the principles of the settlement, ending it thus, "We are founding a New Norway, consecrated to liberty, baptized with independence, and protected by the Union's mighty flag." Then further to bless the occasion he played his violin far into the night.

In due time about one hundred Norwegian immigrants, whose passage had been paid by Ole Bull, arrived on the *Incognito*. Meanwhile the new Utopia's leader set out by way of Williamsport for Philadelphia for the purpose of becoming an American citizen. One might ask how it was possible for him thus to transfer his loyalty from Norway, but for him the answer was simple. *Was not a piece of Norway being here implanted?* From an account in a Williamsport paper we get a vivid picture of the violinist-turned-pioneer: "There was the white hat—the tall, commanding form—the muscular limbs—the flowing locks—the keen, impassioned eye—the countenance all truth, all love, all sympathy, all brotherly kindness."

Overcome by his reception in this town, he spontaneously offered to give a concert that evening in the Court House. Imagine the excitement caused by this announcement! Needless to say the hall was filled to its capacity and Williamsport bade him good night with reluctant hearts.

Arrived at Philadelphia, it was not possible for Ole Bull to receive his powers of citizenship like any ordinary mortal. He must take the oath with accompanying ceremony underneath the statue of George Washington at Independence Hall! Accordingly, hand on heart, Ole Bull declared, "I wish to be found worthy of this great privilege and shall spare no exertion in order to deserve it."

During the month of October he remained for the most part at Oleana. Rising early in the morning, generally atop a magnificent horse, he directed the emerging capital of New Norway. Then off to New York he went; but, with his little community ever in mind, he purchased twelve dozen high silk hats and had them sent back to the new general store at Oleana. Fifty years later they were still on the merchant's shelves; and they might still be there had not some enterprising person auctioned them off to lumberers then come to the once-Ole Bull-land.

Having become reluctantly convinced that the Oleana project required a vast amount of money, he decided to start out on a money-making tour. Accordingly, he came under the management of Maurice Strakosch, whose wife's little sister, Adelina Patti, then eight, appeared with the violinist on what he called his "farewell concerts in America before retiring from his artistic career." Though by no means his "farewell concerts" they were gloriously successful and continued for about a year.

On May 17, 1853, he returned to Oleana to celebrate Norwegian Independence Day. The colonists and their leader enjoyed the occasion to the full; Ole Bull, as always, playing on into the night. Hopes still ran high for the little community. Four towns were laid out—Oleana, New Bergen, New Norway, and Valhalla—and plans were discussed for building a foundry to make the government's cannons. Alas! All was destined to remain in the plan-stage; for, following a Fourth-of-July celebration, Ole Bull left for New York to join Strakosch and Adelina Patti—never to return to his newly founded empire. Shortly thereafter, some litigation regarding the title to the Pennsylvania land developed; Ole Bull withdrew from the company in September; his violin was seized to help defray the expenses of the law suit; and thus, ignominiously, ended a venture so gloriously conceived.

Meanwhile, after giving concerts in New York during the time of America's first World's Fair and going on to Boston, Ole Bull and little Adelina gave benefit concerts in Philadelphia for "the Oleana Sufferers." The disappointed colonizer is supposed to have played these concerts on a violin that he himself made. Be that as it may, the hardy settlers of Oleana scattered Westward;

while the property, following a period of lumber-prosperity, became a state reservation—known today as Ole Bull Park.

After more traveling they ended their tour at Christmas time at Philadelphia. This was surely one of the "low" periods in the Viking-violinist's career; but, in accordance with his philosophy, he was not "down." Gathering his strength together, he decided to go to California; a decision not so easily arrived at in Ole Bull's time, for the trip was certain to be an arduous one.

Their plans made, he and Strakosch set out in March, giving concerts in Chicago, St. Louis, and other cities on the way. By late spring they had arrived at Panama, where they encountered a situation that contributed to the eventual breakdown of Ole Bull's health. Crossing the Isthmus of Panama by donkey, they entrusted their luggage and the all-important violin to a native who went on ahead. In some way they became separated; the native and donkey disappearing as if by magic. Strakosch went on to San Francisco, but there was nothing for Ole Bull to do but to stay and try to locate his violin. This he eventually did; but meanwhile he contracted yellow fever. Consequently it was mid-July when he finally joined Strakosch at San Francisco.

Though he was still weak from his illness, he threw himself whole-heartedly into the life of the exuberant western community. His first concert given on July 24th was a tremendous success; as usual, he generously responded to the audience's enthusiasm, this time playing the *Carnival of Venice* over and over at the San Franciscans' repeated request.

After two months spent in this exhilarating atmosphere, Ole Bull and his manager started eastward; another scheme already afoot in the Norwegian's mind: This time it was to be the organizing of an Italian Opera Company. And sure enough, on February 19, 1855, Verdi's *Rigoletto* opened under his guidance at the Academy of Music in New York. It was not one of Ole Bull's "up" ventures: The critics were not particularly kind to the performance; and then, to make matters worse, the violinist soon thereafter fell, necessitating his remaining in his room for a period of time. Following a sacred concert at the newly leased Academy of Music an announcement appeared in the papers: "In consequence of insuperable difficulties, the Academy of Music is closed. Ole Bull."

This "down period" of the violinist's life haunted him for another two years. Lawsuits surrounding both the Oleana and the opera projects persisted; and then, on top of everything else, he contracted malaria. One event—the visit of his seventeen-year-old son, Alexander—somewhat brightened these dark days. But at concerts given at Dodsworth Hall in New York during March and April in 1857 he was in such a weakened condition that he had to be helped onto the stage. Notwithstanding he was greeted with all the old enthusiasm; for, to his playing like a God, he had now added what his admirers called "a mournful quality."

Soon thereafter he went to Boston, where he gave some concerts and renewed old friendships, thence through New England to Canada. And now he decided that it was time to return once more to Norway. But before boarding the steamer *America* with his son he was impelled to make another Norway-American gesture. Having been convinced that a certain rock in the Taunton River was the one on which the Vikings had landed, he bought it for fifty dollars with the intention of presenting it to the Royal Society at Copenhagen. So far as history reports, the rock still lies imbedded Northward from Fall River in the Taunton River!

Back in Norway, after leaving his son with his family at Christiania, he traveled on to Bergen in order to take up the direction of the National Theatre where he had left off. Trouble ensued with the current board of directors, but when Ole Bull gave a concert to help raise funds for the Theatre, the people greeted him with spontaneous applause. "Long live Ole Bull!" they cried as of old. At the second concert some members of the dissenting board came prepared with whistles for the purpose of breaking up the event. In the midst of the uproar, Ole Bull stepped on the front of the platform and appealed to the simple understanding of the audience by telling them a story involving an elephant. This Bergen Theatre was his "elephant" and he had no intention of deserting it.

"Ladies and gentlemen," he said, "I have won the elephant, and as I—like the man in London—can neither let it go nor have the heart to destroy it, I must, however expensive it may be, feed it."

"Bravo! Bravo! Bravo! Ole Bull!"

In consequence of this new victory he organized a new board of directors, discovered a brilliant new director—Björnstjerne Björnson, then twenty-five years old—and thus satisfied, set off on a concert tour of Europe. Renewing old friendships including a reunion with Liszt, and making new conquests, he enjoyed this trip immensely. One such meeting was with the great Joseph Joachim, who, after having warmly praised the Norwegian violinist and having arranged for Clara Schumann to appear in a concert with him—deploring the fact that Ole Bull did not "stick to his last"—said, "Ole Bull ought to travel around the world for the sole purpose of playing melodies, instead of doing tricks and performances like a white horse in a circus."

Regardless of such criticism, the beloved performer was greeted in London in the spring of 1861 with tremendous enthusiasm. Over twenty years had elapsed since his appearance there, but the English people responded to him just as warmly as they had on the previous occasion; a situation particularly pertinent in view of the fact that the city was at the time literally packed with great performing artists.

The next winter Ole Bull was saddened by the death of his wife in Norway; for, although during their married life, he had spent little time at home he was devoted to Félicie and his family.

Then, after more touring on the continent, he was again involved in a great scheme; a scheme, which though high in purpose, was destined for short life. This concerned the founding of a national academy of music at Christiania. He poured out his ideas in a long letter-of-invitation, in which he sought to acquire enthusiasts and backers for the plan:

"My business in the world is Norwegian music. I am not a painter, not a sculptor, not a literary man. I am a musician. And as such my nation must believe me when I say that I hear a wonderfully deep and characteristic sounding board vibrating within its breast. The aim of my life has been to draw strings across it and enable it to speak out, so that its deep voice can resound in the hall of the temple and, as Norway's own church music, carry the preacher's word to the hearts of the people; so that, on the battlefield, it may bring the nation's hearths and homes to the minds of our country's defenders; so that it may sound out from orchestras to build up our Norwegian art on a sure foundation; so that it may ring out from pianos all over the country into family life, where the notes will speak to the feelings, shaping and elevating more than all the speech in the world—unsurpassed in charm and clarity. I have spent my life in the endeavor to scale the same grey peak as have the other Norwegian artists, to overcome our denationalized musical sense."

This eloquent appeal brought assistance from the King himself. And in 1867, after many complications, the Academy was finally established—with Edvard Grieg at its head. Though it was to be in existence scarcely two years, it laid the foundation for much good in Norwegian musical life, as well as contributing to Grieg's development. In this connection it is interesting to know that Grieg was fully aware of Ole Bull's influence in his life. His description of their first meeting which took place during the summer of 1858 has often been repeated, but it merits telling here, in part, since it provides such a vivid picture of Ole Bull:

"The end of my school days," writes Grieg, "and with it farewell to my home, came more abruptly than I expected. I was almost fifteen.... Then one summer day at Landås, a rider came galloping at full speed along the road. He approached, stopped his splendid Arab, and jumped off. It was he—the fairy-hero I had dreamt of but never seen before. It was Ole Bull. There was something in me that didn't quite like the hero to jump down with no further ado and behave like an ordinary man; to come into the room and greet us all smilingly. I remember vividly that when his hand touched mine something like an electric shock went through me. But bye-and-bye the hero began to make jokes and then it became plain to me—at bottom to my quiet sorrow—that he was only a man after all. His violin, alas, he hadn't with him. But he could talk. And talk he did. We listened breathlessly to his hair-raising stories of his journeys in America.... When he got to know that I was keen on composing and improvising, there was no saying him nay: I must go to the piano. I do not understand what Ole Bull could find at that time in my naive childish notes, but he grew serious and talked in a low voice with my parents. The result of this discussion was not to my disadvantage. For suddenly Ole Bull came over to me, shook me in his characteristic fashion and said: 'You are to go to Leipzig and become a musician.'"

Thus it was that Edvard Grieg started out on his illustrious musical career, which was destined frequently to touch that of his good-fairy hero.

Despite the failure of his latest dream, Ole Bull continued to tour over

Europe in magnificent fashion, spending the summers with his family at *Valestrand* where he entertained in lavish style. There he rode about on beautiful Arabian horses or surveyed his estate atop an elaborate wagon he had had built in America for the purpose. One such summer was shared with Edvard Grieg, home from Leipzig. Here, when they were not playing Mozart together, Ole Bull regaled his young compatriot with the beauty of Norwegian folk music.

Then, following a particularly wonderful trip to Russia, where he wrote one of his most famous pieces—*The Nightingale,* based on a Russian tune—he set out again for America. His reception then was even greater than on other occasions. Soon he was immersed in the musical life of New York; helping to shape its destinies and involved with his friend John Ericsson, a ship designer, in building a piano with an improved sounding board.

Then while on one of his tours into the Middle West, he encountered a characteristic adventure when, on a trip down the Ohio River, his steamship collided with another carrying oil. Grasping his violin in one hand, he jumped overboard and swam safely to shore!

In the summer of 1869 he took part in one of the most fantastic celebrations ever recorded: The Peace Jubilee in Boston to mark the end of the Civil War. The celebration lasted for five days, on the first of which Ole Bull acted as concertmaster. This fabulous affair which took place in the Colosseum was provided with an orchestra of over a thousand players, a chorus of ten thousand, two hundred violins, and cannon shots from the Boston Artillery to accompany the "Star Spangled Banner." In addition, one hundred firemen in red uniforms struck the anvils during the *Anvil Chorus.*

Late that fall, after a flying trip to Norway, Ole Bull was off on another long tour through the United States; this time under the management of his son, Alexander. At the beginning of the New Year they arrived at San Francisco, where the violinist found the city and people just as generous as he had remembered them. After his first concert one critic wrote, "He stands alone." At the last concert he was presented with a wreath of gold, in which thirty-six pearls were set, together with fifty-six diamonds outlining the violinist's initials within the monogram of the state of Calfornia.

Returning East by way of Virginia City, he stopped for a time with Joseph

Thorp and his family at Madison, Wisconsin. This was to prove one of those fated occasions; for, Sara Thorp, the twenty-year-old daughter of the household, with whom he had been enchanted at a previous meeting, now completely captivated him. The feeling was equally strong on her part; and, though her father was to object to their marriage on difference-of-age grounds, the mother encouraging the union, helped precipitate matters by accompanying her daughter on a trip with the violinist to Norway that late spring. Ole Bull and Sara Thorp were secretly married in June at Christiania; the secret, undoubtedly being not thinly veiled from Sara's mother.

Following a few concerts and an involvement in an insurance company, Ole Bull, with his bride Sara, returned to the United States. At Madison they were remarried by a clergyman; afterward a reception was held at the Thorp home, the like of which the Wisconsin town had not previously seen or imagined. Eleven hundred invitations were sent out; the beautiful grounds were gaily decorated; and Ole Bull's numerous prizes and gifts from all over the world adorned the reception room.

Soon thereafter the over-generous Norwegian turned his financial affairs over to his new father-in-law; so that, though he might be tempted to indulge in some dream-plan, there would be a curb on his impractical spending of money. Meanwhile he bought a home at West Lebanon in Maine, where, in the spring of 1871 his daughter, Sara Oleo, was born.

Back at Madison in the winter, he found a congenial friend—in a community not particularly in tune with his temperament—Rasmus Anderson, a Norwegian instructor at the University. And upon discovering that there was no Scandinavian literature in the University Library he gave a benefit concert to raise funds for remedying the matter. Then he, Rasmus Anderson, and Mr. Thorp set out for Europe to select the books.

While at *Valestrand* Ole Bull carried out a resolution made in his earliest youth. Often while spending his summers at *Valestrand* when a boy, he had longingly looked at an island lying across the way from his father's place. As a matter of fact, he had not only *looked*, but, frequently crossing the body of cold, blue water, he had scrambled hither and yon about the hills and crags of this enchanted spot, some times playing his violin and listening to the echoes it made. One day he would own that island! And now the day had come.

Lysöen—"island of light"—six hundred and fifty acres of wonderful Norway! On this magic island he built a fantastic house, inspired by all the countries that he had visited; and in it he spent every summer and one winter until his death.

Back and forth he went between Norway and America; much of the time, giving benefit concerts for this fund or that, including several for a Lief Ericson memorial to commemorate the "discoverer of America."

Shortly after little Oleo's third birthday, which was celebrated at Mentone where they were spending the winter, the child's adoring father, having presented her with a tiny fiddle, was off on a concert tour to Italy. In Rome he saw Franz Liszt once again; visiting Florence, where he had been so warmly received many years before, he again met with great enthusiasm: At his last concert there, he graciously told the Florentines, "I am so thankful that I have not disappointed my old friends."

On his 66th birthday Ole Bull, following a jesting hint of King Oscar of Norway, carried the Norwegian flag and his violin to the top of Cheop's Pyramid near Cairo, and, while the natives cried, "Allah! Allah!", gloriously played his *Saeterbesög*.

Later that spring his wife Sara arrived at Lysöen; and henceforth she managed the violinist's affairs. The concerts both in Europe and America continued, but Sara saw to it that her husband had moments of relaxation. The summer of 1879, a particularly happy one at Lysöen, was highlighted by a visit to Lofthus to celebrate Grieg's birthday. As Sara Bull afterward wrote, "The day was as perfect as friendship, music, and lovely surroundings could make it."

That winter upon their return to America the Thorp-Bull family rented the James Russell Lowell house at Cambridge. Ole Bull soon felt completely at home in the cultured atmosphere of the college town, becoming friendly with the Longfellows, William Dean Howells, and other eminent families. Remarking on the violinist's playing at a certain luncheon, Howell stated, "It was wonderful: the fiddle did everything but walk round the room."

On his birthday many of these friends and his family gave him a great surprise party; at which he was presented with a violin constructed of flowers, as well as an oil painting. After giving some concerts in Boston he set out on a tour with Strakosch, his old manager. At the Brooklyn Academy of Music he appeared with the pianist, Teresa Carreño; at the Tabernacle he made his destined last appearance in New York: then on to Chicago, where he was overcome with illness. On May 21, 1880, at the Grand Central Music Hall in Chicago, he played before an audience for the last time in his life; and he fittingly ended his concert and his career with the playing of his *Mountains of Norway*.

When he set sail at the end of June on the *Gallia* he was a desperately sick man. Arrived at Lysöen, he went immediately to bed. And when the news of his illness circulated among his countrymen some of them gathered beneath his window to play their homeland's music. Too sick to respond in any other way, he insisted upon having the Norwegian flag with the stars and stripes in one corner—given to him by the New York Philharmonic Society—hung out of the window.

At noon on August 17, 1880, after, at his request, Sara Bull had played for him Mozart's *Requiem*, the great Norwegian violinist died.

His body lay in state for several days. Then on August 23rd, the funeral, involving the entire town of Bergen, took place. At the service, held in the music hall at Lysöen, Edvard Grieg played the organ; following which, the body was taken by steamer to Bergen. A convoy of several steamers met the boat as it entered the Bergen harbor, while guns from the fort nearby burst forth in mournful salute. Girls dressed in black scattered flowers in the street before the slow-moving funeral procession which included both Björnson and Edvard Grieg. And the whole procession halted at his birthplace, the *Svaneapolthek*, where a song written for the occasion was sung.

At the cemetery both Björnson and Grieg made speeches. Björnson paid tribute to Ole Bull's contribution to Norway's awakening to her national worth. Grieg, who had in the procession carried the gold wreath given to Ole Bull at San Francisco, now placing another wreath of remembrance on his friend's grave, spoke these words:

"Because beyond all others you were an honor to your country—because you raised our people up with you towards the shining peaks of art as no one else has done—because you were beyond all others a pioneer for our young national music, faithful, warm-hearted and a conqueror of every heart as no one, no one else—because you have planted a seed which will grow in the future and for which the coming generations will bless you—with a gratitude that knows no bounds, for all this, in the name of Norwegian music, I lay this wreath upon your coffin. Peace be with you!"

When hundreds of peasants had strewn his grave with pine boughs and flowers, Ole Bull, the Heaven-taught violinist, fittingly, had been put to rest.

JOSEPH JOACHIM

Joseph Joachim, great Hungarian violinist, whose name is forever linked with violin music of the masters, was born two years earlier than his destined-friend, Johannes Brahms, on June 28, 1831, at Kitsee, Near Pressburg, in Hungary.

He was the seventh child of Julius and Fanny Joachim, who, with their large family moved to Pest when little Joseph was two years old. There a chance-observation on the part of a young medical student by the name of Stieglitz started the youngest Joachim, not yet five, on the road to a violinist's career. Noticing the youngster's struggles to accompany his sister's singing on a toy fiddle, Stieglitz, a good amateur violinist, took it upon himself to teach Joseph the rudiments of violin playing. Then convinced that his pupil possessed genuine musical talent, he persuaded the boy's parents—themselves not musical—to send him for professional instruction to Serwacznski, leader of the Pest opera band.

On March 17, 1839, while he was still seven, the future master-violinist made his first public appearance in a concert at which he played in a double concerto with Serwacznski, as well as a set of variations on a Schubert waltz.

Soon thereafter, at the advice of a cousin, Joseph was sent to Vienna, where he studied for a few months with Miska Hauser: and later, with George Hellmesberger, the senior, whose two sons were also his pupils. The story goes that following a concert at which young Joachim, together with the Hellmesberger brothers and another pupil, played a concerto for four violins, Hellmesberger felt compelled to tell the Hungarian youth that he would never become a good violinist.

"You will never learn how to handle the bow," was Hellmesberger's dictum.

There was some justification for the Viennese teacher's unhappy prophesy, for, Serwacznski had permitted a stiffening of the arm to develop in Joseph's bowing. Fortunately this was not to be the final word on the disappointed boy's future. Soon thereafter inspired by hearing Wilhelm Ernst play, Joseph seized an opportunity that presented itself to play before this master thereby receiving from him advice which set him on the road to artistic fulfillment.

"Go to my great teacher, Joseph Boehm," advised Ernst. "He will unravel all the kinks!"

Thus it was that Joachim happened to study under the master who laid the foundation for his eventual incomparable bowing. Boehm also added to his understanding of Beethoven's last quartets, a study begun by Hellmesberger, at a time when this music was scarcely known by the public.

Then, convinced that his highly sensitive and intelligent pupil had learned from him all that he had to offer, Boehm strongly advised Joachim to go to Paris for the finishing touches. But the same cousin, who had been responsible for his coming to Vienna, again provided direction to his destiny. Meanwhile, having married a merchant at Leipzig and having been impressed with the awakening musical atmosphere of her adopted city, this cousin insisted that Joseph come to Leipzig.

Acting accordingly, Joachim arrived there not long after Felix Mendelssohn and several other eminent musicians had founded the famous Leipzig Conservatory. It was Joachim's first intention to enter the newly opened school; but Mendelssohn, on hearing him play, and examining him in various branches of music, recommended individual instruction. Mendelssohn, in fact, convinced of the young violinist's talent, became more or less his musical godfather, arranging for his general education under a tutor by the name of Hering and theoretical study of music with the great theorist, Moritz Hauptmann. At the same time, under the influence of both Mendelssohn and Louis Spohr's most famous pupil, Ferdinand David, Joachim developed into a violinist and musician of unquestioned integrity. From them, aided by his own natural inclinations, he learned the art of interpretating the world's great music according to the composer's intentions: a characteristic, later synonymous with the name JOACHIM.

On August 19, 1843, Joseph Joachim, at twelve, made his first public appearance, as a finished artist, at a Leipzig *Gewandhaus* Concert given by

Pauline Viardot-Garcia, a member of the famous Garcia family of singing fame. He played a rondo by Charles de Bériot; and was accompanied at the piano by his mentor, Felix Mendelssohn.

At the beginning of the next year he set out for England with a warm letter of introduction from Mendelssohn to H. Klingemann of the Hanoverian Embassy in London. The letter eloquently bespeaks the character both of the writer and the budding violinist:

"His manner of playing all modern and classical solos, his interpretation, his perfect comprehension of music, and the promise in him of a noble service to art, will, I am sure, lead you to think as highly of him as I do. But at the same time, he is a capital, healthy, well brought-up, and altogether thoroughly good and clever lad, full of intelligence and very straightforward. Therefore be kind to him, look after him in great London, and introduce him to those of our friends who will appreciate such an exceptional personality, and in whose acquaintance he, for his part, will find pleasure and stimulation."

Curiously enough his first London appearance bears little relationship to the suggestions outlined in this letter. It took place at the Drury Lane Theatre, on what was called a "Miscellaneous Concert," on March 28, 1844, an affair which must have been more like a circus than a concert. Listed as "the celebrated Hungarian boy," he was forced to play the Grand Variations for the violin on a theme of Rossini's *Otello* by Ernst, wedged in between the first and second acts of the opera, *The Bohemian Girl*. But despite the combination of "Hungarian Boy" and "Bohemian Girl," Joachim, by maintaining a dignity and bearing, mature beyond his years, played with compelling intonation and spirit.

He next appeared at a tremendous concert given by the impressario, Bennett, on the 19th of May. Then came his authentic London début on May 27, 1844, at a Philharmonic concert, when he played the Beethoven violin concerto under the direction of Felix Mendelssohn. This event may best be recreated by reading in part what a critic in *The Illustrated London News* had to say on the subject.

After describing Joseph as a boy of thirteen, perhaps the first violin player of both his age and period, the writer continues: "Of late years we have heard some prodigies... but we can safely say that little Joachim is equal to any, or all of them, put together. His tone is of the purest *cantabile* character; his execution is most marvelous, and at the same time unembarrassed; his style is chaste, but deeply impassioned at moments; and his deportment is that of a conscious, but modest genius! He performed Beethoven's solitary concerto, which we have heard all the great performers of the last twenty years attempt, and invariably fail in.... In the *candenzas,* composed by the youth himself, there was as much genius exhibited as in the subject which gave birth to them. Joachim plays from memory, which is more agreeable to the eye of the auditor than to *see* anything read from a music-stand; it seems more like extemporaneous performance, and admits a greater degree of enthusiasm on the part of the instrumentalist. We never heard or witnessed such equivocal delight as was expressed by both band and auditory."

Small wonder that this prodigeous prodigy, with the *cantabile,* or singing, tone, was welcomed in England for ever after!

After appearing in one more concert and spending many a stimulating evening playing Beethoven's quartets with friends many years his senior, Joachim returned to Leipzig. On November 25, 1844, he took part with three mature violinists—Wilhelm Ernst, Antonio Bazzini and Ferdinand David—in a performance of Mauer's Concertante for four violins at a *Gewandhaus* concert.

Soon thereafter, following Joachim's appearance in a *Gewandhaus* subscription concert, a critic, writing in the famous musical journal, *Allgemeine Musikalische Zeitung,* revealed not only unusual perception but the powers of a prophet. When we read the review in the light of Joachim's ultimate career we are tempted to believe that it was written three generations later than it actually appeared: for its summing up of his qualities as an artist were to befit the crowning of his triumphs, while the hopes expressed for his future behavior were to be wonderfully realized.

Thus this Leipzig critic, like a seer gazing into a crystal, wrote: "Of great interest was the playing of the fifteen-year-old Joseph Joachim. [We should forgive this small mistake; he was still fourteen.] Our Leipzig public knows already from earlier appearances the beautiful, full tone that he gets from his violin, as well as the great dexterity and certainty, and it has fully recognized and encouraged these qualities before now. What Herr Joachim gave us this time was doubly surprising, for he not only gave evidence of the important advance he has made in technical skill, but also showed that he has developed so far as to grasp the spiritual meaning of a work of the highest artistic importance. The manner in which he performed the difficult and inspired concerto of Beethoven, precludes every doubt as to his vocation for the musical profession, and sets him far above the mere virtuoso in the ranks of the artists. In this connection may be noticed that the two *candenzas* introduced by him into the first and last movements of the concerto respectively, which are built most cleverly upon the chief themes of the work. Herr Joachim's playing is so round and certain, his tone so broad and elegiac, and so pure in intonation even in the highest and most difficult passages, his style is so natural yet so independent, that it is only by looking at his youthful form that one can realize his age. May the young man, who last year had a triumph in England, long preserve his childlike, modest nature, and may he not desist from his unwearied work and advancement, whether tempted by the great success that followed all his efforts on this as on every other occasion, or by the assumption that he already stands on the apex of perfection! He has a great and honored future before him, and will most assuredly be numbered among the great artists."

But lest we assume that the young violinist was wholly without human qualities it is reassuring on that score to read what Hector Berlioz has to say about a performance, in which Joachim and one of the Hellmesberger boys appeared in Vienna. "The young Joachim, whose name is beginning to appear," writes Berlioz and then continuing in reference to the two youths, "as befits their age, rash and impetuous, ambitious of producing novel effects, indefatigably energetic and refusing to believe in the impossible." Berlioz, however, apparently reluctant to have this initial impression of Joachim stand unqualified for future generations to read, added this footnote to his *Memoirs*, "Joachim is now the first violinist in Germany, indeed one might say in Europe."

Fortunately neither Joachim nor his parents were anxious to push his career as a virtuoso. Accordingly he remained for a number of years under the guidance of David and Mendelssohn at Leipzig, sharing the leadership of the *Gewandhaus* orchestra with the former. Meanwhile he made occasional trips to England and other places; including Paris, where he was warmly received in a concert directed by Berlioz.

Then in 1849, two years after the death of his Leipzig-music-father, Felix Mendelssohn, Joachim accepted the post of concertmeister, or leader, of the Grand Duke's band at Weimar. He was at first fascinated by the "new music" being produced under Franz Liszt, recently settled at Weimar as conductor of the opera and concerts—and soon to become general guardian of the musical world. Joachim found working with Hans von Bülow and the musician whose first two names were exactly like his own—Joseph Joachim Raff— tremendously stimulating; notwithstanding, Joachim soon realized—largely because of Liszt's fantastic symphonic ideas—that the "new music" aimed at something poles apart from his Mendelssohn-trained ideals. Consequently he gladly accepted in 1853 the invitation of the King of Hanover to become leader of his band, as well as solo violinist at Hanover.

Meanwhile in the late spring of that year at Goettingen—where Joachim often attended university lectures—he met, for the first time, Johannes Brahms after a concert in which Brahms appeared with the Hungarian violinist, Eduard Reményi. Now it was Joachim's turn to prophesy correctly concerning a young artist's future, although he himself was only two years older. Delighted with their performance, Joachim hastened backstage after the concert, congratulated the touring musicians and offered to give them letters of introduction to Liszt at Weimar, to Count Platen at Hanover, and later to Schumann at Düsseldorf. Needless to say his offer was gleefully accepted. And the letter, concerning Brahms, which Joachim then wrote to his friend, Heinrich Erlich, is strikingly like a pocket edition of the Leipzig critic's article about his own talents and future:

"Brahms has an altogether exceptonal talent for composition, a gift which is further enhanced by the unaffected modesty of his character. His playing, too, gives every presage of a great artistic career, full of fire and energy, yet, if I may say so, inevitable in its precision and certainty of touch. In brief, he is the most considerable musician of his age that I have ever met."

It was, as we can planly see, a matter of one artist with "an altogether exceptional talent" recognizing the divine spark in another.

Following their appearance at Weimar, Brahms and Reményi discontinued their tour; Reményi, remaining at Weimar; Brahms, returning to Goettingen, where, staying with Joachim for some time, he also attended the university lectures. Then late in September, armed with Joachim's letter of introduction to Robert Schumann, Brahms set out on foot for Düsseldorf. Arrived at the Schumann's home, a travel-weary young man, he was immediately received into this musical household; Joachim having meanwhile dispatched a letter to Schumann concerning Brahms' compositions.

It so happened that Albert Dietrich, another celebrated musician, was staying in Düsseldorf at this time; and he and Brahms becoming fast friends, often took breakfast together. One day while discussing the expected arrival of Joachim for the purpose of giving a recital at Düsseldorf, the three musicians—Brahms, Dietrich and Schumann—hit upon the idea of writing a joint-sonata for violin and piano in his honor.

Accordingly, on arriving at Düsseldorf, Joachim was presented with the newly composed sonata on the title page of which Schumann had written, "In anticipation of the arrival of our beloved and honored friend, Joseph Joachim, this sonata was written by Robert Schumann, Albert Dietrich and Johannes Brahms."

Scarcely able to contain themselves, the three composers eagerly awaited Joachim's reaction as he hastily scanned the score.

Who wrote each part? they asked in unison.

To which Joachim, without a moment's hesitation, supplied the correct answer.

Three years later another combination of three—this time, Dietrich, Joachim and Brahms—were to walk together behind the coffin of Robert Schumann.

The link between Brahms and Joachim became increasingly strong and was apparently unaltered by Joachim's marriage on June 10, 1863, to Amalia Weiss, a celebrated contralto singer, especially, for whom Brahms wrote songs and duets. In 1866 the two friends toured together through German-Switzerland and the following year assisted each other in concerts given at Graz and its neighborhood in Styria.

Meanwhile Joachim had made several trips to England, playing there for the first time in 1859 his famous Hungarian Concerto which had been written in its original version the previous year. In its revised form it was first played by Joachim in 1860 at a Düsseldorf Festival: later, in 1863, at a Concert of the Musical Society of London. We get a particularly apt description of this work by reading the program notes concerning it, written on the occasion of one of Joachim's subsequent appearances at a Saturday Popular Concert in London, at which, Madame Joachim also sang.

The program-writer, after describing the general outline of the concerto as being in the form of those of Mozart and Beethoven, particularly Beethoven's great violin concerto, and describing the various themes, continues: "These themes are announced in the long *Tutti* which opens the Concerto, and afterwards developed and elaborated in the successive solos for the instrument, which occur in the prescribed scheme of the movement. . . . The treatment throughout, both of the orchestra and Solo Violin, though elaborate, and, in the latter, of extreme difficulty, is always broad and noble, animated by a never-flagging spirit, and rising at times to the height of passion."

Then, after comparing the spirit of the first movement to that of Beethoven's great Choral Symphony, the writer goes on: "The instrumentation of the whole work is masterly—full of variety and color (with a pleasant predilection of the Horns, of which there are four in the score); and might tempt one to believe that Mr. Joachim, instead of being the great executant that he is, had passed his life in composing for the orchestra.

Following this statement we are privileged to witness the critic's opinion of Joachim's playing, when we read—after his praise of the movement's Cadence, or ornamental passage—"The only drawback to the cadence is the doubt it suggests whether anyone but its author will ever be able to play it satisfactorily."

And, in referring to the most familiar portion of the composition, he writes: "The Finale—a Rondo, *alla Zingara Allegro,* is the most brilliant and spirited part of the Concerto"; adding about the Hungarian Concerto in general, "It is only necessary further to say that the difficulties of this work, slight as they may appear in the hands of Mr. Joachim, are enormous, and perhaps greater than those of any other composition for the Violin."

In connection with these Saturday Popular, or "Pops," Concerts, as well as the Monday Popular Concert, to which they were supplementary, it is interesting to know that Joachim's name was associated with them from the beginning. During their opening year Joachim introduced the *Chaconne* of Bach, and the Beethoven quartets, commissioned by Count Rasoumovsky, which contain subtly hidden Russian folk tunes. Also, for a great part of each succeeding season, Joachim led the "Pops" Concert Quartet, thereby thoroughly entwining himself within the hearts of the English people.

On Good Friday, April 10, 1868, Joachim and his wife joined their friend, Johannes Brahms, in the celebration of one of Brahms' greatest triumphs—the first complete performance of his *German Requiem* at the Bremen Cathedral. Madame Joachim sang "I Know That My Redeemer Liveth" and Joachim played Schumann's *Abendlied*. It was a glorious occasion, after which about a hundred of the composer's friends—including the Joachims, Clara Schumann, the Dietrichs, Max Bruch and others—gathered at the Bremen Rathskeller.

That same year was to see Joachim established at Berlin, the city with which his name is most often associated. Invited there to help found a new department of the Royal Academy of Arts, he became its director. And soon this new *Hochschule für ausübende tokunst*, or High School for Musical Execution, became a magnet for students from all over the world. Heretofore Joachim had chiefly taught through the example that he set in his own playing, but now eager pupils worked under his guidance; gaining especially, thereby, some of his insight into the world's great violin literature.

That the Joachim home became a gathering-place for musicians whose ideals coincided with their own is readily discovered by reading the memoirs of various artists of the period. One of these—Sir George Henschel, celebrated singer, composer and conductor—has written that he was a frequent guest at their home, "participating in the many musical gatherings happening there, and if, needless to say, I grew more and more gratefully conscious of the privilege of a closer acquaintance with so great a musician as Joachim, I confess I hardly to a lesser degree appreciated the wonderful art of his wife."

In 1874 at a great music festival at Cologne, Henschel, Brahms, Joachim and many other distinguished musicians had a wonderful time together. Concerning this occasion, Henschel modestly writes, "I hope I was duly appreciative of the privilege of being in the company of such men." Later that summer he joined the Joachims in the Austrian Alps, where they had taken a little villa for the season; and we have a vivid picture of the way the friends spent their days in Henschel's words:

"I do not know which I enjoyed more: a day's wanderings with the great musician, often starting at five o'clock in the morning... or accompanying on the piano, his playing of his own Hungarian Concerto and those of Beethoven, Spohr, and sonatas by Locatelli, Tartini, Handel—he practiced every day for some time—or singing with Frau Joachim songs and duets for hours at a time."

Following a Düsseldorf Festival in 1876 at which Joachim conducted Handel's oratorio, *Hercules,* he acted as chief conductor of a festival at Kiel in northern Germany. And since his birthday occurred on one of these festival-days it was the occasion of great celebration. We can practically attend the party in retrospect by again referring to Henschel who was one of those present. He writes: "There were special 'goings on' after the concert that night. The banquet was rendered particularly interesting by the presence—quite a rare event then—of an admiral of the United States Navy and his officers, whose ships were anchored in the roadstead of Düstenbrook." And he goes on to say that the party that lovely, moonlit, June evening lasted until dawn, when some of the young men took a dip into the sea on their way out to Düstenbrook.

Meanwhile, during the same year that the High School for Musical Execution was established, Joachim founded the famous Joachim Quartet, destined to become *first* among ensemble-groups. Although the personnel of the Quartet was to change over the years, one factor remained constant—the never-changing sympathy of its members with Joachim's high ideals.

From its beginning in 1869, The Joachim Quartet gave an annual series of concerts in Berlin and annual concerts in Vienna; frequent appearances were made in various German towns, Budapest, Paris, London and the English provinces; and at Rome in 1905 the Quartet presented the sixteen quartets of Beethoven in the Farnese Palace, where each member of the illustrious Quartet played on a fine Stradivarius violin: consequently, the resulting tone was not only pure, owing to the players' artistic skill, but uniform, because of the common ancestry of their instruments.

Although Joachim was not an artist to seek honors, honors were bestowed upon him from all quarters: knighthood from princes, degrees from universities, and various other marks of distinction. One such honor came in 1877, in England, when the Degree of Doctor of Music was conferred on him at Cambridge University. Both he and Brahms had been invited to write new compositions for this occasion at which both composers were to be granted the honorary degrees. Brahms, while declining the invitation to be present, offered up his first symphony for this event; Joachim wrote his *Elegiac* Overture, composed in Memory of Heinrich von Kleist. The Program book of the Cambridge University Musical Society included the following in the discussion of the new work:

"Not the least interesting characteristic of this composition is the manifest kinship of its ideas, which seem to spring from a mind actuated indeed by varied emotions and different impulses, but controlling all with a unity of purpose and marked individuality, a mind that, with a particular object in view, suffers this to color each incident that precedes its accomplishment. Equally worthy of remark is the continuity that pervades the whole, each succeeding division of the work growing out of its predecessor and becoming in its turn the generator of the matter that succeeds it."

Then, after analyzing the work in detail, the program sums up Joachim's compositions with glowing praise:

"The present is not the first work of its class that has sprung from the earnest mind of our new graduate; he has written Overtures to Schiller's unfinished 'Demetrius,' and to Shakespeare's 'Henry IV,' and 'Hamlet,' and the world would be richer if it knew them better and bore them in thought. The same serious spirit marks his Concertstück in G. minor, his great Hungarian Concerto, and his Concerto in G, all for Violin with Orchestra, his Hebrew Melodies for Viola with Pianoforte, and his many vocal songs. It needs not the evidence of these symmetrical and fully artistic efforts, nor of the piece which is now to be first judged, to prove Dr. Joseph Joachim's right to his musical pre-eminence; every incident of his career attests the obvious fact, proves him worthy to stand at the head of the musical branch of the Berlinese High School of Art. and makes it an honour to Cambridge to offer him its acknowledgment."

Oxford and Glasgow also honored him with their degrees, so that he became, indeed, *Doctor* Joseph Joachim.

Two years after the Cambridge occasion there occurred other Joachim-Brahms events of tremendous importance to them both: First came the initial performance of Brahms' great violin concerto by Joachim, on January 1, 1879, at the *Gewandhaus* in Leipzig; then, in November of the same year, Joachim played Brahms' G major violin sonata at a Hellmesberger concert in Vienna. The response in each instance amounted to an ovation; an ovation, quite as much for Joachim as for Brahms, the composer. And on the latter occasion some of the applause was directed at the celebrated Joachim Quartet, chiefly responsible for introducing Brahms' chamber music to the public.

Another landmark in the two great musicians' careers occurred in the fall of 1887 when Joachim and Robert Hausmann, violinist in the famous Quartet, played Brahms' concerto for violin and 'cello, usually called the Double Concerto, at a concert in Cologne. The following New Year's Day it was repeated at Leipzig under Brahms' direction; in February came a performance at a London Symphony Concert. Not only did Joachim perform each of Brahms' works, written with the violin in mind, but he contributed specifically to their composition, as well as others of Brahms' compositions, by advising his friend in the matter of the violin's possibilities. For many years Joachim was the only interpreter of Brahms' violin concerto; while today the *cadenza*, most frequently heard in it, is credited to this master violinist.

The year 1889 was made memorable by one Joachim celebration after another; for it marked the fiftieth year of the violinist's professional career: Fifty years spent in sincere devotion to music, particularly to its faithful interpretation. One of the most important of the events naturally occurred at the Berlin *Hochschule* where—following a performance of a cantata by Bach, a speech by the eminent Dr. Spitta, and a presentation of a bust of Joachim— a concert, devoted to three of Joachim's works, took place. First came his "Hamlet" and "Henry IV" overtures, then the Hungarian Concerto, each movement of which was played by a distinguished Joachim pupil.

This was only one of the many ways in which the people of Germany sought to show the illustrious musician their appreciation: Funds to help poor students at the *Hochschule* were raised in his honor; and he was made honorary president of the recently organized "Beethoven House Society" at Bonn; thus becoming active in the organization of the Bonn Festivals.

Another celebration in the much-loved violinist's honor took place on April 16, 1889, in England, when he was presented with a splendid Stradivarius violin, and a Tourte bow that had belonged to the musical writer and collector, Raphael Georg Kiesewetter.

But Joachim, by no means one to rest on his laurels, continued to play the violin, teach, and compose quite as though these celebrations had marked half of fifty years. On reading various musical accounts of the period, we find that scarcely any important musical event in all Europe took place without the assistance of Joachim or his famous Quartet. And not only did he adorn state occasions but the drawing rooms of various friends and relatives where he joined others in playing music just for the fun of it. One such home was that of his brother and sister-in-law, the Henry Joachims, in England, where on his annual visits he always made music to their friends' delight.

When we find the name of Brahms we are almost certain to find that of Joachim; as for instance, in the fall of 1895, at the opening of the new *Tonhalle* at Zürich, Switzerland, Brahms conducted and Joachim, together with some of his associates, assisted. But in April, two years later, Joachim was to lose forever this revered friend: Johannes Brahms died at the age of sixty-four at Vienna. At Meiningen, in December 1899, Joachim it was who made the speech when a statue to Brahms was unveiled.

The sixtieth anniversary of Joachim's professional career was the occasion of even greater celebration than the fiftieth. In Berlin a great concert took place, at which his pupils past and present—one hundred and sixteen violinists and violists, with twenty-four violoncellists who had attended his classes—played under the direction of Fritz Steinbach, a conductor particularly noted for his interpretations of Brahms' music. The great moment of the celebration came when Joachim, without the slightest hesitation, responded to the spontaneous request to play the Beethoven Concerto.

Then in 1904 at Queen's Hall in London occurred what England called Joachim's "Diamond Jubilee" celebration. He was presented with his portrait, painted by the noted artist, J. S. Sargent; a concert was given by the Queen's Hall orchestra under the direction of Henry J. Wood—Joachim conducting his own overture to "Henry IV" and again playing the Beethoven Concerto with great skill and understanding; and then came an address by Sir Hubert Parry which wonderfully expresses England's appreciation of the great violinist's unique gifts:

"At a time known only by hearsay to most of us, you first brought before an English audience the promise of that performance which has been eminent among two generations of men; which, in gaining an unrivalled wealth of experience, has had no loss to count but that of novelty; which we still welcome as a continuous delight, and which will remain for many generations more as a tradition and example to be prized by those who are born too late for the happiness of immediate knowledge. It was under the auspices of Mendelssohn that you played the Beethoven Violin Concerto at the Philharmonic concert of May 27, 1844. No combination could have been more prophetic of your career, though neither its duration in time nor the singular quality of its achievement was then within any probable foresight.

"At that day the fine arts, and music among them, languished in this country. It was not understood that the function of art is to be not merely the recreation of a privileged class, but an integral element of national life. We have now learnt to know and to do better. Opportunities of becoming acquainted with the music of the great masters have been multiplied tenfold, and the general competence of both execution and criticism has been raised beyond comparison."

Now let us read carefully what Sir Hubert Parry had to say regarding Joachim's place in this improved state of affairs:

"This great and salutary change which we have witnessed in the course of the last generation is largely due to your exertion. Learning from Mendelssohn and Schumann, and working with Brahms in the comradeship of lifelong friends, you have devoted your whole energies, as executant and as composer, to continuing the tradition and maintaining the ideal of classical music."

Continuing, he thus addresses Joachim:

"We now hold it fitting that the sixtieth anniversary of your first appearance here should not pass without a special greeting. The welcome we offer you is alike for the artist who commands every power of the trained hand, and for the musician whose consummate knowledge and profound reverence for his art have uniformly guided his execution in the path of the sincerest interpretation. Your first thoughts as a performer have ever been for the composer and not for yourself. In no hour have you yielded to the temptation of mere personal display, and the weight of your precepts in one of the greatest musical schools of Europe is augmented by the absolute fidelity with which your example illustrated them."

Joachim was to live three years longer, shedding light on things musical to the day of his death which occurred on August 15, 1907, at Berlin.

In violin playing, composing, teaching, and particularly in quartet playing, Joachim was the consumate artist; although, as one of his biographers, J. Fuller Maitland, has stated, "he could have excelled in mere virtuosity, as proved in the solo part of the Hungarian Concerto." And the eminent Sir Donald Tovey refers to Joachim's "elasticity and phrasing—resilience of rebound in the sequence of the notes." J. Fuller Maitland further describes Joachim's bowing characteristics, which, as he states, he never successfully passed on to his pupils—"Its chief peculiarity is the union between a perfectly firm grasp of the bow with the thumb and middle finger, and complete suppleness in the wrist and arm," producing, according to this author's words "a kind of ethereal quality to his execution of rapid passages." He continues, "Closely allied to this power is the player's ability to produce the maximum of tone with the minimum amount of bow."

"Another of his secrets," writes Mr. Fuller Maitland, "is that he knows, as the violinists say, "every inch of his bow, and realizes fully at which part of its length the effect he desires can best be obtained."

Such technical achievements, together with an unusually acute ear, served merely as handmaidens to the great violinist in his relentless search for truthful interpretation. And today perhaps the quality-of-Joachim is best remembered in our own artist-violinists' just interpretations of great music, exemplifying Sir Hubert Parry's words addressed to Joachim: *Your first thoughts as a performer have ever been for the composer and not for yourself.*

HENRI WIENIAWSKI

Henri Wieniawski—occasionally called the Chopin of the Violin—was born on July 10, 1835, at Lublin, Poland. Born twenty-five years later than Chopin, the Poet of the Piano, Wieniawski, like his illustrious countryman, early left his native land for Paris.

His father, a physician, and his mother who had been reared in a musical family, soon recognized an unusual musical talent in their young son; and, unlike many parents, who prefer that their children pursue more "solid" careers, they encouraged the boy's natural inclination.

At the age of eight he was taken by his mother to Paris, where he was put in the hands of Clavel at the Paris Conservatory, preparatory to his entering Joseph Lambert Massart's master classes. Progressing rapidly, he easily achieved this goal within a year and soon became known as Massart's star pupil, although he was the youngest in the class. This happy state of affairs, however, did not magically assert itself, for a friendly kind of tug-of-war prevailed between master and pupil. Massart, an excellent teacher, was particularly insistent as far as drill was concerned; while young Wieniawski, a born violinist, instinctively struck out on his own individual path. But though, like Ole Bull, he might have become a great violinist without proper training in theory, technique and the handling of the bow, he became a finer artist for having had this splendid grounding under Massart.

A significant story is told about this teacher-pupil period: One day Henri when scarcely ten, was called upon to play a certain Rode étude. Though recognized as the outstanding pupil in the class, he played the assigned study very badly; whereupon, Massart then asked another pupil, much older, to play it. And when he had finished Massart said, "That is more like it."

Naturally the favored youth beamed with happiness; for it was not often that anyone in the class won praise over the young Polish boy.

Massart then turned to Henri and said, "See that you play it better next time."

But when the "next time" came there was no improvement. Whereupon the master, evidently thinking that drastic steps should be taken, demanded, "Aren't you ashamed of yourself, letting the other boys get ahead of you that way?"

"I'm afraid," reluctantly confessed young Wieniawski, "that I haven't studied Rode lately."

"What have you been up to?" asked his teacher.

"I have been dabbling in the caprices of Paganini," sheepishly answered Henri.

"You shouldn't be dabbling in anything; let alone, Paganini caprices. They are much too difficult. Master your Rode; and Paganini will come in due time!" admonished Massart.

"Please, may I play one for you?" asked the reprimanded pupil.

At which, Massart begrudgingly consented. Then astonished at Henri's performance, he impulsively asked, "Can you play the second one?"

"I will try," answered Henri.

And when he had played this one nearly as well as the first, to his amazement, the ambitious student heard his teacher say, "Go on!" Then one caprice followed another, until, after the tenth, Massart declared: "Mon Dieu! Is it possible that you can play all twenty-four?"

"Yes, I know them all!" answered Henri, with pardonable pride.

"It is incredible!" declared Massart, while the other boys in the class stared in amazement at the star-pupil, now so miraculously returned to the master's favor.

At eleven young Wieniawski won the first prize in violin playing; and soon thereafter he set out on a concert tour through Poland and Russia. Meeting with tremendous success wherever he appeared, he might easily have rested on his laurels, consequently, perhaps, never becoming more than a child prodigy. Fortunately an innate artistic sense cautioned him to cease appearing in public until he had corrected certain defects in his playing and had gained more fundamental knowledge in music.

Accordingly he returned to Paris, where burying himself in study, he concentrated particularly in harmony and composition. Then at fifteen, secure in his own mind that he was now an artist, Henri Wieniawski began his brilliant career in earnest. Appearing in all the important towns of the Netherlands, France, England, and Germany—sometimes with his young brother Joseph, a pianist—the young Polish violinist was greeted with tremendous enthusiasm. Soon he was being sought after by all the leading musical societies of the time and honored by many monarchs; living proof that he was indeed a great artist, for at that time there was keen competition from established violinists.

Possessed of unequalled perfection of technique—subserviant to his passionate temperament—Wieniawski injected new life into the Ernst-Ole Bull-Joachim-Vieuxtemps-De Bériot world, which had lately been deprived of Paganini.

In 1859 Wieniawski modestly wrote to Franz Liszt at Weimar asking for the privilege of appearing under his baton: "The terms are quite indifferent to me," the letter reads. "It is the honor of playing before you and your opinion that I desire." Thus it was that still another artist became associated with the great music master at Weimar.

During the following year, after a very successful tour in Russia, Wieniawski was appointed solo violinist to the Czar of Russia, a position which he held for twelve years. Making his home in St. Petersburg, it was natural that he should become associated with Anton Rubinstein, who, two years after Wieniawski's appointment to the Czar, founded the Imperial Conservatory of St. Petersburg, where Wieniawski taught the violin for five years.

Anton Rubinstein in his *Autobiography* has set down in no uncertain terms his evaluation of the fiery Polish violinist. Referring to a tour which they shared in the United States, Rubinstein writes: "Wieniawski was then undoubtedly the finest violinist. His playing was extremely brilliant; he was a bright, witty man, but somewhat feeble."

This trip to America took place in 1872, at a time when only two Russian artists had previously visited the United States. Consequently Rubinstein and

Wieniawski, looking forward to the trip with no little misgivings, took great care that the terms agreed upon with their American manager left no loop holes to chance. According to their contracts not only was the extent of their tour limited, but one half of the stipulated amount of money guaranteed for the concerts was immediately deposited in the bank by the American manager. And despite the fact that Rubinstein was to deplore the unusual conditions under which the two artists were obliged to fulfill their engagements in the various American cities, he records in his Autobiography, "It may be interesting to note that the contract was fulfilled to the letter."

They often gave two or three concerts in different cities in the same day; concerts, which were fantastically successful wherever they went, though the audience-reaction or expectation might be different from that to which Rubinstein and Wieniawski were accustomed in Europe. For instance, at Memphis, Tennessee, just before Rubinstein was to appear in his first number, an attendant, familiar with minstrel shows rather than musical concerts, warned the great pianist that it was time for him to black his face! Notwithstanding the two artists, despite their fear of becoming "automatons" in this New World atmosphere, frequently inspired by the pioneer, primitive spirit, openly vied with each other for applause.

Wieniawski stayed on in America after Rubinstein returned to Europe, and continued to give concerts. While touring in California he received an invitation to take Henri Vieuxtemp's place as head of the violin department at the Brussels Conservatory. Accordingly, heading Eastward to assume this position left vacant by Vieuxtemp's having broken his arm, Wieniawski stopped off in New York long enough to fall prey to financial misfortune: Whereas Rubinstein had returned to his native land with the foundation of his prosperity snugly established from his American tour, Wieniawski lost all that he had earned in a bad investment.

This becomes both pertinent and sad when we learn that despite Wieniawski's natural tendency to abide by impulse rather than caution he had rigorously lived up to the letter of his American contract; hoping, no doubt, to emulate Rubinstein in establishing a substantial nest-egg to withstand future events. Alas, how far from this goal was his eventual path fated! From

Rubinstein's words we realize how well the impetuous violinist, despite hardship, held to his contract:

"Wieniawski, a man of extremely nervous temperament, who, owing to ill health quite often failed to meet his appointments in St. Petersburg—both at the Grand Theatre and at the Conservatory—never missed one concert in America. However ill he might be, he always contrived to find strength enough to appear on the platform with his fairy-like violin. The secret of his punctuality lay in the fact that by the terms of the contract he must forfeit one thousand francs for every non-appearance."

But as we have seen, despite this display of Herculean will-power, the Polish violinist, with his "fairy-like" violin, was destined to arrive at Brussels, enriched by experience rather than earthly goods. And this unfortunately was to be his fate till the end of his days; for his warm-hearted, impetuous nature, together with a passion for gambling, kept him from ever attaining a goal of security.

One particularly significant gambling incident is supposed to have resulted in the combined authorship of a well-known composition. This is the gist of the story: One night at Brussels, when he and Henri Vieuxtemps were vying with each other at the gambling table, Wieniawski, after losing every cent of money that he possessed, together with some borrowed money, finally lost his violin to Vieuxtemps. Whereupon the French violinist said to Wieniawski, "If you will let me publish your composition, which you played for me today, under my name, I will return your violin and call the matter square."

Relieved at the thought of both having his violin back and not being indebted to Vieuxtemps, Wieniawski readily agreed to the proposition.

Vieuxtemps delighted, according to the story, after making a few changes, writing a showy cadenza and finale, published the famous "Ballade and Polonaise" as agreed upon. Tremendously successful when it first appeared, it is still one of the standard works in violin literature.

Wieniawski remained at the Brussels Conservatory only two years, at the end of which time Vieuxtemps reassumed the position; and the Polish violinist, though quite ill, set out on extended concert tours. Arrived at Berlin, a desperately sick man, Wieniawski was forced to rehearse his newly composed D minor concerto in a sitting position. This he managed without too much discomfort; but attempting to stand while playing at the concert itself, he broke down completely and had to be carried off the stage. Joseph Joachim, who happened to be in the audience, immediately stepped to the platform and generously substituted for the stricken violinist by playing the Bach *Chaconne* in his inimitable manner.

Henceforth, though Wieniawski continued to give concerts, he was forced to play sitting down. And soon city after city heard the fine, spirited, violinist for the last time. At Paris, that same year, after making his last appearance at a Lamoureux concert, he was heard to say, "*Ça ne va plus, Ça ne va plus.*"

Growing steadily weaker, he returned to Russia where he attempted to give violin lessons as a means of earning his living. Then eventually some of his friends persuaded him to make a public appearance. Alas, it was destined to prove even sadder than the unfortunate Berlin incident. For a few minutes he played the "Kreutzer" Sonata with characteristic spirit. The audience was enchanted. Suddenly his violin crashed to the floor of the platform. Then the violinist himself crumpled after it. As he was carried off the stage in a dead faint, his place was taken by the violinist, Arno Hilf, who courageously attempted to finish the interrupted sonata.

Meanwhile the proud Wieniawski, discovered to be penniless, was carried home by some of his friends. It soon became necessary to put him in a hospital where he remained for some time. Fortunately a few days before his death Madame Nadejda von Meck, who so generously befriended Peter Ilyitch Tchaikovsky, took the dying violinist into her home, where he received every care that loving kindness and unlimited funds could offer.

On April 2, 1880—a few months before the death of Ole Bull—Henri Wieniawski at the age of forty-five died at Moscow. He was given a funeral befitting an artist of his rank by Madame von Meck, and all Moscow mourned the loss of one of the world's greatest violinists.

Among Wieniawski's compositions are: the famous "Legende," which he is supposed to have played with a divine spark; his popular D minor concerto; the "Souvenir de Moscow," which during his lifetime was so much admired that he formed the habit of leaving it off his programs, knowing that it would be demanded as an encore; the Fantasie on Gounod's "Faust," and two popular polonaises.

Perhaps the outstanding characteristic of Wieniawski's compositions is their suitability for the violin. George Bernard Shaw, when he served as a music critic under the name of Corno Di Bassetto, made the statement that he was always inclined to believe in a violinist who could play Wieniawski; for though Beethoven and Mendelssohn were great composers of music for the violin, Wieniawski was a great composer of violin music.

A gifted teacher, as well as a violinist and composer, Wieniawski numbered among his pupils the great Belgian violinist, Eugène Ysaÿe whose naturally robust style in playing gained immeasurably from Wieniawski's refined teaching.

Henri Wieniawski will always be remembered as a violinist of rare sensitivity, one whose playing and compositions sprang from a unique combination of musicianship, passionate nature, and graceful good taste.

PABLO DE SARASATE

OLE BULL was thirty-four and Niccolo Paganini had been dead four years when, on March 10, 1844, Pablo Martín Melitón Sarasate y Navascuez—known as Pablo de Sarasate—the third of the modern world's great violin virtuosos, was born at Pamplona in Navarre, Spain. Whereas Paganini evoked mysteries from his fiddle, and Ole Bull brought forth songs from his, Pablo de Sarasate's violin was not only to amaze and to sing but to *dance!*

The little Spanish boy, like most destined virtuoso players, began early to study his chosen instrument; in his case, the violin. His father, a military bandmaster, gave him his first lessons. At eight Pablo made his public début at La Coruña. At ten he began to take lessons from Manuel Rodriguez at Madrid. And two years later he gave a concert at the Madrid Royal Opera House, revealing even at this young age a unique quality of warmth and color in his playing.

A child with this much natural talent deserved the best in musical training! Accordingly Pablo's mother set out with him for Paris. But it was not to be her privilege to carry him far on his destined path, for she died, during their journey, at Bayonne. Fortunately the young boy's reputation was sufficiently established to attract assistance in his hour of unhappiness. Taken under the wing of the Spanish Consul at Bayonne, he soon received funds from various persons—including Queen Isabella—which enabled him to carry out his resolve to study in Paris.

Arrived in France, he immediately found friendly encouragement; and on January 1, 1856, he entered the Paris Conservatory, where he became the favorite pupil of Jean-Delphin Alard. The following year he won first prizes in violin and theory. He then entered the harmony classes of Napoleon-Henri Reber, but though he progressed more than satisfactorily—winning a high prize in 1859—the future concert virtuoso had by this time discovered where both his greatest talent and inclination lay. He would be a famous violinist! He would travel to all parts of the world—but unlike Ole Bull, he would travel not to carry the message of his native land to the far corners of the earth but to establish himself as an artist of the Universe!

Time was to see him do both. For in addition to becoming recognized as a great artist, he helped considerably to popularize "the Spanish Idiom" throughout the world.

Soon after having made his decision, Sarasate set out on a concert tour, the first of many which were always to be successful and eventually to extend to the farthest reaches of Europe, Africa, the Orient, and the two Americas. He made his first appearance in England in the year 1861; his first American one, in 1870, and the last, in 1889. Meanwhile he had taken Europe by storm, traveling from the tip of Portugal to the top of Norway, and criss-crossing the entire continent until he arrived at St. Petersburg as the guest-artist of the Russian Musical Society.

Leopold Auer, in his fascinating book, *My Long Life in Music,* has set down a wonderful account of Sarasate's Russian visit. After explaining the custom of inviting foreign artists to take part in the Imperial concerts, Auer states that Pablo de Sarasate was one of the most interesting of these famous guests. Arrived from brilliant successes in Germany, the Spanish violinist enchanted his Russian hosts; and, from Leopold Auer's description, we get a splendid picture of Sarasate at that time:

"He was a small man, very slender, and at the same time very elegant; his face framed in a fine head of black hair, parted in the middle, according to the fashion of the day. A departure from precedent was his habit of displaying on his chest the grand cordon and star of the Spanish order with which he had been decorated.... From the very first notes he drew from his Stradivarius ... I was impressed by the beauty and crystalline purity of his tone. The master of a perfected technique for both hands, he played without any effort at all, touching the strings with a magic bow in a manner which had no hint of the terrestrial."

Leopold Auer then goes on to say that the ethereal tones seem to have been produced by nothing so material as "hair and strings." Both he and the audience were delighted; and the public, immediately after his first concert, sought desperately to gain admittance to the succeeding ones. To accommodate further the eager public, and more particularly the members of royal society, the Imperial management arranged for Sarasate to play during intermissions of the Opera at various theatres.

But according to Leopold Auer, Sarasate much preferred the companionship of congenial musical friends to that of the wealthy nobility; often spending his evenings with Auer, Charles Davidov, noted violoncellist—then director of the St. Petersburg Conservatory—and the famous piano teacher, Theodore Leschetiszky.

"Always merry, always smiling and in good spirits," writes Auer about Sarasate, "and bursting into peals of delighted laughter when he was fortunate enough to win a few roubles from us at a modest game of cards. He was invariably gallant toward the ladies, and carried with him a number of small Spanish fans, which he was accustomed to present to them."

During this St. Petersburg visit Davidov persuaded Sarasate and Auer to attend a *musicale* at the home of the Grand Duke Constantine, at which Henri Wieniawski, who happened to be passing through the city, was to be present. Arrived at the Duke's marble palace, after responding graciously to the nobleman's greeting, and warmly addressing himself to Wieniawski, Sarasate retired to an inconspicuous seat. During one of the intermissions of the afternoon's recital, the Grand Duke, taking Davidov aside, directed him to ask Sarasate to play something for the assembled guests. Poor Davidov, shy by nature, hesitated to carry out the Duke's suggestion, realizing at the same time that he must do so, inasmuch as the request amounted to a command. Finally, abetted by both Auer and Wieniawski, Davidov mustered enough courage to ask this favor of the visiting artist. After a moment's hesitation, Sarasate sent his accompanist and secretary off to the hotel by sleigh to get his violin and music.

Then according to Auer's account, "When the secretary, Mr. Goldschmidt, returned with the precious Stradivarius and a package of music under his arm, Sarasate played some of the pieces of his repertoire with that ease and tonal charm which were peculiar to him, standing like a marble statue, his entire vitality seemingly concentrated in his eyes, often lowered to his fingers, which moved with astonishing dexterity."

After cordially shaking Sarasate's hand and thanking him, the Duke called upon Wieniawski, as "one of his family" to return Sarasate's favor by playing something in turn. What matter that the Polish violinist had no violin or music with him! "You can use Sarasate's violin," said the Duke. And that was that! And, when Wieniawski had beautifully played the famous "Legende" and one of his polonaises on an unfamiliar violin, Sarasate was the first to embrace and congratulate him.

After a wonderful dinner as the Duke's guests, followed by an evening of memorable conversation, the party broke up with the host's assurance that he would always remember those few hours. And as Leopold Auer adds, "We might have all said the same, for within one and the same hour we had heard two of the greatest violinists of all times."

The above reference to Sarasate's eyes, together with one made by George Bernard Shaw later in England, affords striking proof of one of the Spanish violinist's chief features. Writing about Sarasate, after hearing him play Mendelssohn's concerto in 1889, Shaw, who had on another occasion called Sarasate a brilliant exception to all rules, defines in delightful fashion the secret of Sarasate's power over an audience. After mentioning that Sarasate might just as well have been playing "Pop Goes the Weasel" as far as interpretation was concerned, in that he never interpretated anything but played everything beautifully, Shaw states that Sarasate created the illusion of being a black-haired young Spaniard with "his fine eyes alone." And he goes on to say that there was no affectation about him; that "the picturesqueness of that pluck of the string and stroke of the bow that never fails to bring down the house is the natural effect of an action performed with perfect accuracy in an extraordinary short time and strict measure."

In other words, though Sarasate might give the impression to his listeners that the music he evoked from his Stradivarius violin came straight from Heaven, the precision of his mind and hand, together with the expression of those "fine eyes," contributed generously to this Heaven-sent quality!

On another occasion, Shaw paid tribute to Sarasate's precision of tone by advising the aspiring singing artist among other things to study the violinists "culminating in Sarasate." On still another occason, Shaw wrote that Sarasate "left criticism gasping miles behind him." And still again, this same critic refers with unstinted praise to Sarasate's dance tunes and national airs; Sarasate, representing the South as Ole Bull did the North.

After the year 1870 the Spanish virtuoso by no means confined himself to fantasies and dance tunes, being recognized as "a new star" when he began including the classical violin music in his repertory. But though he played the standard music "beautifully," as Shaw stated, he remained to the end of his career the romantic player; evoking, as one contemporary said "the song of the nightingale" from his fiddle; another, "glorious birdsong and golden sunshine."

And something there was about this "golden violinist," which inspired many a musician to compose music especially for him: Édouard Lalo wrote his first violin concerto and the exquisite *Symphonie espagnole*, with Sarasate both in mind and with his guidance. The latter was performed by the honored violinist for the first time on February 7, 1875, at Paris. Max Bruch composed for Sarasate his second violin concerto and the *Scottische Fantasie;* and the English composer, Sir Alexander Campbell wrote for him the *Pibroch* suite. Camille Saint-Saens' first violin concerto was given its first performance by Sarasate in 1873 at Paris.

From the beginning of his glorious career Pablo de Sarasate annually returned to his native city, where the people celebrated the occasion as a public festival. And at his death he bequeathed to Pamplona the many gifts that had accumulated over the years, for which his countrymen prepared a special museum. One of his greatest hobbies was the collecting of canes. Among the several hundred canes of all kinds, many of them gifts from royal monarchs, were at least twenty from Queen Christina of Spain.

He owned two fine Stradivarius violins, one of which was given to him in his early youth by Queen Isabella. And he is supposed to have had a copy made of it by the violin maker Vuillaume, for rehearsal purposes. Fittingly, he bequeathed one Stradivarius to the Madrid Conservatory; the other, to his second Alma-Mater—the Paris Conservatory.

The "Golden Violinist" continued his concert career to the time of his death, which occurred on September 20, 1908, at Biarritz. A fixed star in the firmanent of violinists, Pablo de Sarasate shines alone, shedding the radiance of his unique quality through his own compositions; particularly in the Spanish Dances. Among his other characteristic compositions are the *Zigeunerweisen* for violin and orchestra; *Navarra* for two violins; the caprice, *Peteneras;* and the *Jota de San Fermín.*

Sarasate, ethereal genius, who used his bow in the most natural manner, wielded his left hand with the wand of a wizard, touched the strings with exquisite precision, and danced with grace on his Stradivarius, not only *stood* alone among violinists, but *shines* eternal in Memory!

LEOPOLD AUER AND HIS PUPILS

LEOPOLD AUER, destined to teach a whole galaxy of modern violinists, was born on June 7, 1845, at the little Hungarian town of Veszprem. Inheriting the natural fiddle-feeling of his native land, he was to establish both his reputation and influence not in Hungary but in Imperial Russia. For nearly fifty years, official violinist at the court of three different Czars, he, at the same time, projected the name *Auer* into succeeding generations through teacher-association with such familiar names as Heifetz, Zimbalist, Eddy Brown, Mischa Elman and Milstein.

Leopold Auer's father was a house painter, a circumstance that contributed to his son's talents being brought to the attention of some of the aristocratic families of the community, for the elder Auer—actually a decorator—often had opportunities to converse with his various wealthy clients; and what was more natural than that he should occasionally boast a bit about the musical talents of his young son, Leopold.

Owing to the interest aroused on one of these occasions, little Leopold was graduated from tiny precocious drummer to violin student: When he was but three or four, the litle boy—with toy drum slung about his neck, keeping exact time with the soldiers' drum-beats—would lead his playmates at the head of regiments entering his native city. Be they Austrian or Hungarian troops it mattered not to the future violinist. It so happened that the commander of one of the Hungarian units was so much impressed with the little boy's rhythmic sense that he tried to persuade Leopold's father to permit the child-drummer to accompany the regiment for the purpose of arousing national enthusiasm. Fortunately the request was not granted, but this military recognition of his natural musical talent when reported served to provide him with his first little violin. He was now on the winding path that eventually led to the court of the Czars!

Following a short period of study at the grammar school in Veszprem, Leopold at eight was taken to Budapest, where he began to study the violin under Ridley Kohné, leading teacher at the Budapest Conservatory. Taking both class and private lessons, the little Hungarian boy progressed rapidly. At the same time he continued his general education at a boarding school, where, fortunately the authorities, realizing his unusual talent for music, provided him with a separate room where he might study and practice undisturbed.

Soon, to the great delight of his father, Leopold was permitted by Professor Kohné to prepare for his public début. What excitement preceded this auspicious event! Although this appearance at the National Opera House of Budapest did not, as the father hoped, immediately catapult his son into the world of fame and fortune, it did bring him to the attention of certain patrons who arranged for him to continue his studies at the Vienna Conservatory.

This proved a splendid turn of events, for, during his two years' study at Vienna, the foundation of his violin technique, as well as his musical grounding, was laid. Living in the home of Professor Jacob Dont under whom he diligently studied the violin, Leopold also took lessons at the Conservatory from Joseph Hellmesberger, who, as we know, was a great quartet player. In addition he studied harmony, composition, and orchestration, all of which contributed to his distinguished future.

At the end of two years, his funds having been exhausted, Leopold was forced to discontinue his studies at the Vienna Conservatory. Accordingly the elder Auer, assuming the inexperienced role of impresario, set out with his thirteen-year-old son—who was equipped with a diploma from the Vienna Conservatory and a silver medal—to conquer the world! Hale of heart, like traveling gypsies, they literally took to the road, making their first stop at Gran, not far from Vienna. Through the assistance of the local pharmacist, they managed to arrange some recitals, the proceeds of which provided food and lodging for the length of their stay, but scarcely enough to ensure proper food or transportation for the trip to the next objective.

Continuing their journey, avoiding the large cities because of the greater cost of living, they often traveled by wagon. And in this connection, Leopold Auer later in his Autobiography related an amusing, though discomforting feature. Seated on boards, propped up by bales of straw, which grew steadily lower as parts of them were periodically fed to the horses pulling their wagon, the violin prodigy and his manager-father often arrived at their destination lying prone on the wagon's bottom for lack of support to their improvised seats. From such a position, often made worse by stormy weather, how eagerly would Leopold scan the horizon for friendly church spires or house-tops, beckoning them shelter-ward to their next town!

For two long years they kept up this wandering life, chiefly among the Hungarian towns, with an occasional visit to Vienna to add to the boy's repertory. During their travels young Leopold often had an opportunity to meet eminent musicians of the day; most outstanding in its results, being the meeting with Henri Vieuxtemps at Gratz in Styria. Having on their arrival at Gratz, spied the announcement of Vieuxtemps' approaching concert, the Auers immediately purchased tickets for the event. Imagine Leopold's excitement when he discovered that the great violinist was going to play his "Fantasie Caprice," this being one of the Hungarian boy's own specialties!

Finally the great day arrived, and a good half hour before the concert was to begin there sat Leopold and his father in eager anticipation! Though by no means mature in judgment, the youthful violinist listened in rapt admiration to Vieuxtemps' playing; while his father secretly determined to secure an audience for him with the great artist. Already, in his mind's eye, he read in their future advertisements, "Leopold Auer, proclaimed a great genius by Vieuxtemps."

Accordingly, with difficulty, chiefly owing to Madame Vieuxtemps' objections to her husband's being bothered with infant prodigies, a hearing was arranged. Arrived at Vieuxtemps' hotel on the appointed day, the wanderers were cordially received by the celebrated artist, though Madame Vieuxtemps—her husband's accompanist at his concerts—remained exceedingly cool. After asking a few questions regarding Leopold's education, Vieuxtemps kindly requested his frightened guest to play something for him. Madame Vieuxtemps reluctantly sat down at the piano to accompany the youth in her husband's "Fantasie Caprice." Trembling with emotion, Leopold, then a boy of fourteen, poured out his very soul through the tones of his violin. Encouraged by a smile from Vieuxtemps, completely letting himself go, in the midst of a singing phrase in which he was playing with far too much feeling, he was rudely interrupted by Madame Vieuxtemps' abruptly rising from the piano stool.

What could she be doing? Walking back and forth around the room, she peered into this corner then that; and leaning down, she looked inquiringly beneath the piano and below the bureau. It seemed to Leopold that the quaked earth was about to engulf him.

Finally Vieuxtemps, also perplexed, asked his wife, "What in the world are you looking for?"

"Some cats must be hidden in this room," she said in reply. "Don't you hear them miaowing in every key?"

Instantly realizing that she was referring to the oversentimentality of his playing, Leopold fainted dead away. Supported by his father's arm, and patted on the shoulder by Vieuxtemps, he half heard the violinist say, "Don't worry. All will be well later."

Father and son left the hotel with tears in their eyes, and the experience remained with the boy-grown-famous to the end of his life. "From that day on I hated all glissandos and vibratos," is the way he put it.

Despite this unfortunate set-back to their spirits, they continued on, stopping in various German towns; and then, through Holland, to Paris! Arrived there, they immediately went to Jean-Delphin Alard, Sarasate's master at the Paris Conservatory, who agreed, after hearing Leopold play, to give him private lessons. Meanwhile the eager youth had an opportunity to make the acquaintance of various eminent musicians, including Gioacchino Rossini and Hector Berlioz. He was also privileged to attend the unfortunate first performance of Richard Wagner's *Tannhäuser* at the Paris Opéra, the one which, though badly received by the French audience, prompted Princess Metternich to remark prophetically as she left the theatre, "You laughed at Wagner today; but twenty-five years from now you will cheer him here in Paris."

After a few months, during which young Auer gave several recitals to help defray their expenses, father and son once more set out on a journey; this time, armed with a letter of introduction to Joseph Joachim at Hanover.

Greeted cordially by this great artist and teacher, Leopold was soon buried in profitable study. Characteristically Joachim opened up entirely new vistas for his young countryman. As Auer later expressed it, "With him I worked not only with my hand, but with my head as well."

Along with his intensive study of the scores of the great masters, he had many opportunities to play chamber music with other students and was often permitted to take part inconspicuously in symphonic concerts under Joachim. One of his greatest joys came in listening to his teacher's occasional Sunday morning quartet recitals. At these he began to penetrate the beauty and meaning of Beethoven, Schubert, and Schumann; and at one such concert he was present at the initial performance of Johannes Brahms' first Sextet for strings. Brahms, then but a youth himself, was present on this occasion and according to Leopold Auer's account "hid in a corner of the room."

Another highlight of these Sunday morning recitals was the performance of Beethoven's "Kreutzer" Sonata by Joachim and Clara Schumann. Hearing it for the first time, and under such favorable circumstances, Leopold Auer was never to forget the impression it made upon him, though he was later to play it hundreds of times in various parts of the world. Not long after this wonderful first hearing of the Sonata, as a matter of fact, Auer himself played it, with the kind assistance of Johannes Brahms, at a recital in Hamburg.

At the end of two wonderfully fruitful years at Hanover under the guidance of Joachim, their all-important funds once again exhausted, the Auers set out again. And since Leipzig at that time was one of the most important cities, musically, they decided to go there in search of further encouragement to Leopold's career. They would try to arrange for his appearance at one of the famous *Gewandhaus* concerts!

Arrived at Leipzig, they sought out the violinist, Ferdinand David—Felix Mendelssohn's colleague and friend—who had previously heard young Auer play at Hanover. And before the young violinist realized what was happening to him he had been invited by David to play at the *Gewandhaus!* On the day of the concert he was so nervous that he could not eat a bite of food. In despair, lest Leopold break down on this important occasion, the senior Auer took along to the hall a bottle of fine wine, and just as his son was about to step onto the stage he forced him to drink a small glass of this stimulant. Fortunately it served the desired purpose. His fears banished, Leopold played with confidence and skill, scoring a success with audience, artists and press. And to his great delight offers for other engagements came tumbling in, including one from Düsseldorf, where he was destined to achieve one of his fondest goals—security!

At that time every aspiring young musician sought some sort of official recognition from one of the reigning German princes; and now Leopold Auer, at nineteen, was made concertmaster at Düsseldorf! Having never known a moment free from money worries since his earliest traveling days, he was particularly grateful and could honestly say that he had "attained his life's greatest ambition." As it happened, his official duties being light, and Düsseldorf being artistically well situated, the young concertmaster gained immeasurably from this opportunity. Not only was he able to continue his own studies without worrying about his next meal, but he was privileged to attend the famous music festivals, held in turn at the three Rhenish cities—Düsseldorf, Cologne, and Aix-la-Chapelle. At one of these—at Düsseldorf—he played a violin concerto, thereby achieving the honor of being the youngest artist to appear on any of the Rhenish concerts.

Several engagements were offered him following this Düsseldorf festival appearance; and because it offered the opportunity of playing the first violin with a new quartet he accepted the invitation from Hamburg. Staying at Hamburg two years, he had an excellent opportunity to study the chamber music repertory, and, as a result of his success in the newly organized quartet, he was asked to substitute for the first violinist in the famous Müller Quartet when that unfortunate member fell ill. Over-joyed at being thus chosen by so eminent a group, Auer hastened to Berlin for the first rehearsal. All went well. And soon he was jogging over the roads once again; this time, a recognized artist in an eminent group. Wrapped in furs, they traveled Eastward through Königsberg, Stettin, Dantzig, and smaller places; everywhere meeting with tremendous success. The members of this famous Müller Quartet had wonderful times together under the leadership of its "youthful and savage" Hungarian violinist.

Meanwhile Leopold Auer dashed back and forth to Hamburg between engagements in order to fulfill his duties as concertmaster and quartet player in that city, sometimes returning to his post with the Müller Brothers scarcely in time to change his apparel before a concert. Despite such interruptions, the Quartet, keeping up its rehearsals, constantly added to its repertory. Steadily the Quartet's reputation grew, so that the traveling artists were not entirely taken by surprise when during a tour in the middle of Germany, they were invited to play at the court of Meiningen. This engagement provided one of the high points in Leopold Auer's young life—another goal-post won!

On the day following the Meiningen concert, the youthful leader of the Quartet was aroused from his musings, on the pomp and ceremony surrounding their court appearance, by a knock on his door. There stood a lackey, dressed in gold-embroidered uniform. Courteously handing the astonished violinist a large envelope, sealed with the Saxe-Meiningen crest, together with a red morocco case, he quickly disappeared. With trembling fingers, Leopold tore open the envelope. Yes! It was true! He had been *decorated!* For that was what the letter contained: the announcement that Leopold Auer had been honored by the Duke of Saxe-Meiningen. And opening the red morocco case, he found the decoration itself—a small cross of the "Order of Ernest." Though the cross could be worn only on state occasions Leopold instantly realized that the decoration carried with it the privilege of wearing a narrow red ribbon, bordered with green, in his button hole. Without further ado he dashed out and bought enough ribbon of the proper kind to decorate the buttonholes of all his wardrobe, including his overcoat!

And that was not all! Further to relish this great joy that had descended upon him, for several nights, after carefully locking the door and lighting all the candles in his room, he stood enraptured before a mirror, which reflected *Leopold Auer* in full evening dress with the cross of the "Order of Ernest" on his breast! Though he was to receive many such decorations in the course of his long career, including that of the French Legion of Honor and the grand cross of the Order of St. Stanislas at St. Petersburg, "not one of them," in Auer's own words, "ever gave me half the pleasure I took in the little Meiningen cross in 1867."

Later that same year Auer accepted the invitation of an American impresario by the name of Ullman to take part in a great series of concerts to be given in Austria, Austria-Hungary, the province of Galicia and the duchy of Bukovina. Auer's violin playing was just one of the "fabulous items" on these circus-like programs, which included singing by Carlotta Patti and Jules Lefort, 'cello playing by David Popper, and piano playing by the virtuoso, Rudolf Wilmers. The concerts, tremendously successful, extended over a period of six weeks; and the artists, "all young and gay," had a wonderful time, despite the fact that on one occasion the violinist was forced to play under the handicap of a raging fever.

Perhaps we should call this tour "Auer's Farewell to His Youth"; for the following year, 1868, was to prove the turning point in his career. After filling some London engagements, he settled down that summer at a little place called Petersthal in the Black Forest. There while thoroughly enjoying the opportunity to practice, read, or study just as he saw fit, he received a letter that contained a clipping from the widely circulated *Cologne Gazette:*

"The violinist, Leopold Auer, is requested to send his present address to the Kreuznach Music Shop in view of an important communication to be made to him."

Desperately curious, he immediately telegraphed the desired information; and soon, he received a request for an interview from Nicolai Zaremba, recently appointed director of the St. Petersburg Conservatory. A few days later, when this gentleman arrived at Petersthal, an important proposition presented itself: a three-year contract as a professor at the St. Petersburg Conservatory and a soloist at the court of the Grand Duchess Helena. Since he would be succeeding no less a violinist than Henri Wieniawski at the Conservatory and filling a post similar to Anton Rubinstein's career-beginning at this court, the "youthful and savage" Hungarian violinist did not long hesitate.

Leopold Auer arrived in Russia at an important moment in her musical history. Up until six years previous to this time there had been but one advanced school of music in Russia—the School of Church Song, connected with the Imperial Chapel. Musicians, otherwise, went to Germany, France, or Italy for training unless they studied privately with foreign teachers, settled in Russia. In 1868 there were two great conservatories—the one at St. Petersburg and another at Moscow: Peter Ilyitch Tchaikovsky, having recently graduated from the first, was now a professor at the latter. Then there was the emerging group of young amateur musicians, eventually to be known as the famous "Five," consisting of Mily Balakirev, Cesar Cui, Alexander Borodin, Modest Mussorgsky and Nikolai Rimsky-Korsakov; Alexander Dargomyzhsky was still living and the great Michail Glinka had been dead only a little more than ten years. Both St. Petersburg and Moscow had their wonderful ballet schools. It was indeed a stimulating situation for Leopold Auer at twenty-three!

Presented to his colleagues at an official dinner, Auer soon felt completely at home in the country, which was to be his *home* until the Russian Revolution in 1917. Charles Davidov, the violoncellist, immediately became his great friend; and it was not long before he was taking part in quartet rehearsals at Davidov's home. As soon as the chamber music of the various contemporary composers was written, it was rehearsed and played by this famous quartet; Tchaikovsky, Borodin, Arensky, Cui, and Anton Rubinstein were all represented. "What glorious days those were!" wrote Auer.

And although St. Petersburg overflowed with famous Russian hospitality, it was at Moscow on periodic professional visits that Auer found even greater warmth of entertainment. Following a Symphony Concert, or a Quartet Recital, he always had an opportunity to attend one of Nicholas Rubinstein's weekly luncheons for his colleagues and friends. Nicholas Rubinstein, the brother of Anton, was director of the Moscow Conservatory; and it was at his house that Leopold Auer would often meet Tchaikovsky, or Sergei Taneieff—one of Nicholas Rubinstein's best pupils—who later accompanied the violinist on his first Russian tour and dedicated a suite for violin and orchestra to him.

Meanwhile the Hungarian violinist, in addition to establishing himself thoroughly as an extraordinary teacher, became "Soloist to His Majesty the Czar," succeeding Henri Wieniawski; a position which entailed the playing of specially written solos at the ballet performances in the Imperial Opera House. Tchaikovsky was, of course, one of the outstanding composers thus to be represented.

Auer also continued his own concert-giving, making occasional trips to London. On one of these trips he especially enjoyed the company of some

French musician-friends who were temporarily living there. Among these were Charles Gounod, Camille Saint-Saëns, Pauline Viardot-Garcia, and her husband. On another visit to London he and the famous singer, Christine Nilsson, informally entertained various members of English and French Society at a reception given by the Russian Ambassador at London; and on still another, he and Joseph Wieniawski—the brother of the violinist—played together Joachim's arrangements of some of Brahms' "Hungarian Dances" at an informal gathering, attended by the typically *Hungarian* violinist, Edouard Reményi.

Returned to Russia from this trip, Leopold Auer was soon once again buried in teaching and musical duties pertaining to the various Imperial courts, including the "Great Court" of the Czar and Czarina. Closely associated with Charles Davidov and Anton Rubinstein, he led a wonderfully rich life, additionally colored by frequent contacts with various foreign artists come to Russia to appear with the Imperial Russian Musical Society. Among these artists were Hans von Bülow and Pablo de Sarasate.

At the same time it was his privilege to appreciate and encourage Russia's own Peter Ilyitch Tchaikovsky, when that composer's name was not as well known as it is today. In turn, Tchaikovsky dedicated to Auer his first composition for violin and orchestra, the *Sérénade mélancholique*. Then one day the violinist was quite overcome when Tchaikovsky appeared with a concerto for violin and orchestra, not in manuscript but already published, bearing the dedication "A Monsieur Leopold Auer." Eagerly scanning the score as Tchaikovsky played a piano version of it, Auer was much impressed with the lyric beauty of certain parts of the music. But upon studying the score at his leisure, he decided that despite its great virtues the concerto required revisions in order to make it more suitable for the violin. Regretting that Tchaikovsky had not consulted him before having the music engraved, Auer, nevertheless, resolved to submit certain changes to the composer.

Unforeseen circumstances were to delay for many years the realization of this resolve. Meanwhile Tchaikovsky, naturally disappointed at Auer's apparent disregard for his concerto, at the end of two years, having recalled the original edition, rededicated the concerto to Adolphe Brodsky, who played it for the first time in Vienna in 1882. Leopold Auer later, in keeping with his word, made certain revisions in the now famous Concerto in D. Played by both him and his pupils, it has been thus published on both sides of the Atlantic.

The immediate cause for delay in carrying out his intentions in regard to the concerto came in Auer's appointment as director of the symphonic concerts of the Russian Musical Society. This was but one more responsibility which, in addition to his regular duties, included directing the orchestral concerts of the Imperial Choir and conducting the orchestral class at the Conservatory.

Leopold Auer, now everywhere recognized as a great master, had for some time been warmly welcomed in various cities whenever a lull in his regular duties permitted him to travel. On one of these occasions an incident occurred which remained lifelong in his memory. While being entertained in a musician's home at Warsaw, he met Apollinaire de Kontski, Polish violinist and director of the Warsaw Conservatory, who invited him to play before the students and teachers at the Conservatory.

Graciously accepting the invitation, Auer arrived at the Conservatory's concert hall at the appointed time amidst great bouquets of flowers and hearty welcome. "Who among your students will accompany me?" asked the violinist. Whereupon Konski beckoned to one of the young men assembled on the platform. The designated youth, fifteen or sixteen of age, eagerly stepped forward, took the music which Auer intended to play, glanced intently through it for a few minutes, and then indicated that he was ready at the violinist's bidding. Though Konski, on introducing the young man, had spoken well of both his playing and musicianship he had in no way exaggerated the student's ability. Leopold Auer in referring to the experience later, wrote, "The whole program was played as though we had carefully rehearsed it in advance." Delighted with this young artist with intelligent eyes, and face framed with a halo of golden hair, Auer warmly thanked him, and having paid no attention to his name when mentioned in the introduction, now asked, "What is your name?"

"Jan Paderewski," answered the youth.

Thus the visiting violinist heard for the first time a name that was to become world famous.

Another happy meeting was the one with Franz Liszt at Weimar. Having looked forward to this moment for some time, Auer was quite overcome when presented to Liszt by Edouard Lassen, conductor of the orchestra of the Weimar Opera. But Liszt, then an old man, with long flowing white hair, soon put the violinist at ease by asking questions about the new Russian music. He then invited Auer to take dinner with him the following day. On that occasion, Liszt, after listening to Auer play some Bach violin solos, accompanied the latter at the piano. Two days later the great Weimar Master dined with Auer at his hotel after having been escorted there by the violinist who was deeply moved by the townspeople's display of devotion to Liszt as they passed through the streets.

Leopold Auer, as a matter of fact, possessed many of the qualities familiarly associated with Franz Liszt. Genuine artist and musician, like Liszt, he also both recognized and developed talent in those about him: a quality, particularly apparent during his conductorship of the Russian Musical Society Orchestra. Assuming the task, previously held by many distinguished musicians, he immediately met the challenge. Conscious that some of Hans von Bülow's power over orchestra and audience lay in his conducting without a score, Auer carefully prepared his first program for presentation in that manner. The result outdid his expectations; for he received a genuine ovation at the first concert. Much to his regret he was forced to give up conducting from memory after the third concert, owing to the lack of time to prepare the scores.

Despite this compromise with his own ideas, the violinist-conductor continued to conduct with spirit and integrity; at the same time, taking particular pride in his choice of visiting artists, as well as music, for these programs. Many contemporary artists—both violinists and pianists—made their Russian débuts under his leadership; and his Liszt-like open-mindedness toward new music was responsible for the first performance in St. Petersburg of such music as: Hector Berlioz's *Requiem*, Robert Schumann's music to Byron's *Manfred* and the Prelude to Wagner's *Parsifal*.

Eventually he added still another responsibility to his crowded schedule— the organization of an entirely independent orchestra. The Russian Musical Society up to this time had been required to rely upon the services of the orchestra of the Imperial Opera; a circumstance, not always convenient either for orchestra or Musical Society. Accordingly Auer, with the assisting advice of Anton Rubinstein, gathered together a group of excellent musicians; the majority of them coming from the two Russian Conservatories; a few, carefully selected through competition at Dresden. It was indeed a proud moment when Rubinstein greeted this infant-orchestra at its first rehearsal; for who more than he realized how much lay behind this achievement! Over thirty years before he had laid the foundation of this Russian Musical Society, together with the St. Petersburg Conservatory; and now, an orchestra had been assembled largely from these beginnings.

Under Leopold Auer's leadership the new group rapidly developed into a working unit. Then came the début of the new orchestra! Great excitement filled the hall on this occasion; some came prepared to praise; others, to pick flaws. But at the end of the second number, orchestra and conductor were extended an ovation. An artistic battle had been won; but, unfortunately, the financial struggle involved in the new venture was perpetually to plague the indefatigable Auer, making it necessary to disband the fine new orchestra at the end of two years. Meanwhile several happy occasions, associated with the orchestra, became fixed in the conductor's memory: one, a Mozart Festival at which Vassili Safonoff played a Mozart piano concerto, and a chorus of six hundred voices took part in the famous *Requiem*; also, two all-Wagner concerts; and finally, a great concert celebrating the fiftieth anniversary of Anton Rubinstein's musical career.

Then in addition to these spiritual rewards, many gifts and honors were showered upon the violinist during his conducting years. Among these were two diamond-adorned batons; a complete library of symphonic scores, presented in a wooden chest; and hereditary nobility rights from the Czar, as well as the cross of the order of St. Vladimir.

Having resigned from his duties as director of the Russian Musical Society, Auer resumed his occasional concert tours; one in 1894, being largely dedicated to the memory of Tchaikovsky who had died the previous year. The first concert of this tour, entirely devoted to the works of Tchaikovsky, played by the Philharmonic Orchestra at Berlin under Auer's direction, was so successful that it was repeated at a popular concert. Then, to their delight, the Berlin Philharmonic and Auer were invited to give the same concert at Leipzig. At the conclusion of this Tchaikovsky-Auer-Berlin association, the visiting conductor presented the Philharmonic Orchestra with his scores of the Tchaikovsky music, played there under his direction.

From Berlin Auer traveled to the beautiful city of Odessa, where he had the honor of conducting the first performance of Beethoven's Seventh Symphony ever given there. Next came a visit to Munich, where a great festival was being held under the leadership of Hermann Levi, celebrated conductor of Wagner's music dramas. At one of the concerts of the festival Auer conducted Tchaikovsky's *Francesca da Rimimi* and played that composer's violin concerto to the warm approval of the Munch public. All in all this festival week was a wonderful occasion, shared with eminent musicians from all over the world, closing with a grand supper in the famous *Hofbrauhaus*.

After this refreshing change from his duties at the Russian court, Auer once again settled down to the routine of teaching and playing. But in the spring of 1902 another interesting opportunity for travel presented itself and was eagerly seized upon. The husband of Madame Gorlenko-Dolina, one of the soloists of the Czar, invited the violinist to accompany his wife on a concert tour, which he would manage through the Balkan capitals. What a wonderful trip this proved to be! They stopped first at Vienna, where an all-Tchaikovsky program was enthusiastically received. From there they traveled to the colorful city of Constantinople. Leopold Auer was delighted with this Ottoman capital, for he had always cherished a desire to visit the Orient. The Turkish city more than fulfilled his dreams of Asiatic splendor. There they gave three concerts at a great hall, provided by the Russian Embassy, then awaited a promised invitation from the Sultan Abdul Hamid II to play at his palace. Meanwhile their previously arranged-for concerts at Sofia and Belgrade had to be postponed, much to the displeasure of the potentates of those small capitals.

Finally the time was set. Two magnificent carriages arrived to carry the artists and the Russian Ambassador to the Royal Palace. Picturesquely attired guards saluted them as they drove through the park leading to the palace; a park, which took about twelve minutes traveling briskly, to cover before reaching the Sultan's palace. Arrived at the entrance, they were met by a horde of black attendants who looked suspiciously upon the violinist's instrument case; and it took some persuasion on Auer's part to keep them from seizing the offending article for examination. Doubtless, they suspected that a bomb abided in it for the purpose of assassinating their over-anxious ruler. That hazard overcome, the artists were invited to partake of a magnificent banquet before playing their concert. Hundreds of wax candles lighted the richly decorated hall where they were served. Golden goblets adorned the table, and delicacies of all sorts were spread before them.

Following the banquet they were escorted to the hall, where the concert was to take place, and after more sniffing at Auer's violin case on the part of the servants, the artists were given specific directions concerning the customs of their court. Under no circumstance could they stop playing or singing, even though they had reached the end of a piece, until the Sultan gave the word! Alas, when Auer's turn arrived, after playing several small pieces, he realized that his violin required tuning. And much to the consternation of those assembled, the violinist stopped and tuned his instrument, despite the fact that the Sultan had not directed him to cease playing. Fortunately this unheard-of behavior met with no tragic results; and after resuming his playing for a short time, and carefully watching for a sign from the Sultan, the violinist was finally permitted, by a smile and a nod from Abdul Hamid, officially, to cease playing.

Before leaving Constantinople two days later both artists were decorated and presented with a bag of gold. Small wonder that the little concert-group left the picturesque Turkish capital with regret and warm memories in their hearts!

Arrived at Sofia, they found that Prince Ferdinand, irked by their delay, had gone off to his summer place. Notwithstanding, their concert was well received in the City-of-Roses. From there they went to Belgrade, where they played at both the Royal Theatre and the Russian Embassy. Following the latter concert they were each presented with the scarf of a commander of the Order of St. Sava, together with a special message from the King, who, like the Bulgarian Prince, had been slightly piqued at the artists' over-long stay at Constantinople.

Returning to St. Petersburg by way of Vienna, where he spent a few days with his former colleague, Theodore Leschetiszky, Leopold Auer soon found himself immersed in some of the richest of his teaching experience. Among his pupils at this time was Efrem Zimbalist, born on April 9, 1889, at Rostov on the Don in Russia. The young Russian violinist eventually finished his studies at the Conservatory under Auer with high honors and made his début, on November 7, 1907, in the Brahms Concerto, at Berlin with brilliant success. A month later he was equally well received in London, and by the next year was sensationally successful wherever he appeared in Europe. His American début occurred in the fall of 1911 with the Boston Symphony Orchestra. On this occasion he played Alexander Glazounov's concerto in A major, giving it its first American performance. Henceforth he toured in various parts of the world; and in 1914, he married Alma Gluck, the singer; and finally he associated himself with the Curtis Institute of Music at Philadelphia.

Mischa Elman was also a pupil of Leopold Auer in this great flowering period. Born on January 20, 1892, at Stalnoye in Russia, the boy at eight had been taken to Odessa to study with a pupil of Adolf Brodsky. Two or three years later when Leopold Auer had arrived at Elizabethgrad, in southern Russia, preparatory to giving a concert, he was informed by a bellboy at his hotel that a gentleman with a small boy insisted upon seeing him. Tired from his trip, and accustomed to appeals from fathers with sons, thought to be geniuses, the violinist, at the same time not wishing to disappoint the man who, he was told, had come from some distance, turned to a former pupil by the name of Halov, who happened to be talking to him, and said: "Take the boy aside somewhere and hear him play. I must rest a bit before dressing for the concert."

Halov soon returned and seriously said, "Professor, you really ought to hear that boy!"

What could the overly-generous violinist do but heed such persuasive advice! "Very well," he replied. "Give them passes to my concert and ask them to come to my hotel tomorrow morning an hour before I have to leave town for another concert."

The following morning, when scarcely out of bed, Auer was greeted by Halov, Papa Elman, and son, come to plead the cause of an aspiring youth; a situation, not so different from one of his own early experiences. While packing his trunk, he listened with astonishment to little Mischa play a concerto with spectacular skill. There was only one thing for him to do: he immediately sat down and wrote a letter of recommendation to Alexander Glazounov, director of the St. Petersburg Conservatory, requesting that Mischa be given a scholarship and placed in his violin class.

Upon his return to St. Petersburg, Auer found that his request had been granted; but poor Papa Elman was enduring all manner of indignities, since he could not procure a permit from the Minister of the Interior to remain in the city to be near his young son. Finally after a great struggle, Leopold Auer secured the necessary permission and little Mischa was free to concentrate on his studies without worrying about what the Russian police would do to his father, if found without the proper credentials. Two years later Mischa Elman made his sensational début at St. Petersburg. Soon, despite his youth, he was triumphantly traveling throughout Europe; then came an equally sensational appearance in London: followed, in 1908, by his first visit to the United States, where, henceforth he made an annual tour. Some American critics immediately expressed the opinion that young Elman, then eighteen, suffered artistically from the handicap brought about by his having been extravagantly received as a prodigy; but, notwithstanding, the young violinist had within his first three seasons appeared with all the important orchestras in the country. And the passing years, during which he was to travel the world over, established him as one of the outstanding violinists of the twentieth century.

Leopold Auer's later years in Russia were enlivened by the privilege of teaching a whole galaxy of future violinistic stars, which included Michel Piastro, Cecile Hansen, Miron Poliakine, Jascha Heifetz, and Toscha Seidel. The latter two, entered at the St. Petersburg Conservatory when quite young, each encountered difficulties similar to that experienced by Mischa Elman and his father. In Toscha Seidel's case his mother and he were obliged to live fifteen miles away from St. Petersburg, in Finland, until permission was obtained for them to reside near the Conservatory. While Jascha's father, who accompanied the talented youth to the Russian capital, skillfully circumvented the law, which would have prevented him from remaining in the city, by enrolling in the classes along with his son.

Jascha Heifetz, one of the world's greatest violinists, was born on February

2, 1901, at Vilna in Russia. A true prodigy, as well as mature artist, he began early to study the violin with his father who was an able violinist. Progressing rapidly, the little boy was soon admitted to the Imperial Music School at Vilna, where, before he was five, he appeared in recitals. At six he made his official début at Kovno, playing Mendelssohn's concerto before an enraptured audience. Soon thereafter he entered the St. Petersburg Conservatory, where, as we know, he came under the guidance of Leopold Auer. At eleven he appeared with phenomenal success with the Berlin Philharmonic Orchestra under Artur Nikisch: the following year he played with equal success at Vienna.

Meanwhile Leopold Auer had established a summer studio at London to accommodate some clamoring pupils; among them, Kathleen Parlow and Mischa Elman; and then, he had held summer classes, first at Oeynhausen in Germany, where Isolde Menges was among his students; and finally, at Loschwitz, near Dresden, where Thelma Given, Alexander Bloch, Jaroslav Siskovsky and many others studied with him during the summer months, several of them following him to St. Petersburg for the winter classes. The high point of these Loschwitz summers came in the annual *musicale* which Auer gave for the benefit of his pupil's relatives and friends. On one such occasion the chief attraction was the wonderful playing of Bach's concerto in D minor for two violins by two young boys in blue sailor suits. Their names were Jascha Heifetz and Toscha Seidel.

The outbreak of the First World War, in the summer of 1914, provided some anxious days for the little violin colony at Loschwitz, but eventually Auer and the greater number of his summer pupils arrived safely at St. Petersburg, where, despite the war, his students strove desperately to become artists. In addition to Jascha Heifetz, Toscha Seidel, and others of his regular pupils, several American violinists studied with Auer at this time, as well as the Norwegian, Maia Bang. In referring to this period, the great violin teacher expressed a thought which was perhaps the most characteristic feature of his teaching—that of encouraging each pupil's individuality. "Often I would ask myself," he wrote in his *My Long Life in Music*, "how I might best help each one of them to preserve his own artistic individuality, and at the same time prevent his losing sight of the end in view, the ideals of truly great art."

At the suggestion of Maia Bang, Leopold Auer spent the summers from 1915 through 1917 in Norway, in the vicinity of Christiania, and learned to love the mountain scenery so dear to the heart of the Norwegian violinist, Ole Bull. At this mountain retreat, the *Voxenkollen*, situated high above the sea, lived several of his pupils, as well as his accompanist, Madame Wanda Stein, who was later to become Madame Auer. Others, including Toscha Seidel, lived in the city of Christiania, where Auer would go twice a week to give lessons.

It was during his first Norwegian summer that he had an occasion to present young Seidel to the public. Having been invited by the management of the *Voxenkollen* to give a *musicale* for the benefit of the hotel's guests, Auer decided to take advantage of this opportunity to introduce his talented young pupil as a solo artist. Genuinely successful, this recital served to win an offer from one of the leading concert managers for Toscha to give several concerts that fall.

Meanwhile Jascha Heifetz had continued his general education, along with his studies at the Conservatory. Although he made a sensational appearance that winter at both Moscow and St. Petersburg, and received many tempting offers to set out at once on concert tours, he was prevented from pursuing such a course by the good judgment of his parents. The following summer, the Heifetz and Seidel families both accompanied Leopold Auer to Norway: and in the fall, Jascha and Toscha each gave concerts at Christiania with likesuccess. The King and Queen of Norway having thoroughly enjoyed the concerts of both boys, conceived the idea of inviting them to give a joint recital at the Royal Palace. Such an invitation was eagerly accepted. First they played the Bach concerto for two violins, previously performed at Loschwitz, and then they generously agreed to please the Queen by playing separate solos.

The fall of 1917 was destined to pull their little artistic world asunder. First of all, Jascha Heifetz and his family set out for America by way of Siberia and Japan: then Auer settled down near Stockholm, from where he awaited anxiously news from Russia regarding the Revolution. Meanwhile he gave several recitals in nearby cities and accepted a few pupils; and then, encouraged by their separate concerts, he and Toscha Seidel decided to give some together. Appearing both at Stockholm and Christiania, they were enthusiastically received; and these Norwegian concerts served to soften for Leopold Auer the devastating knowledge that, owing to the Russian Revolution, he could not return to his adopted country, where he had lived for nearly half a century.

Thus the celebrated violinist found himself at the beginning of 1918, a man without a country, property, funds, mementoes of a lifetime, and a position—previously considered permanent. Fortunately on his last precarious trip to Norway from Russia he had taken his Stradivarius violin. This and rich memories must remain solace for a life now gone!

On February 7, 1918, Leopold Auer, at the age of seventy-three, set out from Christiania for America. Accompanied by several of his pupils, including Toscha Seidel, he was met on the opposite side of the ocean by many others, including Eddy Brown, Mischa Elman, Efrem Zimbalist, Max Rosen, Jascha Heifetz, Alexander Bloch, and David Hochstein who was destined soon to be killed in the War.

Making his American début in New York, Auer appeared in various other American cities, and gave some special courses at the Chicago Musical College, then settled down in New York, where he soon attracted new, as well as old, pupils. And though at times the noise and bustle of New York evoked memories of a quieter past, the celebrated violinist for the most part found the life exhilarating. Had he been less energetic he might have rested on the laurels of his many distinguished pupils; but instead, eventually associated with *The Institute of Musical Art*, he soon attracted a whole new flock of students and musical friends. Among his New York pupils was Edwin Ideler who was to distinguish himself as violinist, ensemble-player and teacher. The Auer household became a meeting place for musicians from all over the world; many private *musicales* and informal musical gatherings were held there; former pupils—now artists—considered it their second home; while the Auers, in turn, often spent their summers with the Josef Hofmann family and always attended an annual Christmas dinner at the home of Jascha Heifetz.

Then in the spring of 1925 came a wonderful celebration at Carnegie Hall in New York City, celebrating Leopold Auer's eightieth birthday. Heifetz, Hofmann, Ossip Gabrielowich, Zimbalist, Rachmaninoff, and many others contributed their talents to the occasion; but above all, it was the great violinist-teacher's triumph.

He lived five years longer, dying on July 17, 1930, at Loschwitz, near Dresden, where he had previously held summer classes. Never did an artist leave a more living monument to his own memory. Listen to the violin playing of Jascha Heifetz, or Nathan Milstein, for instance, and the Master's dictum—"Art begins where technique ends"—gloriously reveals itself. Listen carefully to the playing of his various pupils, and the great teacher's philosophy of bringing out each student's individuality asserts itself; for there is no such thing as a recognizable *Auer pupil*. "Bring out what nature has given!" he would say over and over to himself, as a reminder that a teacher did not *make* artists, but provided a challenge for artistic development.

Since Toscha Seidel's playing, as well as that of Heifetz and others, is incorporated in several motion pictures and that of such artists as Heifetz, Milstein, Zimbalist, Elman and Eddy Brown has been captured on records, Leopold Auer's living monument of artists is privileged to project itself, through modern science, into a distant future.

EUGÈNE YSAŸE

Eugène Ysaÿe—outstanding exponent of the Belgian school of violin playing—was born on July 16, 1858 at Liège, Belgium. Though described as "bumptious" by George Bernard Shaw, when that august author was writing musical criticism under the name of Corno Di Bassetto, the Belgian violinist, nevertheless, possessed an inspired bumptiousness which moved the hearts of his greatest critics.

Beginning to study the violin at five under his father, he progressed rapidly and was soon sufficiently well equipped to enter the Liège Conservatory. There he studied violin under Rodolphe Massart and harmony under Michel Dupuis: eventually, sharing a second prize with a fellow student, Ovid Musin, for playing Viotti's Twenty-Second Concerto.

Meanwhile he had made his first public appearance at a small concert given at Montègnée, not far from Liège, but unlike many of his distinguished predecessors in violin playing, young Ysaÿe did not reveal the exceptional talents of a prodigy. Latent possibilities were apparent, however, and fortunately they were soon to be developed; for it was his good fortune to study, first, with Henri Wieniawski, later, with Henri Vieuxtemps. After studying with the former at Brussels, Ysaÿe so impressed Vieuxtemps with the playing of one of this master's concertos at Antwerp that Vieuxtemps arranged for a subsidy from the Belgian government to enable Ysaÿe to study with Joseph Lambert Massart at the Paris Conservatory.

During his stay in Paris the young Belgian violinist also studied with Vieuxtemps, who, though paralytically handicapped, provided for Ysaÿe his greatest challenge. Something there was in the nature of the older man that awakened the broad, impulsive expression that was to characterize Ysaÿe's mature playing. With Wieniawski, he would gladly agree, "Vieuxtemps is the master of us all."

In later years Vieuxtemps revealed in many ways that he was equally moved by his former pupil's playing. One such evidence occurred, when, recovering from a serious illness at Algiers, Vieuxtemps begged those attending him: "Get Ysaÿe. Listening to his singing tone would make me well!"

This "singing tone," incidentally, was a quality that Vieuxtemps had at once recognized and encouraged; a point particularly pertinent to a story involving Ysaÿe, which the celebrated musician, Sam Franko, has told in his Autobiography—*Chords and Discords*. While Franko was a member of an orchestra conducted by Jules-Etienne Pasdeloup, he was present at a Monday-morning-trial rehearsal at which Ysaÿe, "nineteen years of age, tall and slim, accompanied by his master, Vieuxtemps," played Mendelssohn's concerto. According to Franko, Ysaÿe played it beautifully, on an Amati violin belonging to Vieuxtemps, who, obviously, was delighted with his pupil's performance. The concert finished, Pasedeloup said to the proud master, "No, I cannot let him play it, he has no tone." Anger prevailed over disappointment in this unjustified decision!

On another occasion Vieuxtemps' anger was directed against Ysaÿe himself. Possessed of a keen sense of the ridiculous, and addicted to all sorts of horseplay, Ysaÿe, while taking part in the playing of a new work, obviously worthless, during a rehearsal at Vieuxtemps' home, mischievously poked fun at it in his playing. According to the account of Franko, who also took part in the rehearsal, Vieuxtemps infuriated, chased the offending violinist about the room with a threatening chair and was only prevented from effectively wielding it by the barricade on Ysaÿe's part of Vieuxtemps' own violin! Thwarted in his pursuit, the master finally dashed from the room. A few minutes later he reappeared, and the music was resumed as though never interrupted.

In 1879 Ysaÿe played in concerts given by Pauline Lucca at Cologne and Aix-la-Chappelle. At the same time he made the acquaintance of Ferdinand Hiller, who introduced him to Joseph Joachim. Much impressed with Ysaÿe's playing, Hiller persuaded the great violin master to listen to the Belgian's interpretation of Vieuxtemps' Fourth Concerto. Following Ysaÿe's performance, accompanied by Hiller, Joachim, shaking his head, exclaimed, "I never heard the violin played like that before."

Whereas this remark may have indicated either blame or praise, it is representative of the general reaction to Ysaye's playing. Original in both technique and treatment of the music, he never failed to hold the attention of his listeners; for, from the beginning of his career, he practiced the axiom that first of all the violin must move and charm.

Hiller further contributed to the young artist's developing-career by securing him an engagement to play Mendelssohn's concerto at one of the Gürzenich Festival concerts at Cologne. Following this appearance, still at the advice of Ferdinand Hiller who was held in the highest repute throughout the Rhenish provinces, Ysaÿe went to Frankfurt, where he made the acquaintance of Joseph Joachim Raff, the great friend and colleague of Franz Liszt. While there he also played in concert with Clara Schumann.

Owing to the reputation gained from these appearances, Ysaÿe in 1880 was appointed leader of Benjamin Bilse's popular orchestra in Berlin. Holding this engagement for a year, he gained at the same time his first experience as a conductor. The following year he toured through Norway under the management of Ole Bull's son.

In 1883 he played at the Paris Conservatory under Edouard Colonne and for the next three years, for the most part, he made his home in Paris. There he found a congenial atmosphere in which his exuberant nature developed to the utmost.

Three years later Ysaÿe accepted the post of violin professor at the Brussels Conservatory, a position he held for twelve years. The year of 1886 also marked the event of his marriage; and to his great delight he received from César Franck, as a wedding present, the Belgian composer's violin sonata, written for and dedicated to him.

Though, while carrying on his duties at the Conservatory, Ysaÿe continued to appear in concerts, it was not until his London début that his great fame was established. Playing Beethoven's concerto at a Philharmonic concert, he thoroughly astonished his English listeners, accustomed to Joachim's beautifully restrained rendering of this great work. Once recovered from the shock of this radically different interpretation, the audience responded with wild enthusiasm. The dexterity of his playing was awe-inspiring, and yet he gave the impression of having left the problem of technique far behind in his concentrated effort to charm his listeners with the music.

Appearing later in the season at a Popular Concert, he once again met with tremendous success; and when, on November 16, 1894, he made his New York début with the Philharmonic Society, he created a sensation. Equally successful on his subsequent trips to America, he was, in 1898, offered the conductorship—to succeed Anton Seidel—of the New York Philharmonic, but he chose to decline the invitation.

Back in Europe, the following year he finally succeeded in winning the approval of the Berlin critics, when, appearing in a Philharmonic Concert under Artur Nikisch, he won the hearts of the Berliners through a spectacular performance of Bach's concerto in E. Though his free reading of the concerto was strikingly different from the one to which they were accustomed there was a beauty and aliveness about it that pleased them. "Eccentric and moving," was the verdict.

Meanwhile at Brussels, he had founded the Ysaÿe Orchestral Concerts, of which he was conductor, artist, and manager. Genuinely successful, they were later followed by chamber music concerts. It was during this period—on December 29, 1893 at Paris—that Ysaÿe played in the first performance of Claude Debussy's quartet. Dedicated to the Belgian violinist, it did not immediately meet with approval from audience and critics. Some considered it too orchestral; others, objected to its excessive use of modulation; but Ysaÿe, always open to new ideas, was enchanted with it. Imagine his delight when Debussy expressed his intention of writing a "Nocturne" for him!

The "Nocturne" intended for Ysaÿe, turned out to be one of the *Trois Nocturnes* for orchestra. After Debussy had begun to compose the music his instincts dictated this switch of intention, and there was nothing for the composer to do but act accordingly. Though at first Ysaÿe may have been disappointed at this turn of events, he readily admitted, upon hearing the *Nocturnes* played, that the pictures evoked through the use of diversified instruments could not have been duplicated by means of a solo instrument.

Meanwhile it was Ysaÿe's privilege to act as host to Debussy at Brussels during the time that the impressionist composer was occupied with the writing of his exquisitely beautiful opera—*Pelleás et Mélisande*. They played parts of it over together; and Ysaÿe, fascinated by the music, later sought in vain Debussy's permission to play excerpts from the opera at Brussels before it was given a production.

In 1900, having previously appeared as both soloist and quartet player in London, Ysaÿe joined the celebrated pianist, Ferrucio Busoni, and the violoncellist, Hugo Becker, in the playing of trios in Queen's Hall. Ysaÿe and Busoni had met the previous year in London, when they had both appeared on the same program with Nellie Melba. In referring to this meeting in a letter to his wife, Busoni described Ysaÿe as "a *great* artist and an amusing person." In another letter the pianist mentioned Ysaÿe's "remarkable magnetism" and commented upon the extremes of his nature. Then, after they had appeared together, Busoni visited the Belgian violinist at Brussels and once again expressed himself glowingly of Ysaÿe's "beautiful home, beautiful wife, and beautiful children." During the following year Ysaÿe, Busoni, and Becker again played together in London; and Busoni could refer to their "beautiful" and "clean" playing, as well as his increasing friendliness for Ysaÿe, whose apparent pose he was later to describe as "natural."

During this same year Ysaÿe also took his own group of quartet players to London, at which time he introduced many modern chamber works. Though he was too much the virtuoso to be considered an ideal first violinist in a quartet, he always managed to make the music sound interesting: and he probably had more music dedicated to him than any other violinist who ever lived. Ernest Chausson inscribed to him his symphony; Vincent d'Indy, the *Istar* variations and other works: as we know, César Franck dedicated to Ysaÿe his violin sonata, and Debussy, his quartet; while Theodore Dubois and his pupil Guy Ropartz, Louis Vierne, Guillaume Lekeu, and Sylvio Lazarri all inscribed music to the "bumptious" Belgian violinist.

During the season of 1904-1905 Ysaÿe was once again in America. On December 9, 1904, he appeared with the Boston Symphony Orchestra in New York, playing Bach's concerto in E major, and Bruch's Second concerto in D minor. The music critic, Richard Aldrich, in reviewing the concert, wrote, "Mr. Ysaÿe returns in the plenitude of his powers, which are those of a supremely great master, an interpreter in the highest sense, who glorifies and enobles all he touches with the communicating flame of his ardent musical temperament." Then the critic went on to say that none could pluck the heart out of the mystery of great music like Ysaÿe, and that all thought of technique vanished when he played. The critic also mentioned in this review another characteristic, pertinent to the impression Ysaÿe made in his playing, "The personality of the executant is sunk and merged into immediate communion with the music for its own sake alone." Other observers in watching him on the platform have recorded this characteristic absorption in the music. It has been stated that one could almost see him listen with all his might as he began to play, and then experience with him the sensation of communion with the music, once the contact had been made.

Eight years later when Ysaÿe played in a recital at Carnegie Hall in New York Richard Aldrich could report that he was still the great, master artist. He particularly praised the violinist's interpretation of Mozart's concerto in G major, writing that few could tug at the heart of the concerto's adagio like Ysaÿe, playing, as he said, "with supreme repose and eloquence."

Meanwhile, though he had relinquished his post at the Brussels Conservatory, Ysaÿe had maintained his headquarters in the Belgian city. When the First World War broke out in 1914 he was forced to seek refuge elsewhere. Spending a great part of the War Years in America, he accepted in 1918 the post of conductor of the Cincinnati Orchestra. Having appeared with the orchestra as a guest conductor on two previous occasions the previous spring, as well as during the annual Cincinnati Festival, he came to his new assignment with warm enthusiasm. After holding the position with distinction for four years, Ysaÿe resigned in 1922 and returned to Brussels.

Picking up the thread of his life, broken by the intrusion of war, Ysaÿe resumed his orchestral concerts; later, replaced them with chamber music concerts; continued to give concerts as a virtuoso; and composed a fair amount of music, including an opera—*Pierre Li Howyen*—which was successfully produced in 1930 at Liège.

Though Ysaÿe never regarded himself as a violin teacher, he did, nevertheless, pass on to a number of violinists the benefit of some of his conclusions and experience. Both at Cincinnati and at Godinne on the Meuse River, where he spent his summers when in Europe before the War, he held classes for artist-violinists. These were for the most part devoted to the interpretation of the traditional violin literature of Vieuxtemps, Wieniawski, and other violin masters dear to the Belgian's heart.

Among these artist-pupils was the distinguished musician, David Mannes, who, having heard Ysaÿe play in New York, determined to study with this violinist—in actuality the personification of his own ideals. Carrying out his resolve, Mannes studied with Ysaÿe both at Brussels and at Godinne, gaining an experience that remained permanently inspirational. Transcending technique in his teaching, as well as in his own playing, like the one he wanted most to emulate—Anton Rubinstein, Ysaÿe imbued David Mannes, and the others who worked with him, with his deeply seated conviction that the violin should move its listeners by its warm and vibrant tone. Asked upon one occasion what fingering he had employed to achieve a certain effect in a piece of music, Ysaÿe replied that he really did not remember. This truthful answer was indicative of his unconscious control over technique. Knowing what he wanted the music to express, dictated by the composer's intentions, he had accomplished that end with tools long accustomed to obey their master.

In the matter of interpretation it is interesting to read an account by Neville d'Esterre, an English journalist, regarding the famous sonata performances of Ysaÿe and Raoul Pugno: "The highest level of all interpretations was reached by these two artists: Pugno the ideal interpreter of classical music on the piano; Ysaÿe, perhaps the greatest soloist of his time on any instrument. They played together as one soul. It was impossible for the listener to realize the two individual minds and temperaments at work. A mystic might have supposed that the spirit of Beethoven himself had taken possession of the two artists and was guiding their fingers."

Perfect control of *vibrato* playing and unique use of the bow provided, perhaps, Ysaÿe's most characteristic "tools." Whereas other violinists might sweep and slide with too much sentimentality in employing the pulsating *vibrato*, Ysaÿe, with this wonderful means of transmitting true feeling, would with quick, intense motions, produce his famous "golden" tone. Whereas many violinists—especially exponents of Joachim's teaching—would concentrate on the wrist, keeping it high and stiff in bowing, Ysaÿe, holding his wrist lower in a relaxed position, appeared to place all his bowing attention on the point at which his fingers touched the bow.

Eugène Ysaÿe died on May 12, 1931, at Brussels. He is remembered as one of the world's greatest violinists. Others may have displayed more dazzling feats of technique; some may have been purer artists, but in heart-moving tone, warmth of expression, and unique magnetism, no other violinist has surpassed him.

FRITZ KREISLER

F<small>RITZ</small> K<small>REISLER</small>—the most popular of twentieth-century violinists—was born on February 2, 1875, at Vienna. Although destiny, in the form of two World Wars, was to necessitate his establishing a home in various cities, Vienna remained forever the city associated with his name.

Displaying a talent for music at an early age, he was given violin lessons by his father, an eminent physician and good amateur musician. At seven he appeared in a concert for children given by Carlotta Patti; and in the same year he was admitted to the Vienna Conservatory. While this occurrence indicates that the boy showed unusual music promise—since at that time the Conservatory did not accept pupils under fourteen years of age—contrary to general belief, he was not a violin prodigy. Gifted with the mind and spirit of an artist, he might have become famous in one of many fields: it just so happened that his father started him on a violinist's career.

Enrolled in the class of the celebrated Joseph Hellmesberger, the young student progressed rapidly; though not without continuous urging from his father. Despite his obvious talent, Fritz still found greater enjoyment in playing games with his friends in the wonderful Viennese parks than he did in practicing scales.

Notwithstanding it was while he was studying at the Conservatory that the direction of his musical taste was established. Vienna was indeed the Mecca for great musicians of the day; some of them living there; others, coming to the city of congenial musical atmosphere to give concerts. Imagine living in a city, where, any day of your life, you might meet on the street Johannes Brahms, Hugo Wolf, Gustav Mahler, or Anton Bruckner! Not only was the young Viennese youth privileged to meet them on the street, but it was his great good fortune to associate freely with them through the eminence of his father's position.

Among the visiting artists there were Joseph Joachim, Pablo de Sarasate, and Anton Rubinstein. The playing of Joachim and Rubinstein, particularly, opened a new world to the future violinist. Though opposed to each other in many ways—Joachim, being the great interpreter, Rubinstein, the exponent of moving his listeners before anything else—they represented to young Kreisler the epitome of artistic expression. Both artists, transcending feats of technique, revealed *personality;* and this quality was to be the touchstone of Kreisler's own glorious career.

At ten he won the Gold Medal for violin playing, and soon thereafter he went to Paris where he entered the Conservatory. There he studied violin under Joseph Lambert Massart and theory under Léo Delibes. Two years later he received the Gold Medal—*Premier Grand Prix de Rome*—in competition with forty contestants, all of whom were at least eight years his senior.

During the following year young Kreisler went to America, where he made his New York début on November 10, 1888, at Steinway Hall. Soon thereafter he began to appear in joint recitals in various parts of the United States with the pianist Moriz Rosenthal, who had also recently made his American début. Although the critics were kind to the young Viennese violinist on the occasion of his first visit to America it cannot be said with truthfulness that he made a sensational impression. Consequently, when not chosen for a post in the Vienna Philharmonic upon his return to Vienna, he decided to turn his thoughts from the violin to medicine.

Accordingly, young Kreisler entered the Vienna Gymnasium where he devoted himself to the study of medicine. But the urge for artistic expression must have been seething within him; for suddenly, without apparent reason, he gave up his medical course and turned his attention to the study of painting. Studying first at Paris, and later at Rome, he progressed with not little promise; then, just as suddenly as he had deserted medicine for art, he turned his back on painting to assume the career of a soldier.

Taking a stiff army examination, he soon found himself an officer in the regiment of Uhlans. But once again he had not hit upon his intended career. At the end of a year, military life apparently having lost its fascination,

Kreisler rather reluctantly took up his violin. He was not at all convinced that he wanted to devote his life to violin playing; but he had to do something, and the violin was at hand. This shifting back and forth up various blind alleys, though curious, may have contributed to his eventual development as a human being; for though in later years the word "violin" was to be synonymous with "Kreisler" it by no means expressed the full facet of his personality.

After making a few tentative public appearances, without spectacular success, Kreisler retired to the country and devoted eight weeks to the concentrated study of his chosen instrument. Emerging triumphant, he made his return début on March, 1899, at Berlin, in a program, which included a Bruch concerto, a Vieuxtemps concerto, and the *Non più mesta* variations of Paganini.

At this time there was no question, in the minds of the discerning, that Fritz Kreisler was a great violinist, but it remained for America first to recognize fully his greatness. Returning to the United States in the year 1900, he everywhere met with tremendous enthusiasm, regardless of whether he appeared alone or in the company of other artists. Among the artists who shared the platform with him on some of these occasions was the young pianist, Josef Hofmann.

On May 12, 1901, he made his London début at one of Hans Richter's famous concerts; in the spring of 1904 he was presented with the Gold Medal of the London Philharmonic Society; and he continued to play in England at frequent intervals, until such appearances were interrupted by the advent of the First World War.

Meanwhile America steadily became the scene of his greatest triumphs; and in the year 1902, while enroute to America an event occurred, which undoubtedly set the course of his career for all time. Never again would he waver between this or that decision, for, henceforth, there was to be a staunch friend and advisor at his side to point the way. This all-knowing friend—his future wife, then Harriet Lies—he met on this auspicious crossing when she was returning home to America. They were married in November of the same year; and in later years, Kreisler was the last to deny his wife's often-repeated statement laughingly made in the company of friends: "I made Fritz. Without me he would have been only one among dozens of other violinists; with me, he became *Kreisler!*"

Be that as it may, Fritz Kreisler, soon after his marriage, entered into the kingdom of immortal violinists. The music of Bach, Beethoven, and Brahms came glowingly alive under his fingers and bow, while his playing of small pieces of lesser worth warmed the hearts of his ardent listeners. Above all, he had achieved the Ysaÿe ideal: he could charm and move!

Following several successful tours in the United States between 1901 and 1903, Kreisler returned to Europe, where he added further glory to his name. Consequently, upon his return to America, he was greeted with even greater enthusiasm. Despite the fury of a mid-winter storm, an immense audience awaited his first appearance of the season, on January 4, 1905, at Carnegie Hall; and according to the critics of the day they were in no way disappointed in what they had come to hear.

"He has grown in every way—in technical power, in depth of feeling and poetic insight, in repose, in largeness of view, in breadth of sympathy that puts him upon the level of the highest mastery," wrote Richard Aldrich. Then after commenting on the ambitious choice of his program, which included the Beethoven and Brahms concertos and Tartini's *The Devil's Trill*, this critic used expressions of evaluation that were to be as characteristic of Kreisler's playing in 1945 as they evidently were in 1905. He mentioned "the remarkable fluency and accuracy" of Kreisler's left hand, his "free and firm" bowing, and wrote: "He plays with a delightful positiveness and virility.... He possesses the indefinable quality of style, and there was stamped upon his playing always the mark of unquestionable authority."

Henceforth, until the First War prevented him from doing so, Kreisler traveled back and forth across the ocean, meeting with warm welcome on both sides of the Atlantic. Appearing several times during the season of 1907-1908 in New York, he once again won high praise for the nobility of his playing. "His playing of Bach is supremely noble and imposing, full of vitality and poetic spirit," wrote Mr. Aldrich: and continued to say that in his interpretation of Corelli's variations, *La Follia,* Kreisler "added a sort of rich and sober bravura to his breadth of style and beauty of tone." Various other critics added their words of praise for the Viennese violinist's breadth of conception and warmth of tone; while one and all agreed that he communicated with his audience with wand-like magic.

Then in the summer of 1914 came the event that tore nations asunder and disrupted the lives of individuals all over the world. Fritz Kreisler and his wife were enjoying a vacation at Ragaz, in Switzerland, when war broke out in Europe. Although Kreisler had previously resigned his officer's commission, he realized that this sad turn of events provided for him but one course of action: he must rejoin his regiment. Accordingly, upon learning that the Third Army Corps to which his regiment was attached was being mobilized, he and Mrs. Kreisler set out at once for Austria.

Traveling by way of Munich, they stopped in Vienna to bid Kreisler's father good-bye; then the violinist was off for Graz, the headquarters of his regiment. Arrived there, he was given command of a platoon of fifty or sixty men, stationed at Leoben, a short distance from Graz; and, during the time spent there in organizing and drilling, Kreisler was joined by his wife who insisted upon volunteering for the Red Cross. At the end of a week Kreisler's platoon was on the march; but whereas he and his men thought they were to be stationed for some time behind the lines, where they might engage in further training, they found themselves within the twinkling of an eye in the midst of battle.

In simple and dignified style, Kreisler has set down a record of these war experiences in a little book called *Four Weeks in the Trenches*. Despite the unaccustomed hardships, surrounding the life of a soldier, Kreisler had moments of enjoying the beauty of the night, the feeling of comradeship, and the sense of serving his country. But all such thoughts were thrust to the background when not far from Lemburg, his platoon came face to face with the enemy. The *enemy* in this situation chanced to be Russian; but the curious and awful fact in all wars is that the *enemy* is determined by which side a soldier happens to be fighting on: To the Austrians the Russians were enemies; to the Russians the Austrians were enemies. Fritz Kreisler, the artist, doubtless realized this paradox, for in his recollections he recalls several incidents of warm fraternization with the Russian soldiers during moments of unofficial truce.

Still another of Kreisler's revelations bears witness to the fact that the artist was not entirely buried in the soldier: Once he had recovered from the first tension, caused by the buzzing of shrapnel overhead, he began to make observations of the variations in sound of the bursting shells. Through his trained ear, by comparing the nature of the sound coming from his own regiment's known-varying positions with those coming from the unknown positions of the Russians, he worked out a system which proved useful in determining the location of the opposing batteries.

Meanwhile the violinist's time was by no means devoted exclusively to such pursuits. The horrors of war were everywhere about him, comrades were falling, and his own platoon suffered the additional discomfort of persistent retreat.

Finally the hoof of a Cossack's horse and the rider's lance served to end Kreisler's days as a soldier. Injured in his shoulder and thigh, in the confusion of battle, he was left unconscious in a trench evacuated by the oppressed Austrians. Fortunately Kreisler's absence was soon discovered by his orderly, who, under extremely dangerous circumstances, succeeded in returning to the deserted trench. Consequently, it was the stricken man's good fortune to find his faithful orderly beside him when he became conscious. With no little struggle, the man helped Kreisler out of the trench, after giving him first aid. Then the two of them cautiously wove their way through the night; twice being intercepted by Cossacks, from whom they managed to hide. After several hours' struggle they reached the Austrian lines, where Kreisler—once again having lost consciousness—was revived. First taken to a field hospital, he was soon moved on up the lines, until, to his great joy, he found himself in the station at Vienna. And among the nurses who met the train was the one who meant most to him!

Following treatment in Vienna, Kreisler was transferred to nearby Baden. In November, after an examination before a board of doctors, he was pronounced physically unfit for army duty. Thus, honorably discharged, Fritz Kreisler put his military life behind him.

Soon thereafter he traveled to America, where he resumed his concert giving. On December 13, 1914, in the afternoon, he limped onto the stage of Carnegie Hall amidst the thunderous applause of an audience, which filled every nook and corner of the auditorium and even spilled over onto the platform. The expression on every face was as plain as day, "We're so glad to have you back!" While audience and artist by instinct silently agreed to discount the slight evidence of his wound, Handel's A major sonata, Tartini's *The Devil's Trill*, the famous *Chaconne* of Bach, his own *Caprice viennoise*, a caprice of Paganini, and several smaller pieces made up this memorable program. Never had he played better: warmth of tone, grace and nobility of expression abounded, and to crown the occasion, at the audience's insistence, he generously repeated the *Caprice viennoise*.

Continuing to give concerts, some of them for war relief, Kreisler for the next ten years made New York his home, with the exception of a period spent in retirement. Upon America's entering the War, it became embarrassing for him to appear in public in view of the fact that he had so recently served in the Austrian Army—now become the *enemy* to the country in which he was making his home. With the good taste, so characteristic of his nature, he retired from concert-giving and went to Maine, where he devoted himself to gardening, chess, and the violin.

This routine was only slightly broken by his association with the Letz Quartet, successor to the famous Kneisel Quartet. When Franz Kneisel—the Quartet's organizer and leader for over thirty years—retired, Kreisler was persuaded to join Hans Letz, Louis Svencenski, and Willem Willeke in carrying on the great tradition. At their first appearance in Aeolian Hall, in New York City, it was apparent that though the new Quartet was not the same as the old one it was equally distinguished. An audience, which filled the hall to its capacity, responded with tremendous enthusiasm. This was indeed an important occasion, for, heretofore Kreisler had not appeared as an ensemble player: great though he might be as a solo player, this did not guarantee excellence when playing with a group. With characteristic good taste, Kreisler gallantly met the challenge. Despite the fact that his personality dominated the performance, he had obviously taken seriously this new role of playing with others, and he by no means exploited his own part in the proceedings.

His share in this concert, as well as others given by the Quartet, went to a charitable fund for the benefit of needy musicians.

Then, after an official retirement of two seasons, on the afternoon of October 27, 1919, Fritz Kreisler once again returned to the platform of

Carnegie Hall in New York City. The tremendous welcome accorded him gave dramatic evidence of the public's love for an artist returned to the fold. Many persons were turned away for lack of room to accommodate them; and midway during the concert, elaborate wreaths were deposited at the violinist's feet.

Concertos by Tartini, Vivaldi, and Viotti made up the greater part of this program, which he played with an aliveness that made the music sound fresh and spontaneous. Transcriptions of parts of Gluck's *Orfeo*, Schubert's *Rosamunde* ballet music, of the "Hymn to the Sun" from Rimsky-Korsakov's *Coq d'Or*, and two of his own dance pieces concluded this rich musical fare; that is, so far as the program was concerned. Needless to say, this did not end his playing: encore after encore was demanded and played; until at last, the lights having been put out, there was nothing for the audience to do but go home!

Kreisler made his first appearance in London after the War on May 4, 1921, at Queen's Hall, and three years later he established his home in Europe. An ardent collector, he eventually made of a villa in Berlin a museum-like home, famous for its fine paintings, porcelains, rare manuscripts, and beautiful tapestries. With genuine reluctance he relinquished this home when another war loomed on the horizon.

Meanwhile he traveled to all parts of the world, including the Orient, where, in Tokyo alone he gave twenty recitals to wildly enthusiastic audiences. Little did he know that the Japanese people, who stopped him in the street to autograph their *Kreisler* records, would within a few years be another *enemy*. What a pity that artists have so little voice in the affairs of men!

Once while in another part of the world Kreisler discovered that his violin was better known than he himself; a situation that provided a tale which he often amusingly retold. Browsing among some old violins in an antique shop in Antwerp one day, he selected a nondescript fiddle, and, approaching the picturesque old man who owned the shop, he asked the price. Then, impulsively removing his own violin from its case, he asked the dealer if he would like to buy it. Whereupon the man, after precise examination of the instrument, said, "I am not rich enough to buy it." Then he added: "Just wait here a few minutes. I'll fetch a violin which will interest you."

In place of a violin the keen shopkeeper returned with a policeman, declaring: "Arrest this man! He is trying to sell Fritz Kreisler's violin."

Without avail did Kreisler protest that he was *Kreisler;* and as bad luck would have it, he had no means of identification with him. Finally, struck with a happy thought, he tucked the precious violin beneath his chin and began to play his *Schön Rosmarin.*

"It *is* Kreisler!" exclaimed the astonished pawnbroker.

In keeping with this story is Kreisler's own statement that he never had to worry about losing either of his two famous violins, for they were both so well known: The Guarnerius, with which his name is usually associated, was previously owned by August Wilhelmj; the Stradivarius, with its wonderful golden varnish, he purchased from the famous London dealers, Hill & Sons.

When Hitler came into power and Austria was taken over by Germany, Kreisler received honorary citizenship from the Government of France, previously having been made Commander of the French Legion of Honor. Soon thereafter he returned to New York, his "other" home, where he was received with all the old warmth of welcome.

In 1935 music lovers all over the world opened their morning papers to find screaming headlines, berating their favorite violinist: KREISLER ADMITS FRAUD ON MUSICAL WORLD. When all the smoke had blown away, and critics once again came to their senses, the concensus of opinion was that Kreisler, in pretending that some of his original compositions were transcriptions of early violin music, had created no deliberate crime. The so-called *hoax* came to light when Olin Downes, music critic of the *New York Times*, in attempting to trace the source of Pugnani's *Praeludium and Allegra*, wrote to Kreisler for the information. Kreisler, doubtless relieved at an opportunity to rid himself of a thirty-year-old secret, gladly confessed that not only was it his original piece but that most of his other "transcriptions" were also original.

Kreisler later told friends that the "innocent" fraud had originated in his youth, when he had begun to compose short pieces to fill out his programs. Modest and unknown at that time, he had hit upon the idea of publishing them as "transcriptions." Over the course of years these pieces—supposedly by Couperin, Vivaldi, Pugnani, Dittersdorf, and others—had become part of every violinist's repertoire. Small wonder that violinists, critics, and public were at first shocked at the belated disclosure!

But the much-loved violinist was not to remain long in disrepute. Even his severest critics finally called the matter an "indescretion" rather than a "crime": and when, in the spring of 1941, he was hit by a truck, when crossing Madison Avenue on Fifty-seventh Street, enroute from Carnegie Hall, a kind of hush settled over New York City. For days he lay unconscious, his wife constantly at his side at the hospital. Persons meeting on the street would ask each other, "How is Kreisler?" Bulletins were eagerly awaited in the papers. Suggestion after suggestion was made for restoring his vital self. And legend has it that VIOLIN PLAYING proved the healer.

What a wonderful moment it was for music lovers when the announcement came that Kreisler was well enough to play again. And play, he did, with all the old warmth and magic. Soon he had resumed a life, vibrant with interest, and, future-looking.

Those who had an opportunity to observe him when he was concentrating on the selection of music or intently studying a score saw a great artist at work.

A great artist, a great personality, aglow with gracious charm and vitality—*Kreisler!*

ALBERT SPALDING

Albert Spalding—outstanding American violinist—was born on August 15, 1888, at Chicago, Illinois. Growing up at a time when it was rare that an American-born musician reached eminence in his native land, and further handicapped by a family name associated with sporting goods rather than music, Albert Spalding, with no air of defying the situation, but, with modest persistence, mounted the heights of Violindom.

He and his brother Boardman—named after their mother whose name was Marie Boardman—spent their earliest years in the very heart of New York City: in a towering apartment house of nine stories called the Navarro Apartments. From its upper floors the little boys could catch glimpses of the trees, rocks, and lakes in nearby Central Park; and from one of the windows in the Spaldings' apartment Aunt Sally Guest could watch the traffic in Seventh Avenue to her heart's content.

Soon after their marriage, Walter Spalding—an able young business man, associated with his brother in Chicago—had taken his young wife to New York where he opened a new branch of their sporting goods firm. The lovely young bride was delighted with this turn of events; for, artistic, and musically trained, she found the eastern city enchanting.

Also, impulsive and generous, she soon established a home famous for its charm and hospitality. As Albert Spalding was later to record in his autobiography, *Rise To Follow*, he could not remember a time that the family of four sat down to the table by themselves: Aunt Sally Guest—the permanent "guest"—Grandma Spalding, the other grandmother—known as "Martie," Uncle Charlie, Cousins Harry Walter, and Elsie, together with numerous non-relatives, were likely as not to share the ever-expanding table. Once, to the amazement of Albert and his brother, an honest-to-goodness Indian swami came to dinner. He was the celebrated Vivekananda; and even Aunt Sally—though dubious of the wonders linked with his name—sat fascinated before this Oriental gentleman.

Yes, it was a rich life surrounding the Spalding household; and young Albert drank avidly of it. Honoring and loving both parents for their respective qualities, he was to develop into manhood blessed with a combination of his father's stability and his mother's artistic nature.

One musical evening remained fixed in his memory: Dominating the drawing-room on this occasion, which included the presence of picturesque musicians from various lands, was an old pianist whose name was Villonova. Precise and courtly in manner, the man fascinated Albert. And when, in the playing of some Chopin études and nocturnes, the agility of his fingers appeared tuned to the twitching of his waxed mustache, Villonova held the small boy spellbound.

Pleased by such concentrated attention, he asked Albert, "Did you like it?"

"Oh, yes!" stammered the astonished youth.

Then, after asking Albert if he would like to be a musician and receiving a definite "Yes" for an answer, Villonova warned him, "The road is long, but a nice one."

Soon thereafter, Albert's mother, having becomed convinced by a visit to Florence that the Italian city was the only city in which to live, persuaded her husband to move his telescope-like family there for the winters. Despite Aunt Sally's desperate attempts to keep them on Seventh Avenue, she reluctantly packed her belongings and went along. Street venders and Italian serenaders soon provided her new *windows* with compensating interest.

Aunt Sally's being with the family was to prove important to Albert's future. This is the way it came about: Despite the fact that his mother's miraculous manipulation of the black and white keys of the piano fascinated him, coupled with the fact that the piano was the only musical instrument that he had ever heard played in his home, out of a clear blue sky in 1895, at seven, he asked for a violin as a Christmas present.

"Why a violin?" everyone, except Aunt Sally, asked in unison. "The thing to do is to start with the piano," said his mother. "That's right," advised his father, adding, "when we see how you get along..."

"Pooh!" said Aunt Sally. "The child asked for a violin. Not a piano. He shall have it!"

Accordingly, on Christmas morning, Albert awoke to find a half-sized, gleaming fiddle, bow-accompanied, rakishly attached to the Christmas tree. Aunt Sally, not being over-burdened with worldly goods, had not bothered with a violin case. Little did Albert mind. He had a violin!

Clutching the precious instrument with eager hands, he at once attempted to bring forth music from it. Alas, the results were anything but satisfactory. Just to *have* a fiddle, he soon discovered, did not mean that you could produce the wonderful sounds that the street fiddlers did. Fortunately, among the Christmas callers that afternoon, there was a friend who knew the rudiments of violin playing; and he showed Albert how to hold the instrument and draw the bow across the strings.

This proved fortunate for Albert, who, at least could now approximate intervals of sound from his fiddle, but, unfortunate for the members of his family who were forced to listen to his raucous attempts. Doubtless in self-defense, they soon procured a teacher for him. His name was Ulpiano Chiti. A good violinist, though considered an unduly strict teacher, Chiti immediately won the heart of his new pupil, as well as impressing the parents, by exclaiming, "Alberto has a natural position. How does he know how to hold his bow-arm so free and straight?"

Under these favorable circumstances, Albert progressed rapidly and was soon playing little pieces for admiring guests. There was now not the slightest hesitation in his answer when asked what he was going to be when he grew up. "I am going to be a violinist!" he would say. And that was that. Though such a course was completely foreign to Walter Spalding's notions of what a son of his should become, he never once expressed disapproval; while Albert's mother was, of course, delighted.

Stimulated by Albert's progress, Boardman had, meanwhile, begun to study the violoncello; and though this happily provided a trio in the family, nobody—not even their music-loving mother—thought that Boardman would be anything but a lawyer. Thus the future looked then for each of the Spalding boys; and thus, it proved to be.

The custom of returning home and settling at Monmouth Beach, on the coast of New Jersey, for their summers might have seriously interfered with Albert's practice had he been the son of a less determined mother. Realizing that despite her vigilance Albert was losing ground in his studies, she set out to find a teacher in the vicinity. As luck would have it, Jean Buitrago, who, as the fiery young South American, Juan Buitrago, had taught Edward MacDowell years before, lived near the Spalding family at Monmouth Beach. Taking Albert in hand, he soon had the boy back on the developing path, so that when he returned to Chiti in the fall he had advanced despite the summer vacation.

Back in Florence, the Spalding Trio was occasionally asked to play for various benefit concerts; and at one such, in the presence of visiting royalty, young Albert was forced by the circumstance of his E string's breaking to play the hero. Instinctively realizing that "the show must go on," he transposed the passages from the E to the A string, and in so doing plunged himself into waters far too deep for his wading. No matter! The audience, apparently only concerned with what they could *see*, applauded his efforts with wild enthusiasm.

Though Albert knew that he had not accomplished the feat with half the skill he would have liked, he was deeply grateful to the audience, and at the same time, he arrived at an important conclusion: an audience was his friend, not his enemy. The papers printed glowing accounts of the event; at the same time, predicting a great future for the young man. Fortunately, an innate modesty, plus a sure knowledge of just what he had and had not done, saved him from suffering ill effects from all the furore.

Meanwhile the Spalding family, shifting back and forth between apartment and private dwelling in Florence, lived for one enchanted year, when Albert was twelve, in the lovely *Christina Villa*, surrounded by a great park and gardens. This experience served to quicken the young violinist's growing sense of beauty, a characteristic he was increasingly to value.

Another spurt to his development came in hearing various artists—brought to Florence through the persuasion of his mother and a few other music-lovers. Among these visiting artists were the violinists Pablo de Sarasate, César Thompson, and Joseph Joachim, as well as the pianists Feruccio Busoni and Eugène d'Albert. The young violinist, enthralled by these masters, at once set out to copy the bewitching elegance of Sarasate, the dignity of Joachim, the "thunderbolts" of the two pianists—in addition to the artistry of them all!

He soon learned that a great deal of groundwork was necessary before reaching such dizzy heights. Such experiences did, however, provide goals of approach. He would get there!

At fourteen he arrived at a coveted goal-post with such spectacular success that only his native good sense prevented his being spoiled for all time: On the advice of Chiti, he took the graduating examination at the famous old Bologna Conservatory; and, despite the fact during the ordeal he became so nervous that he broke out in red splotches, he was assured by Chiti and his mother—who had listened surreptiously to his playing—that he had played very well. Mendelssohn, Tartini, and Bach were all a-jumble in his mind. He had no idea himself whether or not he had impressed the judges, who, he knew were prejudiced against him because of his age. Only at Chiti's insistence, supported by the fact that they had found one precedent in the school's long history to justify admitting a contestant so young, had they accepted him for examination.

As they anxiously awaited the decision, one bit of encouragement, suddenly remembered, came to Albert's rescue. His accompanist for the occasion—who later proved none other than the celebrated Ottorino Respighi—had patted him on the back, assuring him at the same time that he had played remarkably well.

Now, all they could do was wait!

The door opened. There were the judges. Before Albert had time to think he was engulfed in embraces. Tears flowed freely; everyone talked at once, "Only once before. . . ."

And still Albert did not know whether he had passed the examination.

Unable to stand another minute's suspense, his mother came to the rescue, "Does that mean that he has passed?"

"Does that mean that he has passed!" repeated Sarti, the senior violin master of the school. "It isn't a matter of his passing, but the *way* he passed. It is possible to make fifty points; thirty points are required for passing. Your son achieved forty-eight points!"

Then, before Albert's mother could express her joy, Sarti continued: "And that isn't all. Only once before in the history of the school has a diploma been awarded to a candidate of fourteen. One hundred and thirty-three years ago, a youth from Salzburg captivated the Bologna board of examiners: His name was Wolfgang Amadeus Mozart."

Miraculously, Albert did not faint; but needless to say, he slept the sleep of no ordinary mortal that night; and, when morning brought extravagant news stories concerning his triumph, followed by generous offers from concert managers on both sides of the Atlantic, it took no little family guidance to keep his feet on the ground.

Fortunately good judgment won over impatience. After two years' study with the celebrated Lefort at the National Conservatory in Paris, in addition to work with Antonio Scontrino at Florence in counterpoint and composition, Albert Spalding, at the age of sixteen, made his début in Paris. Looking slightly more mature than his age, to his great satisfaction, he escaped the epithet of "prodigy"; and was, in fact, greeted with marked enthusiasm.

Again his good sense coming to the fore, he sifted the intelligent praise from indiscriminate acclaim; thereby, gaining for the future. Realizing that some parts of his performance were better than others, he particularly valued Lefort's criticism: some of which bespoke praise, some, blame. Praising him for "being himself," Lefort also warned his precocious pupil to beware of "cheap victories." It was obvious from the first that Spalding had "a way" with audiences: a virtue, potentially good and bad, he must guard against its dangers!

Next came some minor concerts; then, appeared an invitation to take part in a great benefit concert under the direction of the famous orchestra leader, Edouard Colonne. Despite the fact that at the last minute he found himself without an accompanist, he scored a bit of an ovation. The great Adelina Patti, having noticed the predicament of missing accompanist, had graciously lent him her own; and after listening to the grateful young violinist from the wings, she generously put her stamp of approval on him.

Then it was that Spalding's father came forth with some sound advice: "Such ovations are all very well. Honors are fine, but they will never earn you a living. I have never objected to your choice of becoming a musician; but I do insist that you take your profession seriously, avoid the label 'dilettante,' and make a living from the career you have chosen to follow."

Accordingly, Spalding began to combine a long apprenticeship of playing in the provinces with some certain profits—though sometimes meager—with more important honor-engagements in the cities. What a wonderful time he had on these provincial tours: gaining experience in handling ticklish temperaments of lady pianists, learning more about audience-psychology; and, on one occasion, even talking the civic-proud mayor of one town into transporting via white oxen and cart—flag-bedecked—the respectable piano from his town's hall to that of a rival's, when persuaded by the young violinist that thus he might reveal that *his* town possessed a piano with all its ivory keys intact!

Meanwhile Camille Saint-Saëns, having heard a good report about Spalding's playing of his concerto in B minor on the occasion of the American's début, granted Spalding an interview. Warned that the French composer-pianist-organist was likely to be crotchety, Spalding went to the early morning appointment with no little misgivings. His fears proved decidedly unfounded. Saint-Saëns, after cordially greeting him and remarking on the reports of Spalding's playing of his concerto, asked his guest to play for him. Sitting down at the piano, Saint-Saëns played the accompaniments for this impromptu recital. Then on discovering that Spalding was seventeen, in view of the fact that he was seventy-one, he proposed that they play a concert together.

Would he like to play a concert with Camille Saint-Saëns?

Spalding, as in a dream, found himself making plans with his host for such a concert to be given at Florence. And before the interview-rehearsal was over, the young violinist had the additional benefit of some pertinent suggestions on his violin playing from Saint-Saëns. "Sarasate performs that passage thus and so . . . try it . . . try again." Or, "Why do you over-play this passage? Ysaÿe would. . . ."

Walking back to his hotel in a dazed state, various other statements of the French master resounded in his memory: "Patience . . . save the warm colors . . . never let practice become mechanical." Oh, there was so much to learn!

The concert at Florence proved to be a gala affair, ending in a genuine ovation both for SEVENTY-ONE and SEVENTEEN. After bidding Saint-Saëns good-bye at the station, following the concert, Spalding had still further bits of advice to think about; chiefly the one; "Work! Work hard!"

In 1906 the young American made his English début at Queen's Hall in London. The concert went well; everyone was kind, but Spalding knew better than anyone else that there was nothing brilliant about the event: The English press bore out his own conclusions; and yet, as he was reminded, the English were slow to express enthusiasm. After all, wasn't he going to play under the distinguished Hans Richter at one of the London Symphony Orchestra concerts? On that occasion, the concert pleased violinist, audience, conductor, and press. That was more like it!

On the strength of this acclaim he was invited by Richter to play with him at Manchester. Alas, the audience in this town, long associated with the famous Hallé concerts, was icicle-cool in its response. The press the next morning was even more so; but the disappointed violinist had the comforting admonition from Richter: "Don't read the newspapers. You know how you played last night . . . the critics only judge from the surface."

Soon thereafter Spalding made his Berlin début, but this appearance was not as important to him as his specially-arranged recital before Joseph Joachim. Occurring shortly before the latter's death, this meeting was to provide further impetus to the young artist's development. After listening intently to Spalding's playing of the Bruch G minor concerto, the great master expressed his approval to much in the younger man's interpretation, then he proceeded to demonstrate how the opening of the finale should be played. Though, due to his weakened condition, Joachim was forced to make a second attempt in order to illustrate his point, he succeeded well enough to impress the interpretation on Spalding's mind for all time.

Despite the ardent pleas of his guest, Joachim refused to take Spalding as a pupil. Assuring him that he was well on *his own way*—a good one—Joachim further advised him to keep his simplicity of approach. "Work. Develop within yourself!"

There it was again: apparently, the only road to success—work!

Then came more small concerts in England, between which Spalding made several trips to Florence. On these occasions he would resume his lessons in composition with Antonio Scrontini, who stubbornly insisted that Spalding devote himself to composing rather than fiddling. Alas, he was to see his pupil become deeper and deeper involved in concertizing. The spring of 1908 found the violinist enthusiastically working with a new friend—Alfredo Oswald, a young pianist—preparatory to Spalding's début in his native land. Alfredo, whose Brazilian father was an eminent musician, had generously consented to play Spalding's accompaniments on the projected American tour; and many a wonderful rehearsal session they enjoyed together, with Alfredo's father offering pertinent suggestions:

"More fire! More freedom!... No! Not hysteria! Thunderbolts! Not popguns!"

Finally Beethoven's "Kreutzer" Sonata emerged nearer to the revolutionary composer's intentions—even unto rhythm—whereupon Papa Oswald smilingly assured the young artists that they were on the right road. "Now keep on it!" Thus ended the day's lesson—another contribution to a growing reservoir of inspiration.

Back home in America for the summer, Spalding was invited by Walter Damrosch to visit him at York Harbor in Maine. It was under this conductor that the young violinist was to play with the New York Symphony Orchestra in the fall. He must make a good impression at their first meeting! And this he did and more too: Damrosch, ever generous, was wildly enthusiastic about his playing and proceeded forthwith to send out letters-of-prophesy concerning America's "first great instrumentalist."

Then came the Sunday afternoon—November 8, 1908—when Albert Spalding stood before a critical audience of his countrymen at Carnegie Hall in New York City. Never had he been so nervous and never would he be so nervous again. But once he had got in his stride, confidence and previous experience came to his rescue, and soon the audience reacted with the most gratifying response. Recalled time and again, the young violinist was justifiably jubilant when he faced Damrosch and his admiring friends backstage after the concert.

The benign smile on Walter Damrosch's face all but said to the group, "What did I prophesy?" And warmly shaking the débutant's hand, he dramatically assured him that his career was safely launched.

But the next morning upon hearing about the scathing criticism written by the eminent Henry E. Krehbiel of the *Tribune*, Spalding was forced to believe that his course held anything but clear sailing. Had others, as well as himself, not heard the applause of the night before he would have doubted his own ears; for this respected critic had found nothing to praise in Spalding's playing. His tone was *rasping, snarling, raucous*—in fact—everything it shouldn't be! While the gist of the review inferred that the sooner Spalding gave up trying to be an artist the better.

Fortunately all the reviews were not of this character. Some were moderately favorable: others were *glowingly* favorable. Richard Aldrich wrote, "he is assuredly a young man of talent, of high accomplishment at present and of even greater promise for the future." Then after remarking on his technical equipment, this reviewer continued, "There are energy and vitality in Mr. Spalding's playing; and this energy is dominated by a feeling of repose and poise that is altogether unusual for one of his years." After referring to his "sound, wholesome and sane" interpretations, and pointing out both strength and weakness in technique, he informed his readers "that the present achievements of this still very young man were of a sort to promise an uncommonly rich artistic maturity."

But, despite the fact that the Krehbiel review was widely reprinted through the misguided zeal of a rival agency, plus the fact that it was an unusually brilliant musical season, Spalding successfully appeared in fifty or sixty concerts that fall and winter. Mischa Elman, who had made his brilliant début the same year, was his greatest rival; while in opera, such figures as Mary Garden, Geraldine Farrar, and Enrico Caruso competed for the public's favor. One of the great singers of all time—Lillian Nordica—liking both Spalding and his playing, invited him to assist in some of her recitals. Altogether the young violinist could look back to the first season in his homeland with warm memories.

Henceforth he was never to think twice about his father's dictum that he earn his own living in his chosen profession: Returning to Europe, he gave concerts up, down, and across the continent; Russia, Holland, and Finland, where sitting in the dark auditorium during rehearsals was none other than Jean Sibelius. Spalding liked Sibelius. Sibelius liked Spalding and his playing. The Finnish people liked Spalding, providing for him his greatest challenge to date; so much so, that, he could state in his Autobiography that the Helsingfors concert marked "a graduation from triviality, from cheap success."

Spalding's second United States tour came in the season of 1911-1912, during which time his accompanist was André Benoist, who, previously, had been with Lillian Nordica and other noted artists. "Evidences of substantial progress" were found in his playing on October 21, 1911, at New York's Carnegie Hall, according to Richard Aldrich. Then he went on to say that Mr. Spalding had not only gained in technical certainty but in style and musical feeling. "Sympathetic frankness, sincerity and unassuming modesty" found favor with his audience; qualities that were characteristically *Spalding*.

Later that season he appeared at Carnegie Hall with the Theodore Thomas Orchestra of Chicago. On this occasion he had the honor of introducing to New York Edward Elgar's violin concerto, previously played in London by Fritz Kreisler.

Early in 1912 Spalding and Benoist set out on an European tour together, going via the Scandinavian countries and Finland to Russia. To the violinist's great delight Benoist was as enchanted with Finland as he had been on his previous visit, though this visit had doubtful beginnings. "What kind of house are we going to have tomorrow night?" Benoist demanded of Spalding when he could find no notice of the concert in the local papers. And sure enough, on scanning the papers, Spalding could find not a line of publicity. This was particularly annoying considering the amount of advance publicity he had bestowed on Finland! Just wait until he spoke his mind to that man Fazer!

No sooner had this cordial gentleman made his appearance than Spalding began to carry out his threat. "What do you mean by giving us no advance publicity? And tomorrow the concert! What have you..."

"But Mr. Spalding," stammered the astonished Finn, "why spend more money on advertising? Your concert has been sold out for several days!"

Is it strange that both Spalding and Benoist liked Finland?

Then came St. Petersburg, where, once again, the two artists enjoyed themselves to the fullest. Leopold Auer took Spalding under his wing quite as though he "had been one of his students." In addition to inviting the visiting artists to his home, he asked them to attend one of his classes at the Conservatory. "There is one student in particular whom I'd like you to hear," said Auer.

This little wizard-on-the-violin—whose recently acquired full-sized fiddle accentuated his tininess—was none other than Jascha Heifetz!

Meanwhile Spalding's concerts—including some under Alexander Siloti—met with increasing warmth of response: a circumstance particularly gratifying in view of the artistic splendor of Russia at that time. Imagine competing with Chaliapin at the opera, Mengelberg and young Serge Koussevitzky as conductors, and the incomparably wonderful Nijinsky and Karsavina at the ballet!

Armed with all manner of exciting presents—including a special kind of smoked fish, wood-encased—Spalding set out for Western Europe, eventually arriving—fish and all—in Florence.

The early summer of 1914 found Spalding eagerly looking forward to a well-earned vacation. In addition to his regular concerts he had given a series of recitals in Egypt; tours for the next few seasons—including one to South America—were all lined up; now he could relax. Accordingly, though war clouds were clouding the European sky, the Spalding family in mid-July blithely set sail from Cherbourg. Soon after their arrival in the United States War was declared in Europe. Even then, it didn't seem possible, but there it was!

For the next three seasons Spalding gave an average of sixty or seventy concerts a year within the boundaries of his own country. Then it was that he became acquainted with the western part of his homeland; an experience, of great interest to him, as well as rewarding in the matter of concert-giving for his listeners.

At his initial concert of the season in the fall of 1914 at Carnegie Hall in New York City, he was enthusiastically received. Playing a sonata by Porpora an unaccompanied Bach sonata, Mozart's D major concerto, as well as smaller pieces, Spalding revealed great strides in development: "Such an artist as he is one to be reckoned with seriously and is a credit to American art," wrote Mr. Aldrich.

In April 1917, when the United States necessarily became involved in the First World War, Spalding, then in Salt Lake City, immediately set about determining where he could best serve his country. After manifold complications, he became an officer in the Air Service, working under "a dynamo of energy"—Captain Fiorello H. La Guardia, later to be better known in New York City as His Honor the Mayor. In Paris, various parts of Italy, and Spain, Albert Spalding, violinist-turned-soldier, equipped with expert knowledge of several languages, contributed immeasurably to the cause of the Allies; at the same time, both to his superior officer's credit and satisfaction, he emerged from War with his hands intact for Peacetime fiddling.

Resuming the life of a civilian and an artist, Spalding gave his first after-war concert at Rome under Bernardino Molinari. Then, after playing a series of twenty concerts in various Italian cities, the American violinist returned to America, where, on July 19, 1919, at Ridgefield, Connecticut, he married his sweetheart, Mary Pyle. His friend and colleague, André Benoist, and the celebrated violinist, Jacques Thibaud, furnished the music as their "wedding present"; and henceforth, on his tours hither and yon, Spalding was to have a delightful companion, in the person of Mary Spalding, to share his triumphs.

The summer over, one of these tours—extending to the West coast—got under way. André Benoist, who had been accompanying Jascha Heifetz during Spalding's war years, was back in the fold; and this trip proved to be a particularly interesting one for all concerned. At Denver, poor Benoist was fated to shoulder more blame than is the lot of most long-suffering accompanists, when, during the playing of the Mendelssohn concerto, Spalding was seized with one of those blind spots, certain to plague every artist. In his effort to help the violinist extricate himself from his circling confusion, Benoist frantically emphasized some key notes. Finally, just when the situation sounded hopeless, Spalding slid into the sought-after musical stream, and the concert ended in a blaze of glory.

Picture the hero-of-the-day's face when they all read in the local paper that Spalding had never played better, *but what had happened to Mr. Benoist in the first movement of the Mendelssohn concerto?*

In the spring of 1920, Spalding was chosen as one of the two American artists to accompany the New York Symphony Orchestra, under the direction of Walter Damrosch, on its European tour. The first three concerts, given at the Paris Opéra, were gala affairs; as, in fact, were all the succeeding ones whether in France, Italy, Holland, or England. Damrosch was praised; the orchestra was praised; the two artists—Spalding and John Powell the pianist-composer—were praised; and Albert Spalding's playing made a particularly strong impression at Bordeaux and Florence. Their appearance at the Paliteama Theatre in Florence amounted to a home-coming celebration for the violinist; while after the concert, a large reception was given in the visiting orchestra's honor at the home of Spalding's father.

After spending the summer in England, Albert and Mary Spalding returned to New York where Spalding thereafter, became involved in the new medium of concert-giving with which his name will forever be linked—that of radio. Now his audiences were suddenly increased from hundreds to millions: At first it was difficult for him to feel a contact with these maybe-listeners, but, as a growing response to his radio concerts revealed that people were listening, he became aware of their existence. Later he was to add the role of commentator to that of violin playing; and in both capacities, the quality of imparting direct communication with his audience was his chief characteristic.

Meanwhile he continued to give concerts in various parts of the world— the United States, Holland, England, Hungary, and finally—many years after his original plans—South America. In 1923, as the first American to be a member of the Jury at the Paris Conservatory, he helped award the first violin prize.

And, when once again War came to the world, Albert Spalding, dropped the role of violinist for "soldier"; this time, assisting in psychological warfare in Italy.

Following a concert tour in Brazil during the summer of 1945, Spalding made his first appearance of the season in New York on October 15, 1945, at Carnegie Hall. Given for the benefit of the Musician Emergency Fund's reconditioning program for veterans, he played before a grateful audience, quick to recognize the qualities characteristically his: fluency of tone, refinement of expression, and complete frankness.

Proof of the fact that his teacher, Antonio Scontrino, did not entirely lose out to the violinist, rests in Spalding's various compositions: Two violin concertos; a sonata for violin and piano; suite for violin and piano; *Etchings* (theme, variations and improvisation), for violin and piano; Theme and Variations for orchestra; four "Serious Pieces" for piano; many violin pieces, including "Alabama"; and songs.

In history, Albert Spalding—America's "first great instrumentalist"—belongs among the artists of One World.

INDEX

INDEX

Albinoni, Tomasso, 36
Amati, Andrea, 26, 35
Amati, Anthony, 27
Amati, Jerome, 27
Amati, Niccolo, 27, 28, 32
Anet, Baptiste, 39, 53
Auer, Leopold, 44, 162, 169, 224

Bach, Johann Sebastian, 39, 47, 57, 60, 61
  Chaconne, 47
Baillot, Pierre, 40, 41, 44, 76, 77, 109
Balthasard, Beaujoyeulx de, 36
Baltzar, Thomas, 36
Baltzarini, 36
Bang, Maia, 186, 187
Bass bar, 13
Bazzini, Antonio, 140
Beethoven, Ludwig van, 47, 79, 101, 140, 144
Belgioioso, Baldassaro da, 36
Bergonzi, Carlo, 29
Beriot, Charles Auguste de, 25, 44, 114
Berlioz, Hector, 79, 88, 90, 92, 105, 141
Biber, Heinrich, 36
Bloch, Alexander, 186, 188
Blocks, 13
Boehm, Joseph, 43, 138
Bow, 18
Brahms, Johannes, 43, 47, 137, 142, 143, 145, 147, 148, 149, 173
  Double Concerto, 148
Bridge, 11
Brodsky, Adolphe, 178
Brown, Eddy, 44, 45, 169, 188
Bruch, Max, 47, 165
Bruni, Antonio Bartolomeo, 40
Bull, Ole Borneman, 25, 46, 109, 153, 158, 161
  Mountains of Norway, 133
  Saetarjentens Söndag, 121

The Nightingale, 130
Butler, Henry, 37

Campbell, Sir Alexander, 165
Castrucci, Pietro, 39
Chanterelle, 15
Concerto grosso, 53, 61
Conforti, Antonio, 40
Coperario, 37
Corelli, Arcangelo, 35, 38, 40, 42, 49, 57, 71, 79
  Concerto Grossi, opus 6, 54
  La Follia, 39, 54, 204
Cremona violins, 14, 26

da Belgioioso, Baldassaro, 36
Dancla, Charles, 42, 47
da Salò, Gasparo, 24, 25, 26
David, Ferdinand, 42, 107, 138, 140, 173
da Vinci, Leonardo, 23, 24
de Beaujoyeulx, Balthasard, 36
de Beriot, Charles Auguste, 25, 44, 114
Debussy, Claude, 46, 194
de Kontski, Apollinaire, 179
de Sarasate, Pablo, 46, 161, 178, 216
Dounis, D. C., 47
Duiffoprugcar, Gasparo, 24, 31
Dvořák, Antonin, 47

Elgar, Edward, 47
Elman, Mischa, 44, 169, 184, 186, 188
Enesco, Georges, 46
Ernst, Heinrich Wilhelm, 43, 112, 113, 138, 140

Farina, Carlo, 35
  Cappricio Stravaganta, 35
Farinello, Cristano, 38
Ferrari, Domenico, 40
Finger board, 15
Fontana, Giovanni Battista, 38

Franco-Belgian school, 44, 46
French school, 40, 42, 44

Gabrieli, Andrea, 35
Gabrielowich, Ossip, 188
Gaviniés, Pierre, 42
  Twenty-four Matinées, 42
Geminiani, Francesco, 39, 53
German school, 36, 38
Gibbons, Orlando, 37
Given, Thelma, 186
Glazounov, Alexander, 47
Guadagnini, Lorenzo, 29
Guarnerius, Andrea, 27
Guarnerius del Gesù, Joseph, 27, 30, 31

Habeneck, François-Antoine, 42
Handel, Georg, 47, 51
Hartmann, Arthur Martinus, 46
Haydn, Joseph, 40, 47, 59, 74
Heifetz, Jascha, 44, 169, 185, 186, 187, 188, 224
Helmesberger, Joseph, 170, 201
Hilf, Arno, 158
Hochstein, David, 188
Hubay, Jenö, 45
  Hyre Kati, 45

Ideler, Edwin, 188

Jenkins, John, 37
Joachim, Joseph, 43, 44, 45, 47, 137, 158, 172, 192, 197, 216, 220
Joachim Quartet, 146, 149

Kontski, Apollinaire de, 179
Kreisler, Fritz, 45, 46, 201
  Caprice viennoise, 207
  Schön Rosmarin, 209
Kreutzer, Rodolphe, 40, 42, 45, 77, 103
  Forty Etudes or Caprices, 41
Kublík, Jan, 47

Index

LaFont, Charles Philippe, 86
Lahoussye, Pierre, 67
Lalo, Édouard, 47, 165
Laurenti, Bartolomeo Girolamo, 38
Legrenzi, Giovanni, 36, 39, 57
Letz Quartet, 207
Linings, 13
Liszt, Franz, 44, 79, 88, 118, 142, 179
Locatelli, Pietro, 39, 42, 53, 84
Loeffler, Charles Martin, 46
Lolli, Antonio, 42
Lully, Jean Baptist, 38, 50
Lyra, 4
Lyra da gamba, 6

Maggini, Giovanni Paola, 25
Mannes, David, 197
Mannheim school, 41
Marini, Biagio, 35
Massart, Joseph Lambert, 45, 153, 191, 202
Matteis, Nicola, 37
Mendelssohn, Felix, 43, 47, 104, 138, 139
Menges, Isolde, 186
Menuhin, Yehudi, 47
Milstein, Nathan, 44, 169
Modern Franco-Belgian school, 44
Modern French school, 40, 42
Modern school, 40, 71, 77
Monteverdi, Claudio, 35
Mozart, Leopold, 41
Mozart, Wolfgang Amadeus, 38, 40, 47, 71, 98, 218
Müller, Quartet, 174, 175

Nardini, Pietro, 40, 41, 67, 68
Neck of violin, 11
New Russian school, 44
Nut, 15

Paduan school, 39, 63, 67
Paganini, Niccolo, 30, 42, 43, 79, 97, 102, 107, 161
  Napoleon Sonata, 85
  Scene amoureuse, 85
  Twenty-four Capricci, 89
  Witches Dance, 95
Pagin, Andre Noel, 67
Parlow, Kathleen, 44, 186
Pegs, 15
Piastro, Michel, 185
Piedmontese school, 39, 53
Poliakine, Miron, 185

Polledro, Giambattista, 40
Powell, Maude, 47
Prokofiev, Sergei, 47
Pugnani, Gaetano, 40, 72
Purcell, Henry, 38
  Golden Sonata, 38

Rebec, 4
Reményi, Eduard, 43, 142
Rest, 15
Ribs, 10
Rode, Pierre, 40, 42, 43, 77, 99
  Twenty-four Caprices, 41
Rolla, Alessandro, 80
Roman school, 35, 38, 47, 49
Rosen, Max, 188
Rosin, 19
Rossini, Giocchino, 87, 102
Rubenstein, Anton, 155, 176, 178, 181
Russian school, 44

Saint-Saëns, 47, 165, 178, 219
Salò, Gasparo da, 24, 25, 26
Sarasate, Pablo de, 46, 161, 178, 216
  Jota de San Fermin, 166
  Navarra, 166
  Peteneras, 166
  Zigeunerweisen, 166
Sauret, Emil, 45
Schumann, Robert, 142, 143
Scroll, 11
Seidel, Tsocha, 185, 186, 187, 188
Sevčik, Otaker, 47
Sibelius, Jean, 47
Simpson, Cristopher, 37
Sirmen, Maddalena Lombardini, 67
Siskovsky, Jaroslav, 186
Somis, Giovanni Battista, 39, 40, 53, 61, 72
Sonata da camera, 54
Sonata da chiesa, 54
Sound post, 13
Spalding, Albert, 213
  compositions, 227
Spohr, Louis, 42, 88, 97, 111, 117
  Alruna, 100
  Calvary, 104
  Das befreite Deutschland, 102
  Faust, 102
  Jessonda, 104
  Scena cantante, 102
  The Consecration of Sound, 104

The Fall of Babylon, 104
The Last Judgment, 104
The Lovers' Duel, 101
The Seasons, 106
Zemira and Azor, 102
Stainer, Jakob, 31, 37
Stradivarius, Antonio, 13, 14, 27, 28
Strings, 15
Szigeti, Joseph, 45

Tailpiece, 15
Tail pin, 15
Tartini, Giuseppe, 39, 63, 72, 79, 86
  Miserere, 68
  The Devil's Trill, 39, 65, 204
Tchaikovsky, Peter, 47, 158, 176
Telmányi, Emil, 45
Torelli, Giuseppe, 38
Tourte, François, 18

Varnish, 14
Veracini, Antonio, 38
Veracini, Francesco Maria, 39, 66
Vienna school, 43, 44
Vieuxtemps, Henri, 45, 156, 157, 171, 191
Vinci, Leonardo da, 23, 24
Viol, 3
Violin
  construction, 9
  history, 3
  makers, 23
  music, 35
  players, 35
Viotti, Giovanni Battista, 40, 41, 42, 44, 71, 98, 103
  Symphonies concertantes, 74
Vivaldi, Antonio, 39, 40, 53, 57

Walther, Johann Jakob, 36
Wieniawski, Henri, 46, 153, 163, 176, 191
  D minor concerto, 158
  Legende, 158
  Souvenir de Moscow, 158
Wilhelmj, August, 43, 209
Wood in violin construction, 10

Young, William, 37
Ysaÿe, Eugène, 45, 159, 191

Zimbalist, Efrem, 44, 169, 184, 188